Why Obama Won

The Making of a President 2008

Why Obama Won

The Making of a President 2008

By Greg Mitchell

Copyright 2008 by Greg Mitchell
All rights reserved, including the right to reproduce this book or portions thereof in any form whatsoever.

ISBN: 1-4392-1831-5
ISBN-13:9781439218310

Published January 2009 by Sinclair Books

Portions of this book were previously published, in a different form, by *Editor & Publisher*, its web site or E&P Pub blog.

Editor & Publisher is a division of Nielsen Business Media, Inc., which retains the rights to the articles or postings in their original form in the print magazine or online.

The name "Editor & Publisher" and its accompanying logo, are exclusive trademarks of Nielsen Business Media, Inc. All Rights Reserved.

Other parts of this book were previously published at The Huffington Post, Daily Kos, and the author's personal blog, Pressing Issues. The Introduction was written for this book.

Additional copies of this book may be ordered via Amazon.com and other sites, or from the author directly. He can be contacted through his personal blog, http://gregmitchellwriter.blogspot.com/ , or by email at epic1934@aol.com.

The author's previous books include: *The Campaign of the Century, Tricky Dick and the Pink Lady, Joy in Mudville, Hiroshima in America* (with Robert Jay Lifton), *Who Owns Death?* (with Robert Jay Lifton), *Acceptable Risks* and *Truth and Consequences*

Huffington Post: http://www.huffingtonpost.com/
Daily Kos: http://dailykos.com/

Printed in the U.S.A.

For Andy and the Millennials

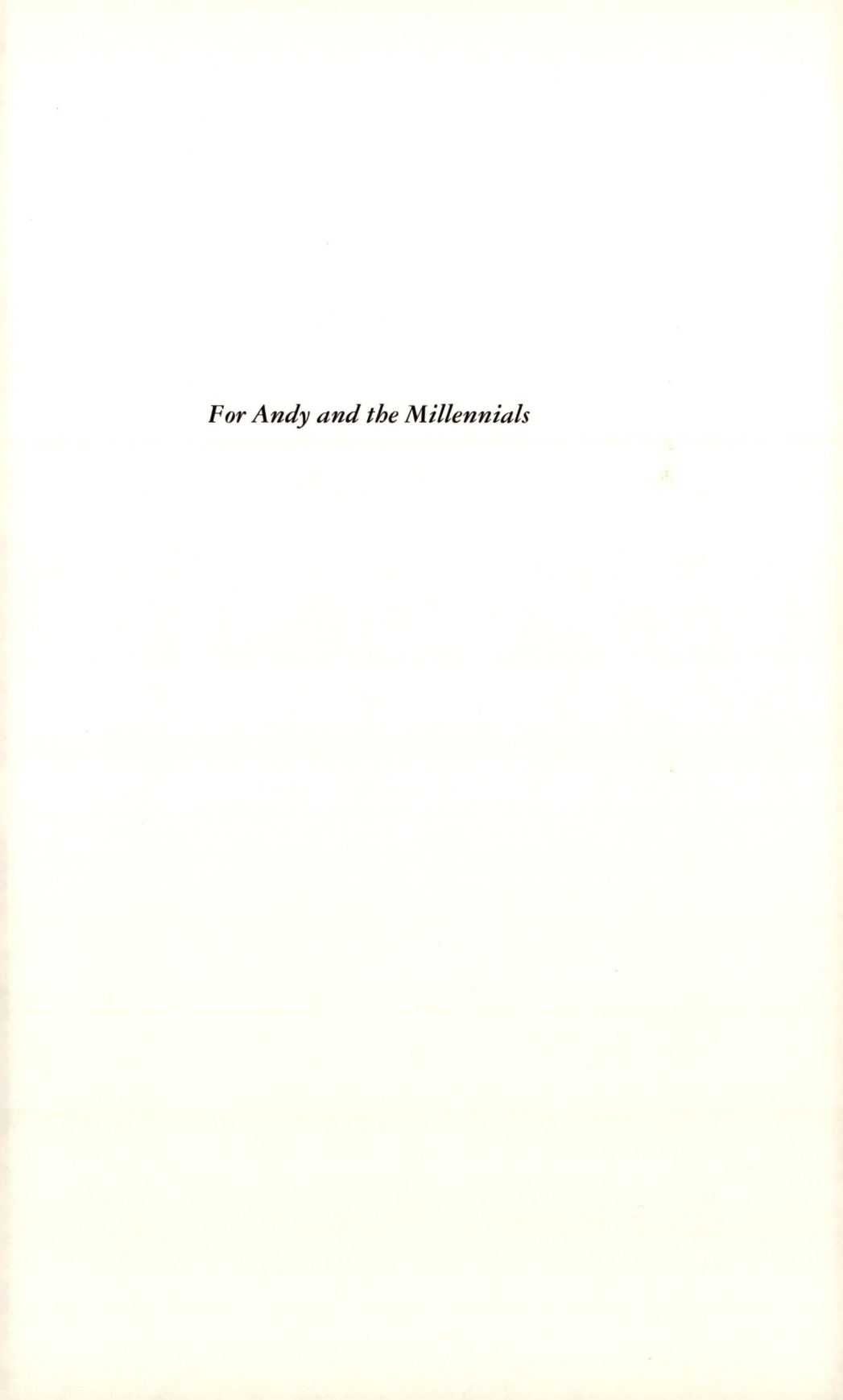

Contents

Introduction i

2007

November 1
December 9

2008

January 17
February 41
March 55
April 65
May 77
June 83
July 89
August 99
September 117
October 143
November 183

About the Author

Greg Mitchell is the editor of Editor & Publisher, *the "bible" of the newspaper industry, and its popular Web site and E&P Pub blog, and also blogs at other sites. His acclaimed book* So Wrong for So Long: How the Press, the Pundits – and the President – Failed on Iraq, *was published in March 2008 by Union Square Press, and included a preface by Bruce Springsteen and a foreword by Joseph L. Galloway.*

Since the 1980s, Mitchell has written eight nonfiction books, all for major publishers including Random House, Putnam, Viking, Pocket and HarperCollins. Among his best known books are Tricky Dick and the Pink Lady: Richard Nixon vs. Helen Gahagan Douglas *(a New York Times Notable Book) and* The Campaign of the Century: Upton Sinclair's Race for Governor of California and the Birth of Media Politics *(winner of the Goldsmith Book Prize and a finalist for the Los Angeles Times Book Award).*

He wrote two influential books with Robert Jay Lifton, Hiroshima in America *and* Who Owns Death?, *which explored capital punishment. He also authored the popular 2001 memoir,* Joy in Mudville.

Mitchell's articles have appeared in every major section of The New York Times *and dozens of other leading newspapers and magazines. He has also served as a consultant on two films based on his books. He lives in Nyack, N.Y. He can be contacted at: epic1934@aol.com. His personal blog is:* http://gregmitchellwriter.blogspot.com//

Introduction

When the nearly two-year race for the White House ended on November 4, 2008, the solid win for Sen. Barack Obama of Illinois, a vote for hope and change, no longer seemed a surprise. Certainly it was judged historic and profound but Obama's triumph had come to feel almost inevitable in the final weeks. John McCain's pathetic last ditch efforts – painting Obama as a "socialist," adopting "Joe the Plumber" as his campaign pet, appearing on *Saturday Night Live* with Tina Fey as she continued to make his running mate a national laughing stock – could not stem the tide.

Going back one year, however, as we do in this book – and finding Hillary Clinton labeled the clear frontrunner – puts the Obama victory in perspective. Joe Scarborough wasn't the only pundit back then to pat Obama on the head for a nice effort and tell him to prepare to get ground up and "spit out" by the unstoppable double-Clinton machine. Instead, Obama, with the help of an unprecedented grassroots funding and organizing effort, battled that machine to a standstill, then knocked out McCain a few months later.

How did that happen? As *Why Obama Won* makes clear, the Democratic insurgent made few poor moves, remained calm while avoiding, or wiping off, the mud thrown at him, and continually surprised the pundits, who overestimated both Clinton and McCain (and Sarah Palin) past the point most voters abandoned them. This book provides an illuminating, if at times humorous, way to really appreciate what transpired, by reliving the final year of the campaign almost day-by-day, sometimes hour-by-hour. You may recall that Bill Clinton helped drive his wife's campaign off the tracks – and that Palin clearly doomed McCain – but here's how that became clear (to some of us). Along the way, a full cast of inspiring or unlikely characters appears, from Sam Brownback and Chuck Norris to Bill Ayers and Bruce Springsteen.

The hundreds of sometimes brief, sometimes substantial, pieces in this book, presented in chronological order starting in November 2007, come from my many columns, articles and postings at the *Editor & Publisher* site and blog, leading political sites Huffington Post and Daily Kos, and my own blog, many of them reduced in length or slightly revised. I followed the campaign from an almost unique perch: Very much within the mainstream (*E&P* has been the "bible" of the newspaper industry for 125 years) but at the same time as a regular commentator at two of the most popular "new media" blogs in the world.

I also brought to the 2008 race a long connection to American political campaigns, as an activist, a journalist, and historian. I've been a campaign junkie all of my life. At the age of eight, I paraded in front of my boyhood home in Niagara Falls, N.Y., waving an "I Like Ike" sign. A few years later, in 1960, I argued for Richard Nixon for president against John F. Kennedy in a junior high school debate (the vote went 20-3 against me, surely Nixon's fault). In 1968 I got a chance to cover my first presidential campaign when one of Sen. Eugene McCarthy's nephews came to town, before the state primary, and I interviewed him for the *Niagara Falls Gazette*, where I worked as a summer reporter during college. (I had been chair of the McCarthy campaign at my school.) A few weeks later, as I describe much later in this book, I ended up in Chicago for the notorious Democratic National Convention, witnessing the "police riot" that broke out in the streets.

In the decades that followed, I wrote or edited numerous magazine articles about political campaigns. Then, in the 1990s, I wrote two books on landmark California elections for Random House: *The Campaign of the Century: Upton Sinclair's Race for Governor of California and the Birth of Media Politics* and *Tricky Dick and the Pink Lady: Richard Nixon vs. Helen Gahagan Douglas*. Arriving at *Editor & Publisher* in 1999, I focused tightly on the contested 2000 and 2004 contests. By early 2008, I was blogging almost daily about the campaign at several sites. Many of those pieces are collected here to provide one of the first book-length histories of the 2008 race.

The nomination of an African-American for president by a major party, and the Republicans' first selection of a female candidate for vice-president, were not the only historic aspects of the 2008 election campaign in the United States. This was also the first national campaign profoundly shaped – even, at times, dominated – by the new media, from viral videos and blog rumors that went "mainstream" to startling online fundraising techniques.

James Poniewozik, the *Time* magazine columnist, observed at midyear that the old media are rapidly losing their "authority," and influence, with the mass market. "It's too simple to say that the new media are killing off the old media," he declared, while highlighting a pair of influential scoops for Huffington Post by a hitherto unknown "citizen journalist" named

Introduction

Mayhill Fowler. "What's happening instead is a kind of melding of roles. Old and new media are still symbiotic, but it's getting hard to tell who's the rhino and who's the tickbird." He concluded, with an oblique reference to the late Tim Russert: "Maybe we'll remember this election as the one when we stopped talking about 'the old media' and 'the new media' and, simply, met the press."

Simply put: The rules of the game have been changed forever – by technology. It was more than the "YouTube Election," as some dubbed it, or "The Facebook Election," or "hyper-politics." James Rainey, the longtime media reporter for the *Los Angeles Times,* declared that there is a "new-media revolution that is remaking presidential campaigns. Online videos can dominate the evening news. Or an unpublished novelist 'with absolutely no journalism training' can alter the national debate," a reference to Mayhill Fowler.

This book reveals – and reflects – the growing influence of the new media, but also offers "equal time" to traditional TV and print coverage, highlighting their ongoing strengths and shortcomings and exploring how they are now so deeply influenced by, and responsive to, the Web.

Case in point: In June, the alleged Obama "terrorist fist bump" went from viral to *The View* in just three days. Fortunately, the candidate was able to laugh it off, which was certainly not the case after the Rev. Wright videos went viral – another example of the unpredictable power of Web politics. More evidence: After wrapping up the nomination in June 2008, the Obama campaign launched an extensive Web site devoted solely to shooting down viral rumors and innuendo.

"What's different this year is that the entire political and media establishment has finally woken up to the fact that the internet is now a major player in the world of politics and our democracy," said Andrew Rasiej, co-founder of the TechPresident blog and annual Personal Democracy Forum. "We are watching a conversion of our politics from the 20th century to the 21st."

How did sites with names like Politico and FiveThirtyEight and Eschaton and Crooks and Liars collectively come to rival the three television networks in influence, even if partly by influencing the networks themselves? It's been more than thirty-five years since "The Boys on the Bus" were anointed and celebrated. Now Huffington Post's "Off the Bus" site often made headlines with on-the-scene bulletins and audio/video snippets from some 3000 contributors. It was there that Mayhill Fowler's two major scoops in the campaign were posted.

Defending her second one – on Bill Clinton's "sleazy" attack on Todd Purdum of *Vanity Fair* captured along a rope line in South Dakota – Jay Rosen, who runs that section of the Huff Post site, said, "Professional reporters are going to have to decide whether they want to view citizen journalists as unfair competition, which is one option, or as extending the news net to places that pro reporters can't, won't or don't go, which is another – and I think a better — way to look at it."

Online influence in political campaigns pre-dates the current race, of course. Who can forget the Web-organized "meet-ups" that helped spark Howard Dean's insurgent drive in 2004? Daily Kos was backing Dean and many Democrats in Senate and House races – while losing almost every key contest, it should be noted. The blog phenomenon had barely begun, YouTube was not yet born, social networking sites were in their infancy or still a glimmer in the eyes of entrepreneurs.

The "swiftboating" of John Kerry was mainly carried out in the traditional ways – TV spots, print ads and interviews on Fox News. The other major controversy surrounded a network TV report: the infamous Dan Rather segment on *60 Minutes* about George W. Bush's National Guard service (or lack of). It was fatally critiqued by conservatives on the Web but bloggers were still only in a reactive mode, not making the news themselves.

Two years later, the "tickbird" really started…ticking, with the 2006 elections, in which the Democrats took back Congress – thanks, quite significantly, to the activism and funding generated by liberal blogs and their allied groups. This reversed the poor new media/netroots record in the 2004 campaign and signaled that the "revolution" had really arrived.

YouTube had burst on the scene. The most revealing single incident: Sen. George Allen's "macaca" moment. This was when he uttered a distasteful slur at an obscure campaign rally, which happened to be caught on video and soon watched by millions on the Web, and millions more when picked up (in the usual manner) by cable TV.

This was unthinkable – even impossible – until recent years. Allen lost narrowly to Jim Webb, the Democrat. Then the liberal Web-backed candidates triumphed in several special elections in 2007.

Introduction

That same year, Obama's online fundraising prowess, I suggest, was a key to his eventual victory, for several reasons: It gave him a quick start in the spending race; the millions of small donors gave him credibility as a broad-based candidate and provided the mainstream media with a catchy story line; it showed party leaders and super-delegates – and the press – that he might be the most powerful nominee; and it allowed his followers to feel they were intimately linked to his fortunes (in both meanings of the word).

But let's not forget that the wildly passionate, if not exactly successful, Ron Paul phenomenon was purely a product of the Web. On the other hand, other candidates—such as Rudy Giuliani and Joe Biden – faltered badly partly because they had little or no life online. Hillary Clinton's Web operation was largely viewed as old-fashioned and "square," and she did not get her online fundraising act together until too late in the game. Her most "hip" moment of the whole campaign came early when she filmed a video spoof of the final episode of *The Sopranos*, with her husband in a diner. It was viewed by millions but she never followed up on that type of success, even though she had hired a former blogosphere ace, Peter Daou. Clinton was mocked by many for campaign videos that had a saccharine "Up with People" quality, while more cutting edge acts put together hot Obama tunes.

At the same time, many of the candidates had to repeatedly answer charges or respond to embarrassing videos posted on the Web. Giuliani had to put out almost weekly flash fires about his record and his mistress/wife; Mitt Romney had to defend making his dog ride on the roof of his car and claiming that his sons were doing their part in the war on terror by campaigning for him; John McCain was captured singing the old Beach Boys tune with new lyrics: "Bomb-bomb-bomb, bomb-bomb Iran." And John Edwards had to endure the constant replay of him fluffing up his hair before a TV appearance four years earlier.

I would argue that videos featuring Bill, not Hillary, Clinton led to the true turning point in the primary race, when on three separate occasions he was caught making what some took to be "racial" remarks and/or losing his temper with voters or reporters – all in informal settings captured by amateurs or small town reporters and then beamed to millions. Countless Democrats, and particularly African-Americans, who had always revered the Clintons, switched to Obama in the space of a week or two. Even if they still liked Hill they did not want another four or eight years of Bill. Obama won eleven primaries in a row and the race was all but over.

Early in the final Obama-McCain showdown, the number one campaign charge from the Democrats was that the Republican wanted to stay in Iraq "for 100 years." What was the source for this? An amateur video of McCain making a remark to that effect at a small campaign gathering months earlier, spread widely on the Web – in the usual fashion, first by liberal bloggers, then by the Obama campaign itself. Soon it turned up frequently on network and cable TV shows and even in Democratic commercials.

From the GOP side, Rev. Wright's Greatest YouTube Hits perhaps peaked too early, quickly grew stale and were not utilized widely in the fall until the final days of the campaign . Some Republicans lamented that McCain was getting killed on the Web – and he didn't help his image any when he admitted that he was still an internet neophyte. In June, when Obama passed the magic barrier of one million Facebook friends – a measure that didn't exist four years ago – it was noted that McCain only had 150,000.

And we haven't even mentioned Obama Girl.

In the autumn, the turning point for the entire campaign might have come when McCain's gamble, picking Sarah Palin as his running mate, was undermined by the CBS interview with her by Katie Couric and the *Saturday Night Live* parodies starring Tina Fey. Yes, they were generated in the mainstream but they gained tens of millions of additional viewers online in the days that followed.

Today, old media still plays a strong role, of course, but even when it is at center stage, which is often, it now comes under withering review from the world of the Web – and in turn, responds to those critiques, and the cycle goes on and on. Even mainstream figures such as Couric, Brian Williams, and Keith Olbermann write blogs, which are quite popular.

And all of the top newspapers now choose to break campaign news every day not merely on their Web sites but on (multiple) campaign blogs fed by longtime reporters, such as Adam Nagourney at *The New York Times* and Chris Cillizza at *The Washington Post*. Imitation of the blogosphere has become a sincere form of flattery – or, at times, desperation.

Yes, the networks and cable news outlets hosted almost all of the candidate debates, but this year they were joined by partners such as Facebook

Introduction

and YouTube. The YouTube debate provided some of the best, and goofiest, questions of the whole primary season (who can forget the query about global warming from a melting snowman). One of the lowlights of the primary season for the networks was the public flogging of ABC anchor Charles Gibson for his often inane questions during one debate. The uproar from the Web was so strong that Gibson had to respond – on the air the next night.

And recall what happened after the Democratic debate in February. Everyone remembers the *Saturday Night Live* sketch a few days later – but what sparked that? For days after the debate, the Web was alive with charges that the all-male panelists had piled on Hillary and given Obama a free pass. The *SNL* segment was credited with helping to spark Clinton's "comeback" in primary voting that spring.

As the final week of the campaign approached in October, Howard Kurtz ventured out on the campaign trail for a few days for *The Washington Post* and then asked: Have the Web and the digital age doomed the "boys on the bus"? He sketched Obama about to speak to 10,000 screaming fans at a state fairgrounds but observed that before he "took the podium, the text of his speech arrived by BlackBerry. The address was carried by CNN, Fox and MSNBC. While he was still delivering his applause lines, an *Atlantic* blogger posted excerpts. And despite the huge foot-stomping crowd that could barely be glimpsed from the media tent, most reporters remained hunched over their laptops.

"Does the campaign trail still matter much in an age of digital warfare? Or is it now a mere sideshow, meant to provide the media with pretty pictures of colorful crowds while the guts of the contest unfold elsewhere? And if so, are the boys (and girls) on the bus spinning their wheels?"

A few days later, a new Pew poll found that online had now overtaken newspapers as a way to keep up with the campaign this year. Newspapers remained flat in popularity since 2004 while Web climbed 23% and seemed poised to challenge TV as the prime source next time around.

Then, on the morning of Election Day, *The New York Times* presented, as its banner headline on the front page, "The '08 Campaign: A Sea Change for Politics As We Know It." Adam Nagourney opened it with, "The 2008 race for the White House that comes to an end on Tuesday fundamentally upended the way presidential campaigns are fought in this country, a legacy that has almost been lost with all the attention being paid to the battle between Senators John McCain and Barack Obama.

"It has rewritten the rules on how to reach voters, raise money, organize supporters, manage the news media, track and mold public opinion, and wage — and withstand — political attacks, including many carried by blogs that did not exist four years ago."

So blogs, which rarely drew wide notice in 2004 and were derided by some as a silly, passing fancy, now earned a place in the second paragraph of the top *Times* story on Election Day 2008. "I think we'll be analyzing this election for years as a seminal, transformative race," said Mark McKinnon, a senior adviser to President Bush's campaigns in 2000 and 2004, in that *Times* article. "The year campaigns leveraged the Internet in ways never imagined. The year we went to warp speed. The year the paradigm got turned upside down and truly became bottom up instead of top down."

Terry Nelson, who was the political director of the Bush campaign in 2004, said that the evolution would continue in 2012 and beyond. "We are in the midst of a fundamental transformation of how campaigns are run," Nelson said. "And it's not over yet." As Sarah Palin might say: You betcha.

NOVEMBER 2007

November 4

Only One Year to Go!
After ten months of campaigning in the race for the White House, one year somehow still remains until election day. Polls show that voters are already complaining about the media's "horse race" focus with the finish line barely visible on the far side of the track. News coverage of the campaign so far has centered on just five candidates, offered very little information about their public record or what they would do in office, and focused more than 60% of stories on political and tactical aspects of the race, according to a Project for Excellence in Journalism study.

It's hard to really know for sure (did Sam Brownback just drop out?), but about ten Republicans and ten Democrats remain in the race, and that's not counting Stephen Colbert. Yet the more Americans complain about the media, old and new, the more they seem to tune in, or click through, for campaign coverage.

A lot of old boys, such as David Broder, remain on the bus, but citizen journalists are rising to prominence using their own transportation. One of the new twists this time around is the rise of blogs at major newspaper sites maintained fulltime by veteran political reporters. Joe Strupp at *Editor & Publisher* decided, for fun, to ask five of them to predict what might happen in the next twelve months. Here is the scorecard. Hillary Clinton is the unanimous pick on the Democrats' side with Mitt Romney earning a narrow win for the Republicans.

James Pindell, *The Boston Globe:*

Most Crucial Campaign Issue: Iraq
Expected Democratic Nominee: Hillary Clinton
Expected Republican Nominee: Can't choose now
Dark Horse: Mike Huckabee

Frank James, *Chicago Tribune:*

Most Crucial Campaign Issue: Iraq
Expected Democratic Nominee: Hillary Clinton
Expected Republican Nominee: John McCain
Dark Horse: John McCain

Kate Phillips, *The New York Times:*

Most Crucial Campaign Issue: Iraq
Expected Democratic Nominee: No Choice
Expected Republican Nominee: No Choice
Dark Horse: Mike Huckabee

Chris Cillizza, *The Washington Post:*

Most Crucial Campaign Issue: Iraq
Expected Democratic Nominee: Hillary Clinton
Expected Republican Nominee: Mitt Romney
Dark Horse: Mike Huckabee, John Edwards

Andrew Malcolm, *Los Angeles Times:*

Most Crucial Campaign Issue: Iraq
Expected Democratic Nominee: Hillary Clinton
Expected Republican Nominee: Mitt Romney
Dark Horse: John Edwards

November 8

Stephen Colbert, We Hardly Knew Ye!
Now that his quixotic race for the White House has suddenly ended, it's time to review the highlights of Stephen Colbert's brief but meaningless venture into electoral politics. Colbert has pulled out of the upcoming primary in South Carolina, despite topping Bill Richardson and closing in on Joe Biden in one national poll.

November 2007

Colbert had kicked it off during an appearance on Larry King's show last month to promote his new book, *I Am America (And So Can You)*. The Comedy Central star was accused by the host of using the book as a platform to run for president. Colbert happily confirmed this, saying that he would likely seek the nomination from both parties. When King said this was a "cop out," Colbert said that it actually demonstrated true "courage" because "I could lose twice."

Likely he will launch his grassroots crusade in his native state, South Carolina, as a "favorite son." Colbert refused to knock any of his competitors, but did allow that Fred Thompson's campaign slogan should be, "Do Not Disturb." He pointed out that Mike Huckabee had already offered him the veep spot if the former Arkansas governor gets the GOP nomination.

Soon, a major South Carolina public TV station offered Colbert airtime to officially announce his candidacy. The Colbert bump kept growing when, on October 14, Maureen Dowd turned over her *New York Times* column to him for the day. Colbert revealed, "While my hat is not presently in the ring, I should also point out that it is not on my head. So where's that hat?"

Keeping nothing under his missing hat, he went on to describe his platform. On gender: "The sooner we accept the basic differences between men and women, the sooner we can stop arguing about it and start having sex." On race: "While skin and race are often synonymous, skin cleansing is good, race cleansing is bad." On the elderly: "They look like lizards."

And finally: "I don't intend to tease you for weeks the way Newt Gingrich did, saying that if his supporters raised $30 million, he would run for president. I would run for $15 million. Cash. Nevertheless, I am not ready to announce yet — even though it's clear that the voters are desperate for a white, male, middle-aged, Jesus-trumpeting alternative."

Two nights later, after nearly a solid week of dropping hints, Colbert did find, and throw, his hat in the ring. On his own show, *The Colbert Report*, with balloons falling, he screamed, 'Yes, I'm doing it!" Then he welcomed CBS political analyst Jeff Greenfield to analyze his impact on the race "in the past three minutes."

Greenfield said it was "astounding."

Colbert took out one of the "Colbert/Stewart 2008" bumper stickers that have circulated for awhile and cut out the Stewart part, saying that he might replace Jon Stewart as a possible vice president with someone named

"Huckabee" or even "Putin." To finance his campaign, he threatened to sell advertising patches on his suit, like a NASCAR driver.

Questions quickly rose about his ballot status in South Carolina but the situation there appeared murky. Stewart signed a contract extension for his *Daily Show*, explaining, "I love doing this show. . . . I look forward to using this extension to having great fun at President Colbert's expense."

Stephen, in fact, was already threatening to overtake the lesser-rans on the Democratic side. The Public Opinion Strategies national poll in mid-October found him drawing 2.3 percent in the Democratic race. This put his ahead of Richardson (2.1 percent) and Dennis Kucininch (2.1). He trailed Biden by just a tad (Joe's at 2.7 percent).

A week later a Rasmussen poll showed that his surge was continuing. In a projected three-way context against frontrunner Hillary Clinton and Rudy Giuliani he was pulling 13% of the vote (28% of the 18-to-29 demo). At *E&P* we predicted: "If he keeps gaining over 10% a week, Colbert should be leading the field before November is out."

Meanwhile, a Facebook group titled "1,000,000 Strong For Stephen T. Colbert" had attracted more than 880,000 members in just over a week – making it the most popular political group on Facebook by far. And that was before he, improbably, appeared on *Meet the Press* with Tim Russert on October 21. From the transcript:

RUSSERT: *You've thought this through.*

COLBERT: *That's a generous estimation. Thank you.*

RUSSERT: *The press reaction to your announcement has been mixed. Here's one headline.*

COLBERT: *OK.*

RUSSERT: *This was on Thursday. "Electile Dysfunction: Colbert Running For President."*

COLBERT: *That's good work. That's good work.*

November 2007

RUSSERT: Are they, are they questioning, shall we say, your stamina?

COLBERT: I don't know. I think a lot of people are asking whether—they say is this, is this real, you know? And to which I would say to everybody, this is not a dream, OK? You're not going to wake up from this, OK? I'm, I'm, I'm far realer than Sam Brownback, let me put it that way.

RUSSERT: Would you consider Senator Larry Craig as your running mate?

COLBERT: I would.

RUSSERT: Have you had conversations with him?

COLBERT: Define conversation.

RUSSERT: Have you spoken to him?

COLBERT: No, no.

RUSSERT: Have you met with him? Have you been in the same room together?

COLBERT: Sorry, my lawyer's telling me to say no more.

Colbert visited Columbia, S.C. and received the key to the city from the mayor on "Stephen Colbert Day." The local newspaper, *The State*, published a side-by-side comparison of its two native son candidates, Colbert and John Edwards. The latter's hair was described as "naturally fluffy" while Colbert's was "very stiff." Colbert, perhaps angered by that, was quoted saying of his opponent: "John Edwards left South Carolina when he was 1 year old. He had his chance. Saying his parents moved him — that's the easy answer."

But just as momentum was building uncontrollably in early November, the state's Democratic party ruled that he was not "viable" enough to be awarded a spot on the ballot. Colbert was reduced to citing – and showing on the screen – an article in *E&P* to prove that he was, indeed, not merely a joke candidate for president. The audience roared its approval of *E&P* as potential kingmaker.

Too bad, he said, he wouldn't get a chance to run, waving a thick file of papers – he had an exit strategy for Iraq all mapped out.

November 9

A Tip from Hillary Clinton
Hillary Clinton, it turns out, does know how to leave a good tip. The Democratic frontrunner's tipping skills were called into question Thursday after National Public Radio aired an interview with an Iowa waitress who served a sandwich to Clinton during a recent campaign visit, two months before the critical caucus. Anita Esterday waited on the senator and her entourage at a Maid-Rite restaurant in Toledo, Iowa. The waitress posed for photos with Clinton and described her challenges as a single mother forced to work two jobs to make ends meet.

Clinton later incorporated Esterday's story into her campaign stump speech. Pictures of their meeting appeared in newspapers and on TV newscasts. In the NPR interview, however, Esterday said that while she had enjoyed meeting Clinton, she hadn't gotten much out of her minutes of intimacy. "I mean, nobody got left a tip that day," Esterday said, adding, "I don't think she understood at all." Esterday's comments were potentially harmful, undermining Clinton's appeal to working class voters, especially women. Rival campaigns quickly e-mailed the story to reporters, as did the Republican National Committee.

But Brad Crawford, manager of the Toledo Maid-Rite, said Clinton campaign aides paid the bill for lunch and left a tip to be divided among the servers, "and everything was good." Crawford said he didn't know why Esterday may not have received any of the money. "If she got left out it wasn't because they meant to leave her out," Crawford said. "If something happened with the disbursement, it's probably my fault."

Esterday said she did not understand what all the commotion was about, *The New York Times* reported. "You people are really nuts," she told a reporter during a phone interview. "There's kids dying in the war, the price of oil right now – there's better things in this world to be thinking about than who served Hillary Clinton at Maid-Rite and who got a tip and who didn't get a tip." Good advice as we look to the next twelve months.

November 18

Robert Novak Leaks Again

A throwaway item in a Robert Novak online column inspired a strong reaction from Barack Obama today. Novak had suggested that Clinton was sitting on "scandalous" information on Obama but had not made it public. The columnist did not say what the info was or his source for this claim.

Rather than just let that sit out there and possibly fade away, Obama brought it center stage with a strong rebuttal. He said in a statement, "The cause of change in this country will not be deterred or sidetracked by the old 'Swiftboat' politics. The cause of moving America forward demands that we defeat it." He called on Clinton to release the alleged information – or renounce the whole thing: "She of all people, having complained so often about 'the politics of personal destruction,' should move quickly to either stand by or renounce these tactics."

According to a story at *Politico*, Howard Wolfson, Clinton's campaign communications director, said she has "no idea" what the item is about. "Once again Sen. Obama is echoing Republican talking points, this time from Bob Novak," he said in an e-mailed statement. "This is how Republicans work.... Voters should be concerned about the readiness of any Democrat inexperienced enough to fall for this. There is only one campaign in this race that has actually engaged in the very practice that Sen. Obama is decrying, and it's his."

Obama campaign manager David Plouffe replied in a statement that Wolfson's comments represented the "Washington art of evasion and deflection."

November 28

Rudy's 'Love Nest'

His friend Bernie Kerik had his Ground Zero "love nest." Now *Politico* reveals today that as New York mayor, Rudy Giuliani "billed obscure city agencies for tens of thousands of dollars in security expenses amassed during the time when he was beginning an extramarital relationship with future wife Judith Nathan in the Hamptons, according to previously undisclosed government records.

"The documents, obtained by *Politico* under New York's Freedom of Information Law, show that the mayoral costs had nothing to do with the functions of the little-known city offices that defrayed his tabs, including agencies responsible for regulating loft apartments, aiding the disabled and providing lawyers for indigent defendants. At the time, the mayor's office refused to explain the accounting to city auditors, citing "security.'

"The Hamptons visits resulted in hotel, gas and other costs for Giuliani's New York Police Department security detail."

A Giuliani spokeswoman, Sunny Mindel, declined to comment on any aspect of the travel documents or the billing arrangements. A Giuliani aide refused to discuss his visits to Long Island but denied that the unorthodox billing practices were aimed at hiding expenses, citing "accounting" and noting that they were billed to units of the mayor's office, not to outside city agencies. *Politico* editor John Harris said they were standing by the story.

DECEMBER 2007

December 11

Many Say They Won't Vote for a Mormon
A new Gallup Poll finds that better than one in six Americans, including similar numbers of Republicans and Democrats, indicate they would not support their party's nominee for president if that person were a Mormon. The poll was conducted from Dec. 6 to 9, immediately following the major speech by Republican presidential candidate Gov. Mitt Romney in which he addressed voter concern about his Mormon religion. The percentage of Republicans who now rule out voting for a Mormon, 18%, is just one point lower than it was in March.

This stand against voting for a candidate based on *one* such factor is unusually high. Gallup observes: "Four percent of Americans (including 3% of Republicans) say they would not vote for a Catholic, 5% would not vote for a black, 12% would not vote for a woman, and 12% would not vote for a Hispanic." Earlier this year, however, Gallup found 28% of Americans saying they would not vote for someone who is on his or her third marriage.

December 12

Huckabee Wants the Stones to Roll at His Inaugural
After the AP leaked a quote from the story last night, *The New York Times* today put up its entire mammoth profile of Mike Huckabee coming in this Sunday's magazine. One passage: "Huckabee ordered soup and a sandwich without drama or comment and began talking about rock 'n' roll. This is his regular warm-up gambit with reporters of a certain age, meant to convey that he is a cool guy for a Baptist preacher. Naturally I fell for it, and asked who he would like to play at his inaugural. 'I've got to start with the Stones,' Huckabee said.

"The governor regards 1968 as the dawning of 'the age of the birth-control pill, free love, gay sex, the drug culture and reckless disregard for standards.' The Rolling Stones album *Their Satanic Majesties Request* provided the soundtrack for that *annus terribilis*. But Mike Huckabee wanted me to know that he believes in the separation of church and stage.

"The governor's musical wish list also included John Mellencamp, who, he noted, would be welcome despite their differing political views; the country duo Brooks & Dunn; Stevie Wonder; and, surprisingly, Grand Funk Railroad. 'That's a groundbreaking group,' he said earnestly. 'The bass player, Mel Schacher, is very underrated.'"

<u>December 14, 2007</u>

Bill Clinton On Obama: 'No Dice'
In a surprisingly frank interview with Charlie Rose on his PBS show late Friday night, former President Bill Clinton declared that his wife was not only far better prepared to be president than her chief rival Sen. Barack Obama – "it's not close" – but that voters who disagreed would be rolling the dice if they chose Obama. Repeatedly dismissive of Obama (which could come back to haunt the Clinton campaign) the former president at one point said that voters were, of course, free to pick someone with little experience, even "a gifted television commentator" such as Rose who would have just "one year less" experience in national service than Obama.

Clinton also said, with a laugh, "It's a miracle she even has a chance" to win in Iowa, adding he was not just "low-balling it." He said John Edwards might well win. He praised Obama's intelligence and "sensational political skills" but repeatedly suggested that, unlike his wife and some of the other candidates, he might not be ready for the job. Clinton pointed out that when he was elected president in 1992 at about the same age as Obama, he was the "senior governor" in the U.S. and had worked for years on international business issues. Viewers could draw their own conclusions.

Asked if Obama was ready to be president, Clinton passed: "Well the voters have to make up their mind." He added that "even when I was a governor and young and thought I was the best politician in the Democratic Party, I didn't run the first time. I could have." Later he said that his friends in the Republican Party had indicated that they felt his wife would be the strongest candidate, partly because she had already been "vetted" – another subtle slap at Obama. The most important thing to judge was who would be "the best agent for change" not merely a "symbol for change....symbol is not as important as substance."

He also hit back at the charge that experienced politicians had helped get us into the Iraq war, saying that this was "like saying that because 100 percent of the malpractice cases are committed by doctors, the next time I need surgery I'll get a chef or a plumber to do it."

One more dig at Obama: He said that Edwards had first run for president after just a few years in the Senate, but then completed his term and went out and conducted a serious study of poverty. "I guess I'm old fashioned," he said, in wanting a president who had actually done things for people. Some people, of course, could "risk" taking someone who had served just a year in the Senate if they chose.

When Rose said that all this seemed to add up to Clinton hinting that people would be "rolling the dice" if they picked Obama, the former president replied: "It's less predictable, isn't it?"

If a call had gone out from his wife's campaign to pull back any critiques of Obama, her husband clearly did not get the memo. He did say that he gets "tickled" watching Obama because of his attractiveness and political skills. "I like all these people," he said. "I have nothing bad to say about him or anyone else."

Obama responded on Saturday in Iowa by pointing out that Clinton himself had said in 1992 when he ran for president that a candidate can "have the right kind of experience or the wrong kind of experience." He also noted that he had been "involved in government for over a decade," mainly in Illinois, and had the right kind of experience to "bring people together." He decried "slash and burn" politics and said Americans are "not interested in politics as a blood sport."

December 16

Mitt Has a Hole
Mitt Romney on *Meet the Press* today turned emotional as he recalled the day in 1978 he learned over his car radio that his Mormon church had finally dropped its full membership barriers to blacks. He may have even shed a

tear on camera, or as Drudge has it in a headline at the top of his site: MITT TEARS ON MTP. He had cried that day in 1978, too, allegedly so happy the black ban had finally collapsed. You'd hardly know that, in fact, Romney had done absolutely nothing about fighting this racist barrier before his epiphany in his car.

The Mormon Church considered blacks spiritually unfit as a result of a biblical curse on the descendants of Noah's son Ham. Some prominent Mormons — including Morris and Stewart Udall – had publicly called for an end to the doctrine, the same kind of pressure that had earlier led to the end of approved polygamy. Mitt Romney, a former missionary and in an influential position as son of former Gov. George Romney of Michigan, said absolutely nothing.

"I hoped that the time would come when the leaders of the church would receive the inspiration to change the policy," Romney told *The New York Times* a few months ago. "The way things are achieved in my church, as I believe in other great faiths, is through inspiration from God and not through protests and letters to the editor."

Now today he says, "I was anxious to see a change in my church...it's very deep and fundamental in my life and my most core beliefs that all people are children of God. My faith has always told me that." But, actually, his faith – as a Mormon – told him the opposite. Tim Russert gave him a chance to say that his church was wrong, but Romney would only reply, "I told you exactly where I stand. My view is that there's no discrimination in the eyes of God." Yet, queried repeatedly today by Russert, he heartily embraced the support for his candidacy by Rev. Bob Jones.

December 17

Kerrey a Torch?
The big 2008 campaign kerfuffle today concerns remarks about Obama by former Sen. Bob Kerrey in endorsing Hillary Clinton yesterday. He told reporters, "It's probably not something that appeals to him, but I like the fact that his name is Barack Hussein Obama, and that his father was a Muslim and that his paternal grandmother is a Muslim. There's a billion people on the planet that are Muslims, and I think that experience is a big deal."

December 2007

After some charged that Kerrey was only the latest Clinton backer to stab Obama – this time with the word "Muslim" instead of "cocaine"– he asserted that his words were only meant in praise for Obama's potential to communicate abroad. Critics came back with: Why, then, the use of his middle name "Hussein," a favorite game of the far-right?

<u>December 20</u>

Drudge Rumor Draws Response from McCain
A top-of-the-page (though without siren) story on the Drudge Report today declares that Sen. John McCain is appealing to *The New York Times* to halt an upcoming story that, allegedly, links him to some sort of improper activities involving a lobbyist. Drudge headlines the story: "McCain Pleads with NYT to Spike Story."

The McCain response comes from Communications Director Jill Hazelbaker: "It is unfortunate that rumor and gossip enter into political campaigns. John McCain has a 24-year record of serving this country with honor and integrity. He has never violated the public trust, never done favors for special interests or lobbyists, and he will not allow a smear campaign to distract from the important issues facing our country.

"Americans are sick and tired of this kind of gutter politics. John McCain is the most experienced and prepared to lead as commander in chief, and he will continue to run a positive campaign on the issues."

Drudge also suggests that McCain "has hired DC power lawyer Bob Bennett to mount a bold defense against charges of giving special treatment to a lobbyist!" Now the story has gone "mainstream," with full reports by The Associated Press and Howard Kurtz in *The Washington Post*. Kurtz reports, "Bennett is preparing answers to written questions submitted by a team of *New York Times* reporters who have spent weeks investigating questions about the senator and the lobbyist; she has also retained a lawyer, according to a knowledgeable source who asked not to be identified because he was discussing legal matters.

"McCain called *Times* Executive Editor Bill Keller earlier this month to deny the allegations and to complain that he was not being treated fairly by the *Times* reporters, who have not yet interviewed him, the source said."

December 20

Ron Paul Falling Behind...Alan Keyes?

While it's true that the media has been slow to cover Rep. Ron Paul's fundraising success, the notion that the press is missing a true grassroots surge for Paul in the race for president is questionable. A new Gallup Poll out today shows that his support among Republicans nationally has actually dropped in the past month, from a paltry 5% to a pathetic 3%. This is after he did get more press and appeared in most of the TV debates. By the way, that 3% total now ties him with new entrant.... Alan Keyes.

Admittedly, Paul is much stronger among independents, but that won't help him in the GOP race, no matter how much money he raises. And do any of the thousands who have donated money to Paul wonder when he will actually start spending a lot of it? He was getting 3% nationally in Gallup back in July, and hasn't gained an inch since. Another surprise in Gallup: Contrary to much media coverage, it suggests that Huckabee has peaked – his 16% is identical to what he polled two weeks ago. And Rudy not only still tops him with 27% but easily beats him (56%-38%) or Romney (57%-37%) in match-ups.

December 31

Obama is Finished?

Or so says Dorothy Rabinowitz of the *Wall Street Journal*. On this past weekend's TV "Journal Editorial Report," hosted by Paul Gigot, she and other panelists were asked to make predictions for 2008. Here is her big one, right off the transcript: "My pick? Well, I think that in very short order Americans are going to be asking, Who is Barack Obama?

"You know, this man has come forward like a Rorschach test for everybody to project this notion of what a Democratic candidate should be. He's the inkblot. And it's becoming clearer and clearer that this mass of platitudinous, high-minded expression pouring forth from Obama as—it is beginning—it's going to sit on people who are going to ask, What's he saying? What does this mean? This started at the convention speech where he gave this strange speech about no one is black, no one is white, no one is this, no one is—"

Gigot: "But people loved it, Dorothy."

Rabinowitz: "Yes, I know, they loved–exactly....Well, I can tell you that this mass of non-meaning, nonspecific feelings, attitudes and programs is going to become unraveled very soon when people look for programs...."

JANUARY 2008

January 2

Ghosts in the Machines

Coming between the Iowa and New Hampshire tallies, this Sunday's cover of *The New York Times Magazine* ought to strike a chord. It shows a man inside an exploding voting booth with a WARNING label over it and the words: "Your vote may be lost, destroyed, miscounted, wrongly attributed or hacked."

The massive Clive Thompson article, titled "The Bugs in the Machines," is quite chilling. "After the 2000 election," it opens, "counties around the country rushed to buy new computerized voting machines. But it turns out that these machines may cause problems worse than hanging chads. Is America ready for another contested election?" One key passage: "The earliest crtiiques of digital voting booths came from the fringe – disgruntled citizens and scared-senseless computer geeks – but the fears have now risen to the highest levels of government."

One expert says that "about 10 percent" of the devices fail in each election.

The piece focuses on the newly-popular "touch-screen" machines, noting that "in hundreds of instances, the result has been precisely the opposite" of the intention to add "clarity" to results: "They fail unpredictably, and in extremely strange ways; voters report that their choices 'flip' from one candidate to another before their eyes; machines crash or begin to count backward; votes simply vanish. (In the 80-person town of Waldenburgh, Ark., touch-screen machines tallied zero votes for one mayor candidate in 2006—even though he's pretty sure he voted for himself.)"

During this year's primaries, about one-third of all votes will be cast on touch-screens. The same ratio will likely hold this November, even with some states junking the devices. The *Times* notes that "what scares election observers is this: What happens if the next presidential election is extremely close and decided by a handful of votes cast on machines that crashed?"

In the same issue, David Frum, the conservative writer and former Bush White House speechwriter – currently working for Rudy Giuliani – says in an interview, "What I am terrified of is that the Republican Party is heading into a period of political defeat....I am terrified that we can lose the election in 2008. We can lose in 2012, and it will take us half a dozen years to do the rethinking we need to do." He also tells Deborah Solomon, "What I am saying is that there is exhaustion, intellectual exhaustion on the part of Republicans and conservatives."

January 3

Peggy Noonan 'Pyles' On

The big winners, it turns out, in the Iowa caucus vote: Barack Obama and Mike Huckabee. Peggy Noonan at the *Wall Street Journal* says people better not underestimate Huckabee. He's "hometown" but *not* Gomer Pyle – more James Carville than Jim Nabors. Well, yes, like Carville he *is* married to a Republican.

Favorite media errors, out of many (including Chris Matthews claiming the Iraq war is now in its 7th year instead of its 5th): *The New York Times* still has a special editorial board comment from yesterday afternoon posted near the top of its home page. It includes this graf: "The Iowa caucuses are an extreme case of putting up barriers to voting. It is no wonder that turnout today is expected to be so low." Of course, it ended up smashing all records. Matthews also predicted McCain would do much better than he did, and promised a major news making announcement in the Hillary concession speech (didn't happen).

Of course, the unstated joke is that so much is being made of this choice by what has been called "a sliver of a sliver of a sliver" of the electorate. Andrea Mitchell on MSNBC agreed with Howard Fineman that "the torch has passed" from Hillary Clinton and she needs to find a reason to even "go forward," as if she has nothing in her favor at all. Indeed, she is in trouble but this same sliver of voters previously rejected numerous future presidents, including her husband.

On MSNBC, Eugene Robinson of *The Washington Post* said the Obama speech was "goose bumps" time for him, watching a black candidate win and sound like Robert Kennedy to boot. Pat Buchanan says Huckabee is for real – and Fox News will just have to come to grips with it. But his margin over Romney is actually the same as Obama's win. And Huck had Chuck Norris out there with him for his victory speech (is this a winning combo?).

Obama, in the final results, has actually "thumped" Clinton by 38% to 29%, with Edwards at 30%. Dodd and Biden drop out – at last! Tim Russert's "headline" for the day is the giant Democratic turnout in a "red" state, topping Repubs by about 2-1.

McCain ends in third place. Ron Paul will not finish 3rd as his supporters predicted. Poll analysis shows 56% of first-time caucus voters went for Obama. But will young turn out everywhere, and in the fall? They often disappear.

January 4

The Morning After

Howard Kurtz at the *Washington Post* looks at the punditocracy: "We in the news business made the same mistake we've made so many times before, overvaluing money and organization. Phil Gramm was going to be huge in 1996 because of his war chest. Howard Dean was virtually guaranteed to win because he had raised the then-unimaginable sum of $40 million. But in the end, message and personality can trump fat checkbooks and precinct workers.

"We cling to those benchmarks because they feel real. We overvalue early polls, which can change in a heartbeat, as Huckabee just demonstrated."

Meanwhile, Andrew Malcolm at the *Los Angeles Times* leads a posting, "Clinton aides hint that now things'll get nasty." It goes on: "While you were sleeping, the chartered jet of the third-place finisher in the Iowa Democratic caucus winged its way from Des Moines to Manchester, N.H. And it sounds like some decisions were made on that plane that may alter the course of that party's presidential race." He recounts an interview with Clinton aide Mark Penn on how she will now target Obama, with Malcolm recalling the hints or rumors put out by Clinton people previously about certain things in Obama's past, whatever that means.

David Brooks in *The New York Times* hails the Huckabee win, feeling (rightly or not) that it heralds a new brand of "compassionate conservatism."

Where have we heard that before? But he still finds a Huck nomination "highly doubtful," and here is why: "The past few weeks have exposed his serious flaws as a presidential candidate. His foreign policy knowledge is minimal. His lapses into amateurishness simply won't fly in a national campaign.

"So the race will move on to New Hampshire. Mitt Romney is now grievously wounded. Romney represents what's left of Republicanism 1.0. Huckabee and McCain represent half-formed iterations of Republicanism 2.0. My guess is Republicans will now swing behind McCain in order to stop Mike.

"Huckabee probably won't be the nominee, but starting last night in Iowa, an evangelical began the Republican Reformation."

And from Politico.com: "The Iowa results, with a victory for a populist social conservative [Huckabee] deeply mistrusted by many people in the Republican establishment, also virtually guarantee that the nomination contest will not simply be a battle over personalities and credentials. Instead, the race will now be a deep and probably intensely negative fight for the direction of the party in the post-Bush era.

"Here's what is still utterly uncertain: Who will emerge from this demolition derby? Iowa's historic role is to winnow the field. In 2008, it has the effect of expanding the number of credible top-tier contenders. There are now five people who can conjure at least somewhat plausible paths to the nomination."

January 6

That Old Time Barack on a Roll
Latest Rasmussen survey has Obama now up 12% on Hillary in New Hampshire. That matches yesterday's 12% in the ARG poll, which seemed high.

Hillary, not coincidentally, went after Obama today, with a *New York Times* blog report opening this way: "A charged-up Hillary Rodham Clinton retooled her stump speech Sunday afternoon to challenge the messages of change from Barack Obama and John Edwards, her chief rivals in the New Hampshire primary, by using their own words and voting records against them." This included attacks on Obama for voting for the Patriot Act, for Iraq war funding (which Hillary also supported, of course), and then there's this:

"If you say that you passed the Patients Bill of Rights, but then forget to add it did not become law, that's not change."

John McCain, meanwhile, is not backing off his statement from three nights ago, when he said that if the U.S. stayed in Iraq for 100 years that would be fine with him. On CBS "Face the Nation" today, asked about this, he added two more zeroes to his number, saying, "The point is it's American casualties. We've got to get Americans off the front lines, have the Iraqis as part of the strategy, take over more and more of the responsibilities – and then I don't think Americans are concerned if we're there for one hundred years or a thousand years or ten thousand years."

January 7

Kristol's New Persuasion
Bill's first column appears today in *The New York Times* and while many of his critics may agree with his opening graf, in which he thanks Barack Obama for hurting Hillary Clinton, they will probably quickly part ways when he says the nation can't afford an Obama presidency.

Like many conservatives and fellow Fox analysts, he is starting to warm to Huckabee (knowing they could be stuck with him) and dreams about a Bloomberg candidacy that would, he claims, draw votes from Obama. In this, of course, Kristol reveals his insipidness – what are the chances that Bloomberg would even run if Obama gets the Democratic nod, and if he did, how many Dems would vote for Bloomberg in that case?

My favorite moment is when he refers to "the writer Michelle Malkin," as if she is David Halberstam or David McCullough or Leo Tolstoy. And Kristol notes, in hearting Huckabee: "His campaigning in New Hampshire has been impressive. At a Friday night event at New England College in Henniker, he played bass with a local rock band, Mama Kicks." What next, Derek Smalls of Spinal Tap for president?

UPDATE: Eight paragraphs into his new stint as a *New York Times* op-ed columnist, Kristol has already made an embarrassing error. His column, which suggests that the Democrats not underestimate Huckabee's chances to win it all, quotes Michelle Malkin as saying, "For the work-hard-to-get-ahead strivers who represent the heart and soul of the G.O.P., there are obvious, powerful points of identification."

There's just one problem: She never said it, as she was quick to point out herself on her Michellemalkin.com site: "Since I never usually appear on the *New York Times* op-ed page unless someone's calling me a fascist, I was pleasantly surprised to see the quote. Unfortunately (or fortunately, depending on how you look at it), I didn't write what Kristol attributed to me. A different MM – Michael Medved – was the author."

Colbert for Veep!
Jon Stewart and Stephen Colbert returned Monday night with writers' strike-oriented shows. Colbert had a number of funny bits, replaying his many faux anti-union statements, then introducing tonight's "Word" – which this time failed to appear. He also claimed that Mike Huckabee's Colbert "bump" from his latest appearance on the show earned him the Iowa win and he showed Huck in three separate slots on the show inviting Stephen to run with him as his vice president.

January 8

Surprising New Hampshire Wins for Clinton and McCain
Following the Clinton upset in New Hampshire, Maureen Dowd at *The New York Times* remains caustic about "the tracks of my tears" moment for Hillary – her brief emotional moment at a campaign stop – while noting it had been pivotal in winning back older female voters: "There was a poignancy about the moment, seeing Hillary crack with exhaustion from decades of yearning to be the principal rather than the plus-one. But there was a whiff of Nixonian self-pity about her choking up. What was moving her so deeply was her recognition that the country was failing to grasp how much it needs her. In a weirdly narcissistic way, she was crying for us. But it was grimly typical of her that what finally made her break down was the prospect of losing."

Chuck Todd, political director at NBC, seems to back the "race" angle in the poll errors (Obama had led), based on previous famous examples of whites telling pollsters one thing and voting otherwise. Asked why this didn't happen in Iowa, he points out that it was a caucus vote, with people having to declare themselves openly. In New Hampshire they could pull the curtain and vote privately.

Andrew Sullivan (a big Obama backer) at his blog at TheAtlantic.com: "There was a backlash by women against the media's coronation of Obama. There may well have been something about Clinton implying that she was an older woman who was being passed over by a less experienced man for a job. That may well have resonated with some women, especially after she seemed actually human in the last two days. Once Clinton was weak enough to ask for their help, they gave it to her. But that's not the kind of thing that happens twice. And she's the front-runner again. For awhile."

At *The New York Times* site, David Brooks makes a rare blog appearance, listing 10 things that happened in New Hampshire, including: "Crying works. I have no data to back this up. But Hillary's human moment must have helped. Expect Romney to cry a river of tears at the next press conference."

Tim Russert sees a huge gender divide, "and that means this race goes on big time." He calls Obama-Clinton another "Ali-Frazier." But who will be Ali? He lost the first fight and then won the next two – then beat George Foreman (John McCain?) to take the crown.

Jon Stewart, as often the case, out-pundits the real pundits. On *The Daily Show,* taped hours before the polls closed, he made fun of those who predicted Hillary's "meltdown" over her "crying" episode. He showed the clip of her getting a little emotional and commented, "That's IT? That has wrecked her candidacy? Are you fucking kidding me?" Turns out he was dead-on.

Rachel Maddow, at MSNBC, says many liberal blog fans are blaming Chris Matthews for pushing votes to Clinton by bashing her so much. James Carville, Bill Clinton's former political strategist, has written a one-page memo to Clinton and her aides urging that she come out of the New Hampshire primary with a fighting message that she is bouncing back from her Iowa loss and will challenge Obama in state after state with an inspirational message of change and readiness for the presidency.

Meanwhile, David Gregory on NBC wonders if McCain won solely due to indies, and he will struggle soon in places where they can't vote in the primary, such as Florida. Also, Romney will be favored in his home state of Michigan. But over on CNN, Bill Schneider says exit polls show McCain actually did slightly better among Republicans than indies. So much for conventional wisdom.

January 11

Did Race Bias Cost Obama a Win?
Why were the polls so wrong in the New Hampshire primary (causing embarrassment for the press and pundits) – and only on the Democratic side? Many theories have been advanced in the media since Hillary Clinton's stunning upset over Barack Obama. One of them has been much contested: that white voters told pollsters they would vote for Obama but couldn't quite pull the trigger for the African-American candidate when the time came to cast their ballots. This allegedly counted for more than any sort of "late female surge" for Clinton.

Maybe when Bill Clinton referred to the "fairy tale" surrounding Obama he meant the fable that massive numbers of whites would actually vote for Obama when they had a plausible alternative. But this has been the elephant in the room almost totally ignored by the media until now. Why did it show up (if it did) in New Hampshire and not in Iowa? The Iowa caucuses were quite public, this theory goes, while voters had a curtain to hide behind in New Hampshire.

An interesting new detail has now emerged seemingly bolstering that theory: not just advance polls, but some exit surveys apparently show that even coming out of the polls, voters in New Hampshire gave Obama about a 5% bulge – if they were being honest. Where did all those votes go? Maybe he never really had them to start with.

Frank Newport, head of the Gallup organization, said that his numbers did not support the idea that huge numbers of older women turned out and were not fully accounted for in the projections. Democratic party membership is now strongly tilted toward women.

"I think it's very naive to dismiss the racial factors in this," said Larry Sabato, professor of politics at the University of Virginia.

The racial theory is far from proven, yet it was surprising to see lengthy probes of the poll debacle – such as one by Ken Dilanian in *USA Today* – that did not even mention the possibility of some sort of modest race effect.

"Anytime you've got white undecided voters pulling the lever choosing between a white and a black candidate, that is when the race issue is most important," Drew Westen of Emory University told Tom Edsall, the former *Washington Post* reporter now writing for Huffington Post. "Both campaigns' internal polls showed a 10 to 12 point Obama lead; to see that evaporate into a three-point loss, when he didn't have any gaffes, that has a ring to it."

Andrew Kohut of the Pew Research Center said, "The failure [of polling] on the Democratic side has to do with the fact that Clinton ran best among groups of voters who most often refuse polls – poorer, less well-educated people. These are also the very people who are reluctant to vote for a black candidate." And Kohut told the Associated Press: "You can't rule this out as an issue." He said the problem had not arisen in Iowa, where "Obama was not the front-runner. He was not such a symbol, perhaps threateningly, to people who don't like blacks, that he might be president." He told NPR he would be drilling deeper into the results this week to see what shows up in this area.

In a *New York Times* op-ed on Thursday, he concludes: "In New Hampshire, the ballots are still warm, so it's hard to pinpoint the exact cause for the primary poll flop. But given the dearth of obvious explanations, serious consideration has to be given to the difficulties that race and class present to survey methodology."

This is not a new phenomenon, of course. It is sometimes called "The Bradley Effect" or the "Wilder Effect" after two well-known black officials whose huge leads in final polls mysteriously disappeared (Mayor Tom Bradley of Los Angeles and Governor Doug Wilder of Virginia). And, of course, if true it would have enormous ramifications for the rest of the primary race, and the general election if Obama did manage to get the Democratic nod.

Matt Yglesias at TheAtlantic.com put it this way, "The pollsters underestimated Clinton's level of support. People who were undecided as of the last round of polling seem to have gone overwhelmingly in her direction." But did many, or most, do this out of reluctance to vote for an African-American?

Jacques Steinberg and Janet Elder for Thursday's *New York Times* try to shoot down the theory by declaring, "public opinion researchers say that is probably an artifact of a time when there were few black candidates running for elective office at any level. At any rate, there was no evidence to suggest that that was at play in New Hampshire, and there was no evidence of it in Iowa, where some earlier polls wound up being closer to the mark."

However, this ignores the fact that no black, until now, has really had a shot a being elected president – this is hardly an "artifact" – and that the very open caucus voting in Iowa was profoundly different than the New Hampshire way of balloting.

Jon Stewart on *The Daily Show* Wednesday night told pollster James Zogby that the only thing we now know for sure coming out of New Hampshire is "Democrats lie." He wasn't referring to the racial controversy but the issue is now out there.

Better Fred Than Dead?
In her *New York Times* column today, Gail Collins points out that Mitt Romney reminds some people of Mr. Potter, the banker in *It's a Wonderful Life*. And: "Fred Thompson reacts stonily to any suggestion that the rich should not always get richer, and it was a real treat to watch him in New Hampshire when a debate moderator asked about a windfall profits tax on oil companies. Fred stared at him as if he'd heard a really foul obscenity, or been asked to convert to Scientology." Meanwhile, "Rudy's actual problem is not that he failed to campaign enough in Iowa and New Hampshire, but that he showed up just often enough for the voters to get a sense of what he's really like when he isn't heroically covered in dust from a terrorist attack."

January 13

Chris Rock Predicts the Next President
On CNN last night, he said it simply *had* to be Hillary or Obama because Bush has been so bad "he has screwed it up for any white man to be elected."

January 14

Media Continue to Study 'Race Card'
After the surprising results on the Democratic side in New Hampshire, race and gender politics have really come to the fore in the media and even, at times, on the campaign trail.

Hillary Clinton, on *Meet the Press* on Sunday, continued to hit *The New York Times'* version of her remarks about the relative roles of Dr. Martin Luther King Jr. and President Lyndon Johnson in passing civil rights legislation. Tim

January 2008

Russert opened the show by reading from *The State*, South Carolina's largest paper, which reported yesterday: "Sharp criticism of Barack Obama and other comments about Martin Luther King Jr. — all from people associated with Hillary Clinton's presidential campaign — have generated resentment among some black S.C. voters."

Clinton replied: "Beats me, because there's not one shred of truth in what you've just read."

The New York Times carried yet another article about the dispute today, and the same paper, at the top of the front page of its Week in Review section, carried huge side-by-side photos of iconic 19th century women's rights and black rights leaders.

John Judis, meanwhile, is out with a piece at *The New Republic's* Web site attempting to debunk the notion that even a small part of the reason for the Obama loss in New Hampshire might be attributed to certain whites telling pollsters one thing and then voting differently. He may be right, but why do so many pundits, particularly on the left, feel it's ridiculous to suggest that race might still be a key factor when Americans go to the polls? It would seem that the only way you could claim that there is no race-tinged voting today would be to hold that racism has been completely wiped out in America. Does anyone seriously believe that?

There's no way it could not have been a factor at all in nearly all-white New Hampshire, or anywhere else where (unlike in the Iowa and Nevada caucuses) votes are cast in private. It's just a matter of the size of it: very modest or fairly significant? Judis feels – really, guesses – it was very modest, at most.

And does anyone really believe that some men (or for that, matter, their wives) simply won't vote for a woman as president right now? In fact, the Obama-Clinton "bias" vote may have simply canceled each other out in New Hampshire. But it is real. I'm glad we've come a long way, baby, but we have a ways to go.

January 15

Pastors of Plenty?
Obama got heat today from Richard Cohen in *The Washington Post* because his pastor said some nice things about Louis Farrakhan. Former reverend

Mike Huckabee, meanwhile, in Michigan yesterday called for amending the constitution to ban abortions and gay marriage, explaining that "it's a lot easier to change the Constitution than it would be to change the word of the living God – and that's what we need to do, is to amend the Constitution so it's in God's standards rather than try to change God's standards."

Romney Wins in Michigan – As Democrats Debate
Mitt Romney won by a comfortable margin over John McCain in the GOP primary in Michigan, with Mike Huckabee trailing badly – and Ron Paul doubling Rudy Giuliani's total. The call was made at 9 p.m. just as the big Democratic debate with Obama, Clinton and Edwards, opened in Nevada.

Two hours later the rather bloodless debate ends with Brian Williams asking when each decided to run for president and why – in each case a little over a year ago. This allows them to deliver a bit of their stump speech and raise central themes. Obama jokes that he thought his family could manage it because "my wife is extraordinary and my children above average."

Earlier, Williams had asked Obama about his "you're likable enough Hillary" quip in the last debate. Obama says he regrets it because it was not received as it was meant, that he was trying to give her props.

January 16

Huckabee Gets Squirrelly, McCain Goes to Woodstock
This morning, Mike Huckabee explained why South Carolinians love him: He shares their tastes, such as eating fried squirrels. Why, he used to bake them in his popcorn popper back in his college dorm! "Too much information," replies Joe Scarborough.

Meanwhile, almost 40 years late, John McCain finally made it to Woodstock today. He has quipped in the past that he never made it in 1969 because he was "tied up at the time." Now he is airing a TV ad in South Carolina that includes that joke but also footage of the music festival as part of his slam at presumably "pro-pharma" (and he's not talking about the big drug companies) Hillary Clinton.

January 2008

January 17

Chris Matthews' Confession
Chris Matthews tonight 'fessed up to charges that he has been somewhat (or very) male chauvinist in regard to Hillary Clinton. On his *Hardball*, he now admits a few failings, after revealing, "Some people whom I respect, politically concerned people like you who watch this show so faithfully every night, people like me who care about this country, think I've been disrespectful to Hillary Clinton, not as a candidate, but as a woman."

Here's the climax: "If my heart has not always controlled my words, on those occasions when I have not taken the time to say things right, or have simply said the inappropriate thing, I'll try to be clearer, smarter, more obviously in support of the right of women – of all people – the full equality and respect for their ambitions. So – I get it." But look what it took for him to "get it."

In other news: Mitt Romney angrily clashed today with an AP reporter questioning him at a campaign stop in South Carolina inside a, yes, Staples store. Romney couldn't believe that the reporter actually thinks that he is misleading people when he says that lobbyists are not helping to run his campaign – when a top lobbyist is often seen by his side and offers advice. "He's unpaid," Romney explained, and then things really got heated.

Plus: a big flap in Denver over a local bigwig joking at a dinner that we'll have to change the name of the White House if Obama gets elected. Actually, they could have changed the name to Bleak House a few years back.

January 19

Clinton and Romney Win Bets in Nevada
Hillary Clinton has won the hotly-contested Nevada caucus over Barack Obama today, and Mitt Romney easily took the GOP prize. Clinton leads Obama by about 9% with Edward a non-factor. Details from the NBC entrance polls: African-Americans – Clinton 16%, Obama 79%. Hispanics – Clinton 64%, Obama 24%. Of Clinton's vote, 58% were women and 42% men.

Apparently about one-quarter of Nevada vote on GOP side came from Mormons, explaining Romney's easy win. Pat Buchanan on MSNBC says that this bodes well for him in "Idaho and northern Arizona" but how that gets him the nomination is anyone's guess. Some funny bits in Gail Collins' column at *The New York Times*: "The number of people in the state who have ever attended a caucus before is probably smaller than the number of people in the state who make their living as Elvis impersonators.....It would have made as much sense to decide who gets the delegates by a roll of the dice, and think of the great publicity for the state's premier industry. (Wayne Newton could emcee!)

"The Republican caucuses have been overshadowed by the weirdness in the South Carolina G.O.P. primary. Remember John McCain's joke about playing Will Smith in the movie where everybody else turns into a zombie? Even McCain probably did not envision an empty-eyed Mike Huckabee lurching around South Carolina, yowling about telling people who don't like the Confederate flag where they can stick their flagpole....

"Really, there's got to be a better way. It's only a matter of time before some state party decides to pick its presidential delegates by counting the number of voters who paint themselves blue and howl at the full moon."

January 20

Chuck Norris: McCain May Up and Die on Us
From CNN: "Chuck Norris brought his tough-guy approach to the campaign trail Sunday, taking aim at John McCain's age and suggesting the Arizona senator might not last even a single term. Norris, an ardent supporter of Mike Huckabee, told reporters he believes serving as president accelerates the aging process 3-to-1. 'If John takes over the presidency at 72 and he ages 3-to-1, how old will he be in four years? Eighty-four years old — and can he handle that kind of pressure in that job?' Norris said, as Huckabee looked on. 'That's why I didn't pick John to support, because I'm just afraid the vice president will wind up taking over his job within that four-year presidency,' added the action star."

Obama to Hit Bubba Tomorrow
ABC News reports tonight that in an interview with Robin Roberts to air Monday on *Good Morning America*, Obama hits back at Clinton – Bill, that is – pretty hard. "You know the former president, who I think all of us have a lot

of regard for, has taken his advocacy on behalf of his wife to a level that I think is pretty troubling," Obama said. "He continues to make statements that are not supported by the facts – whether it's about my record of opposition to the war in Iraq or our approach to organizing in Las Vegas. This has become a habit, and one of the things that we're gonna have to do is to directly confront Bill Clinton when he's making statements that are not factually accurate." Maybe the Big Dog will have to learn some new tricks?

Just my two cents, but: Based on what's gone down the past few days, Obama may sense that a kind of "buyer's remorse" is already setting in, regarding the Democratic nominee, as it usually does in campaigns – but with an odd twist this time.

True, Hillary is a long way from locking it up. The problem for Obama is that huge numbers of Democrats (probably including himself) actually like Hillary and/or think she is a fine candidate. However, a growing number either realize that they never really liked her husband, or never really forgave him, or loved him until recently – when he started acting obnoxious on the stump – or simply are now troubled as they finally realize that they don't really want to live through another eight years of gabby/grabby Bill and the Clintons' marital dynamic.

Anyway: I see all of this playing out on liberal blogs and some mainstream media sites and I wouldn't be surprised to see Obama keep hitting Bill – while sweet-talking Hill.

January 22

The Delegate Count: Obama Leads (Trails)
It gets little attention, but in case you are wondering (since it is, in fact, the most important thing): Obama officially leads Clinton in delegates for the nomination 38 to 36, according to NBC News tonight. But Tim Russert helpfully points out that this doesn't include the "super-delegates" – elected Democrats who strongly back Hillary. She claims about 90 while Obama only names 40 of them, so put it together and she leads by about four dozen right now.

Meanwhile, Bill Clinton said in South Carolina today, "I know you think it's crazy, but I kind of like to see Barack and Hillary fight....They're flesh and blood people and they have their differences – let them have it."

And did you hear? Bill Clinton has announced *he* is running for president. Or so claims *The Onion*. Well, it would at least split the Clinton vote – and he would spend just as much time attacking his wife as he would hitting Obama. The Big Dog, according to the satirical paper, calls Hillary a "wonderful wife and worthy political adversary." But does he have the "constitution" for it?

January 23

Economy Tanking Because of Fear of Democrats?
Jon Stewart tonight played clips of various "experts" on Fox declaring that the main culprit behind our sinking financial picture and the sell-offs on Wall Street is fear of a Democratic victory in November. Stewart's comment: "How bad do the Democrats have to be to pre-fuck the economy?"

He also played statements by numerous pundits hailing Fred Thompson's chances last summer, closing with Bill Kristol calling him truly "formidable." Stewart: "Oh, Bill Kristol, aren't you ever right?" The idea of Fred Thompson as candidate put him way up there in the polls but the reality made the poll numbers plunge. Ergo, now that he is out again, he may rise again and yet become the nominee, Stewart argues. Lending credence to that: a *National Review* article today pointing out that a pro-Thompson uncommitted slate carried the Louisiana caucuses yesterday after he dropped out. The Fredmentum has started!

January 24

Hillary and the 'Hit Job'
An Associated Press report: "Hillary Rodham Clinton, defending her husband's increasingly vocal role in her presidential effort, sidestepped questions about whether Bill Clinton's suggestion that Barack Obama had put a 'hit job' on him was language befitting a former president. 'We're in a very heated campaign, and people are coming out and saying all kinds of things,' Hillary Clinton said in an interview Wednesday." *People*? Or one Big Dog?

And, here is a preview of *Time*'s cover coming tomorrow. Jay Carney writes, "Now having won two important early contests, McCain finds himself burdened with the front-runner label for the second time in a month, the third time in the past year and the fourth time since the 2000 primaries ... Up to this point in McCain's career as a presidential candidate, becoming the man to beat has meant, inexorably, that he was about to be beaten ... If McCain loses Florida, and the nomination, it will be because Republicans couldn't overcome their doubts about him—and because McCain wasn't willing to make it easy for them."

McCain says, referring to potential Democratic presidential nominees, "I am confident we'd have a respectful debate with any of the three ... Why not? I've worked with them all. They're all patriots." Ken Duberstein, a former chief of staff for Ronald Reagan, tells *Time*, "McCain has his flaws, but everyone is starting to recognize that he's the most electable Republican out there."

GOP Debate Goes to War

One high point so far comes when Tim Russert asks if the candidates still back the war going on endlessly despite polls showing that at least 60% of Americans think it was a bad idea in the first place and we ought to get out. Of course, they all say, screw the polls. Huckabee actually says that the fact we didn't find WMD "doesn't mean they weren't there." Romney, ignoring the 60% problem, defiantly declares that the Democratic nominee will really be in trouble when he or she has to tangle with the Republican nominee on this!

At the close of a no-fireworks debate – with barely a jab thrown by anyone – most of the MSNBC analysts called it for Romney, simply because he was able to pretty much deliver his stump speech without having to endure attacks, which generally make him "flinch" and "look terrible," as one put it.

January 26

Caroline Sweet on Obama

The title for Caroline Kennedy's pro-Obama pitch tomorrow is startling: "A President Like My Father." It concludes: "I have never had a president who inspired me the way people tell me that my father inspired them. But for the first time, I believe I have found the man who could be that president — not just for me, but for a new generation of Americans."

Meanwhile, on the *Times*' op-ed page today, Garry Wills, the fine author and historian, comes out against a Clinton "duo" presidency. Among other things, he points out that a somewhat similar arrangement – Bush/Cheney – hasn't worked out so well. After looking at constitutional issues he concludes: "We have seen in this campaign how former President Clinton rushes to the defense of presidential candidate Clinton. Will that pattern of protection be continued into the new presidency, with not only his defending her but also her defending whatever he might do in his energetic way while she's in office? It seems likely. And at a time when we should be trying to return to the single-executive system the Constitution prescribes, it does not seem to be a good idea to put another co-president in the White House."

Colbert King in his op-ed at *The Washington Post* today also lays into the couple he calls "Billary," and wonders if they would have his and hers desks in the Oval Office.

January 27

In South Carolina, It's Obama in a Rout
Barack Obama trounced Hillary Clinton in South Carolina by a surprising 2-1 margin, sending the pollsters and pundits also down to defeat. John Edwards took third. Contrary to predictions Obama took about 1 in 4 votes of whites, and a majority from those under 30. Exit polls were unclear on how much, if any, Bill Clinton's very active campaigning helped push the Obama surge.

Chris Cillizza at *The Washington Post* noted, "Obama's dominance of the black vote in South Carolina is a remarkable accomplishment. But looking ahead to the Super Tuesday states, black voters will not be as dominant.... Obama will need to make gains among white voters to win as convincingly a week from Tuesday."

Obama gave another well-received (by pundits) speech, with Joe Scarborough practically levitating. Joe kept saying his Blackberry is getting clogged with positive reviews by conservatives. The speech had a bit of a harder edge to it, as well, clearly promising to keep fighting back against the Clintons.

January 28

Bill and Ted's Not So Excellent Adventure
Politico reveals that Bill Clinton made a desperate phone call to Ted Kennedy to try to forestall the latter's startling endorsement of Obama: "The announcement stunned Senate colleagues, who had expected Kennedy to remain neutral until the increasingly vitriolic nominating contest with Sen. Hillary Clinton settled out. 'This is the biggest Democratic endorsement Obama could possibly get short of Bill Clinton,' said a high-level Democrat.'"

New York Times on Monday, meanwhile, reveals, "Senator Hillary Rodham Clinton's campaign team, seeking to readjust after her lopsided defeat in South Carolina and amid a sense among many Democrats that Mr. Clinton had injected himself clumsily into the race, will try to shift the former president back into the sunnier, supportive-spouse role that he played before Mrs. Clinton's loss in the Iowa caucuses, Clinton advisers said....Yet some advisers expressed concern that Mr. Clinton might prove difficult to rein in."

A Barry Good Column
Humorist Dave Barry returns with a column about the primary in his native Florida and a review of all the candidates. He concludes: "On Tuesday, it's your turn to stand up and be counted, unless of course you're a Democrat. But whatever you are, you should get out there and vote, even if you have no earthly idea what or whom you're voting for, or why, because that's what democracy is all about. Also, Rudy, if you're reading this: My hedge needs trimming."

The Torch Is passed?
Ted Kennedy, as promised, endorsed Obama at a Washington area rally, and Caroline introduced him, with Obama in attendance – as he had returned to vote (wrongly) on the FISA bill. Obama in his own remarks talked about his father's arrival in this country and "that part of what made it possible for him to come here was an effort by the young Senator from Massachusetts at the time, John F. Kennedy, and by a grant from the Kennedy Foundation to help Kenyan students pay for travel. So it is partly because of their generosity that my father came to this country, and because he did, I stand before you

today – inspired by America's past, filled with hope for America's future, and determined to do my part in writing our next great chapter."

Ratso Rezko
Tony Rezko, the alleged "slumlord" (in Hillary Clinton's phrase) and longtime Obama backer – who also posed for a now-famous photo with Bill and Hill – was arrested early Monday near Chicago on an alleged bond violation, the *Chicago Tribune* has reported. "Investigators had in recent weeks become concerned about the movement of some of his finances," a source said. Rezko is scheduled to stand trial on corruption charges in less than a month.

Meanwhile, the California primary looms large as a key decider, and Obama has just picked up the endorsement of the *San Francisco Chronicle*. And, amusingly, he also gained the backing of novelist Toni Morrison – the woman who dubbed Bill Clinton "the first black president," which led to a question on this matter for Obama at the last debate.

On the GOP side, Florida vote looking like a beauty tomorrow – McCain and Romney are tied in most polls. Rudy may actually edge Ron Paul this time. And then as I wrote one week ago: Goodbye Rudy – Tuesday.

January 29

Precedent Obama: One Kennedy Comparison to Avoid
You can't say that the thought had not already occurred to millions, but still one has to question the tact and taste of CBS morning guy Harry Smith raising today the question of Obama getting assassinated – with Ted Kennedy, no less. Hey, why not send out a printed invitation to all the nut cases out there? According to my viewing of the video, Smith asked, "When you see that enthusiasm [for Obama] though, and when you see the generational change that seems to be taking place before our eyes, does it make you at all fearful?"

Kennedy seemed to not know what Smith was hinting at – although he did stutter a bit – and offered a bland reply about a "new generation." Smith then tried again: "I just, I think, what I was trying to say is – sometimes agents of change end up being targets, as you well know. And that was why I was asking if you were at all fearful of that." This time Kennedy, who certainly does well know, surely understood what he meant but again evaded the question, just referring to Obama as an "agent of change." Good for him. Smith also tried to get Teddy to reveal what went down in his now-famous phone conversation with Bill Clinton regarding the pending endorsement. Kennedy chuckled heartily and said, no way.

Florida Primary: McCain Wins, Rudy Will Quit
McCain wins again in Florida. NBC confirms Rudy to quit tomorrow. Romney will fight on and has the cash to do it. Joe Scarborough and Pat Buchanan had given him hope by agreeing that McCain's platform is (to paraphrase) "no jobs, let the illegals stay, and more wars." Try to run and win on that, they joked. But Chris Matthews points that McCain is "broke" and "looks tired." Can he keep up the pace?

January 30

War Is So Over, Pundits Declare
Even after all of these years of flim-flam and false predictions regarding Iraq, I still find it amusing that so many pundits have declared that the war is no longer a major issue in America, or at least in the 2008 political campaign. They seem to be quoting John Lennon – "War Is Over" – except they mean it in a very different way.

All you had to do, as if you should need any further illumination on this, was to watch Wednesday night's GOP presidential debate at the Reagan Library. All three of the major candidates not only failed to find any fault with the war, they competed to see who could promise to stay there longer and offer the toughest terms for departure. The rhetoric escalated from wanting to make sure the place was "secure" to wiping out every single "safe haven" for al-Qaeda, Hezbollah and god knows who else (Roger Clemens?) to – as Mitt Romney said – full "victory."

Mike Huckabee was asked point blank if he agreed with John McCain that we might have to stay there for 100 years and he wouldn't even reply, suggesting he thought this sound quite sensible, rather than the ravings of a mad man. One might expect a pious man of god to say, "Gosh, that would be unacceptable, think of the lives destroyed," or some such thing, or at least point out the budget-busting catastrophe in that scenario.

In any case, to listen to any of debates in the past months and then say the war is dead as a hot button issue in absurd, considering the stance on the war taken by the two Democratic frontrunners. Now, it's true Hillary Clinton came out against the war too late, and exactly what she and Barack Obama want to do about withdrawing is not precisely clear – and surely open to reality checks once in office. But while the Republicans argue about who is most against any withdrawal (or even any sort of timetable), the Democrats are full-throttle in favor of a phased pullout beginning ASAP.

So the issue is dead? It's hard to believe that some of our leading press and TV commentators could be so vapid as to say that the issue is in retreat simply because it has not been a barn-burner in debates – when the Democrats on their side, and the Republicans on there side, agree with each other (Ron Paul aside).

Even the polls that show that the economy now edges the war as the top issue in many minds do not suggest that the concern about Iraq is fading but mainly that worries about the economy (which influences just about everything in one's life) are understandably rising. And it's a false question anyway: Citizens now have absolutely no confidence that anything will be done about the war for the rest of the year. The president, and Democrats in Congress, have made that clear, even as they promise quick economic relief.

McCain Cruises – Obama Kicks Big Dog
On the heels of his Florida win, John McCain smirked and chuckled his way, rather un-presidentially, through the GOP debate tonight, and reports have him picking up Arnold Schwarzenegger's endorsement tomorrow which, in contrast to Rudy's nod, actually means something. On the other hand, the Democratic contest is about to go to Code Red, with Clinton aides livid over a hard-hitting Obama speech in Denver today.

Obama argued that the Democratic race is a contest of "the past versus the future," and warned against "nominating a candidate who will unite the other party against us," rather than "choosing one who can unite this country around a movement for change." But maybe the blast that set off the alarms is: He mocked the Big Dog himself. "I know it is tempting, after another presidency by a man named George Bush, to simply turn back the clock, and to build a bridge back to the 20th century," Obama said, paraphrasing an old slogan of Bill Clinton. Let's see if his wife can keep him off the campaign trail after that.

On *The Daily Show* tonight, Peggy Noonan really acted stumped by Rudy's fall – she can find "no discernible" reason for it and she hopes "books will be written about it" so we can all figure it out. Jon Stewart, like nearly everyone else in the country, doesn't need to wait for that. Voters, he said, simply decided: "That guy – I don't like him."

The Edwards Exit Speech
Back in New Orleans on a flood-ravaged street, he says it is "time to step aside" and let history be made by one of the two top candidates, with a unified party behind them, that is, he says, if they are willing to take tough stands. Pundits seem divided on whether his exit will most help Obama (uniting the anti-Clinton vote) or Hillary (with women flocking to her plus maybe some others not ready for a black president).

Edwards reveals that he has talked to Obama and Clinton and that they will make ending poverty and seeking economic equality a central part of their campaigns – and their presidency. He waves goodbye, and goes off with U2's "Walk On" ringing out. Atrios at his Eschaton blog notes wryly: "Maybe if Edwards had announced his exit from the race every week he would have gotten more media coverage." Over at Talking Points memo, Edwards' top guy, Joe Trippi (the former Howard Dean honcho) is claiming that people with Obama and Hillary are "banging down the doors" seeking an endorsement.

A 'Hill' of a Victory
Amusing Dana Milbank column in the *Washington Post* today on the Clinton "win" in Florida: "Cheering supporters? Check. Election returns on the projection screen? Check. Andrea Mitchell and Candy Crowley doing stand-ups? Check and check. In fact, the only piece missing from Hillary Clinton's Florida victory party here Tuesday night was a victory.... But in a political stunt worthy of the late Evel Knievel, the Clinton campaign decided to put on an ersatz victory party that, it hoped, would erase memories of Obama's actual victory Saturday night in South Carolina's Democratic primary. 'Thank you, Florida Democrats!' Clinton shouted to the cheering throng. 'I am thrilled to have this vote of confidence.'

"It was a perfect reproduction of an actual victory speech, delivered at a perfectly ersatz celebration at a perfectly pretend location: a faux Italianate palace with lion sculptures, indoor fountains and a commanding view of Interstate 595."

January 31

The Debate: Few Sparks, Clinton and Obama Nearly Hug
Yet another debate ended tonight with the usual "offbeat" final question slot. The two were asked if they would form a "dream ticket." They both had some fun with it and didn't rule it out. But then an amazing moment at end, as Obama gallantly pulled back her chair as Hillary got to her feet. Then they whispered to each other and nearly embraced. It was almost sexy.

Earlier, some fun shots of celebs in audience: Rob Reiner, Diane Keaton, Pierce Brosnan, Jason Alexander, "Ugly Betty," more. Hillary got the biggest applause of night saying, "We needed a Clinton to clean up the mess made by the first Bush and we need another Clinton to do the same after the second Bush," or words to that effect.

The debate opened with the two candidates coming out billed as the first black and woman to ever make the "finals." And it was striking to see the two of them, and two only, up there. CNN reported earlier that tickets were going for upwards of $1,000.

FEBRUARY 2008

February 1

Annie razed McCain

We know the far right is upset with McCain as nominee but this is really going too far: Ann Coulter asserted on Fox News that if he gets the nomination she would not only "vote for" Hillary, she would "campaign for her if it's McCain." She told Sean Hannity last night that Clinton "is more conservative than he is" and added that in that scenario "she will be our girl." As president, Hillary would be "stronger in the war on terrorism" and would not pull the troops out of Iraq – she jumped to her feet at the State of Union speech when Bush said the surge was working.

Hannity countered: "McCain did support the war." She pointed out: "So did Hillary."

Alan Colmes, enjoying it all immensely, said Hillary would likely say "no" to the campaign offer. But Coulter plunged ahead: "Hillary is absolutely more conservative" and moreover "she lies less than John McCain. And she's smarter than John McCain so when she lies she knows it....John McCain is not only bad for Republicans he is also bad for the country." Hannity clearly doesn't fully agree, but like Coulter hates his anti-torture stance.

Adventures in Punditry

David Brooks in *The New York Times* offers friendly advice to John McCain on how to "transition" to frontrunner and beat Obama in the fall. McCain's problem is that he used to be "the happy warrior" but now that is Obama.

Why no longer so happy? What does he have to overcome? Dig this Brooks explanation: "McCain seems to be burdened by the emotional cost of the war in Iraq, by the gravity of young people dying. But F.D.R. was a happy wartime campaigner and to compete with the Democrats in the fall, McCain will have to reconnect with the spirit of this moment. The country, the über-pollster Peter Hart notes, is not in a mood for irritation and anger. It's thirsty for uplift, progress and hope." Right, McCain is so emotionally "burdened" by kids dying that he wants us to fight on to "victory" – and stay there for 100 years if need be.

February 2

Hillary Gaining in Polls – Obama Too Nice?
Conventional wisdom (including my own, such as it is) had Obama slightly "winning" the latest debate, mainly because of the Iraq questions. And certainly his crowds have gotten even bigger and wilder since. But the latest Rasmussen and Gallup polls show that her lead nationally has actually widened since then from about 4 points to about 8 points. Could just be a blip, but analysts such as Markos at DailyKos feel that Obama actually made a mistake in being so cordial at the debate – it was good for the party but bad for him, since he is the one who had to make up ground and needed to hit harder. In this view, he allowed people moving toward him to feel okay again sticking with her. Well, we will see soon.

You've probably seen Charlie Cook of the *Cook Report* quoted a hundred times as a leading political campaign expert/pundit. The *L.A. Times* helpfully looks back today at Cook telling another paper last year that John McCain's campaign was "effectively over. The physicians have left the hospital room, and it's the executors of the estate that are taking over." In other news, we now know that Rudy spent $50 million to gain one delegate. At that pace it would have cost him $60 billion to get enough delegates to win the GOP nod. Even Romney doesn't have that kind of money.

February 4

We Watch the Polls So You Don't Have To
For the first time, a major poll has put Obama ahead of Clinton nationally. Today's CNN survey finds him with a 49% to 46% lead. There's some chance that he is picking up the bulk of former Edwards supporters. Other polls show a dead heat or a Clinton lead. McCain, meanwhile, remains far ahead nearly everywhere, though Romney is doing well in California.

Gossip King/Queen Perez Hilton has endorsed Hillary, saying, "We watched the debates and Clinton just won us over. Barack is great. But Hillary is the better leader, for us." On a somewhat weightier note, as it were, Jack Nicholson is making "robo-calls" for Clinton in California today. In other celebrity news, John Mellencamp has asked John McCain to stop using any of his songs at campaign rallies. George Clooney has reiterated his support for Obama, while Michael Moore says he is still on the fence (it would have to be a hell of a sturdy fence).

<u>February 6</u>

'Super Tuesday': There's Got To Be a Morning After
The big day – the Super day – finally arrived, and we're not talking about the Super Bowl. In more than 20 states, citizens trooped to the polls.

At least one state, New Mexico, was still undecided on the Democratic side, but finally this morning the dust was starting to settle. Salon's Walter Shapiro might have put it best: "Never before in the long history of presidential politics have so many voters in so many states gone to the polls and their caucus sites on the same day – and decided so little. Instead of wrapping things up, the delegate contests in 24 states gave certainty a bad rap."

A favorite post though comes from Andrew Malcolm at his *Los Angeles Times* blog: "Officials in Maryland and Virginia reported hundreds showing up ready to vote, although their primaries are a week away. Apparently the media coverage and citizen interest in the unfolding campaigns had created such interest the would-be voters forgot to check their local dates....Election officials in San Antonio reported more than 1,000 calls about today's Texas primary, which wasn't today but is set for March 4."

The New York Times features at the top right of its home page the all-important "delegate count" from AP, which stands at Clinton 845 and Obama 765. John McCain is far ahead with 613, Romney has 269 and Huckabee 190. John Harwood offers a video analysis of the results, and Adam Nagourney writes: "The Republican and Democratic presidential contests began diverging Tuesday, leaving the Democrats facing a long and potentially divisive nomination battle and the Republicans closer to an opportunity to put aside deep internal divisions and rally around a nominee."

A *Times* editorial warns: "While it is still too soon to tell which candidates will gain either party's nomination, the eventual winners will need to work hard to bridge the divisions that plague both sides."

Maureen Dowd in her column: "Tuesday's voting showed only that the voters, like moviegoers, don't want a pat ending. Even though Hillary reasserted her strength, corraling New York, California and Kennedy country Massachusetts, she and Obama will battle on in chiaroscuro. Her argument to the Democratic base has gone from a subtext of 'You owe me,' or more precisely, 'Bill owes me and you owe him,' to a subtext of 'Obambi will fold at the first punch from the right.'"

At *The Washington Post*, Dan Balz and Anne E. Kornblut look at the battle for the Dems: "The results ensured that the fierce contest for delegates will continue into critical primaries in Texas and Ohio on March 4, and possibly beyond, in what has become the party's most competitive race in at least a quarter of a century." Howard Kurtz in his media review hit the TV networks for – overall – overplaying the early returns, rooting against Hillary, and/or putting too much focus on Huckabee.

The *Post*'s editorial tweaked the "Limbaugh" factor: "Mr. McCain's emergence as the dominant candidate in the Republican field has generated an outcry from some of the party's conservative stalwarts. Rush Limbaugh says a McCain nomination would destroy the Republican Party. We think Mr. McCain, with his moderate views on immigration, his realism about global warming and his willingness to speak out on issues such as torture, would save the party from some of its worst and most self-destructive instincts. Still, Mr. Huckabee's unexpected string of victories underscored the degree to which self-described conservatives remain wary of the Arizona senator."

February 7

Secret Obama Memo Suggests True Deadlock
NBC's political unit is calling it "the political junkie scoop of the post-Feb. 5 news cycle." Apparently an internal Obama team memo was mistakenly attached to a sheet released to Bloomberg News, which now reveals that the Obama managers expect him to sweep all of the primaries in the next few weeks – but then lose to Clinton in the big states of Texas, Ohio and Pennsylvania, which would even out the delegates. NBC thinks this is based on Obama expecting to do well in more "white wine" states while Hillary holds on to more "blue-collar" and Hispanic support. "So it's a very realistic

assessment," NBC concludes. Others have suggested that Obama, with the momentum of a long run of February wins, will then carry at least Ohio and Pennsylvania, possibly wrapping things up...

February 8

Clintons vs. MSNBC – as Shuster Suspended
The Clinton camp is hopping mad over comments MSNBC's David Shuster made last night on Tucker Carlson's show about Chelsea Clinton. He said that she was being widely used by her mother on the campaign trail, even making phone calls, but refuses to talk to the press, and concluded (after also praising her) with a reference to her being "pimped out" for the campaign. NBC said Shuster has apologized – then suspended him.

Clinton spokesman Howard Wolfson is now threatening to pull out of any MSNBC debates, citing other infractions (Chris Matthews) there – and they have the big one in Ohio coming up. Meanwhile, David Brock over at Media Matters has hit today a "pattern" of sexist quips at MSNBC (Matthews in the lead).

February 9

'NYT' Clears Obama of Massive Drug Use – Puts It On Front Page
Wonder what others make of today's front-pager in the *Times* (complete with vintage Obama in Afro photo) which is reminiscent of that infamous *Washington Post* front-pager which focused so prominently on the "Muslim rumors" – with editors later explaining that actually they were trying to merely clear them up. "Friends Say Drugs Played Only Bit Part for Obama," the headline reads today.

The new *Times* story is at least based on fact – Obama has admitted he dabbled in marijuana and cocaine as a young man – but the slant of the story is that his old friends believe that he was the most casual of users, so no big deal. Then why put it on the front page, on the morning of important primaries and caucuses no less? The reporter, Serge Kovaleski, early on even muses that something seems to be off – either Obama's friends' memories are fuzzy or Obama "added some writerly touches in his memoir to make the challenges he overcame seem more dramatic."

Much of the story, in fact, looks at other aspects of his teen and college years in Hawaii and at Occidental, such as what a great dorm room debater he was and how he became involved in activist concerns. The closing quotes a college friend: "I would never say that he was a druggie, and there were plenty there. He was too cool for all that." Then why put it on front page with the drug headline?

February 10

Barack Up Another Win
Obama continued his roll – in this case, a lobster roll? – with another landslide in Maine caucus and at least 15 of 24 delegates snatched. And that was just the beginning of his haul elsewhere. Clinton has now replaced her campaign manager. Meanwhile, Obama won a spoken word Grammy tonight – beating Bill Clinton. The *Baltimore Sun* endorsed Obama. John Edwards is meeting with both Clinton and Obama and may endorse one of them soon. The fun continues.

And CBS News reports tonight: "In the delegate chase, Obama has pulled ahead of Clinton, even when the support of uncommitted super delegates is figured in. According to CBS News estimates, Obama holds a razor-thin lead with 1,134 delegates overall to 1,131 for Clinton." Good thing he carried the Virgin Islands, or he would be down by one....

Obama, in his speech in Virginia following his sweep of all the primary/caucus contests today, produces laughs when he says that, thank goodness, "my cousin, Dick Cheney, will not be on the ballot this November." Then, seemingly ad-libbing, he adds, "that's embarrassing. When people look at their genealogical charts they like to find someone cool."

February 12

Race to the Finish
Liberal blogs and others, such as Mark Halperin's 'The Page," are highlighting a recent offhand comment by Pennsylvania Governor Ed Rendell to the *Pittsburgh Post-Gazette* editorial board. Rendell has long been a big Democratic party boss and Clinton backer. Anyway, he said, referring to the key Pennsylvania primary coming up, "You've got conservative whites here, and I think there

are some whites who are probably not ready to vote for an African-American candidate."

He allowed that this was a relatively small number, but the black columnist at the paper, Tony Norman, who reported it, and now others, have expressed shock and disapproval. As I have pointed out for awhile, it amazes me that so many Obama backers, and media, seem to act like racism ended in the U.S. at some point in the recent past. They have been carried away by Obama's strong showing so far – while ignoring the evidence that, indeed, some whites still are voting against him on the basis of race. I'm not saying that race is the major factor in this campaign but the extent that it is pooh-poohed surprises me.

Rendell never said it was a large number – but a number. Obama himself said in Virginia this week, "Sure, there are some people who will not vote for me because I'm black and there are some people who will vote for me because I am black."

Sometimes I even wonder if one reason so many conservative pundits, such as Bill Kristol, are saying so many nice things about Obama is that secret GOP polling shows that Obama will actually pose a weaker threat in November (for this reason) than Hillary. But if the "new voters" and indies keep flocking to Obama (and actually, for a change, bother to show up at the polls in November) it will indeed be easy for him vs. McCain.

How Sweep It Is for Obama

Instant reaction tonight to big primary wins from Adam Nagourney in *The New York Times*: "The lopsided nature of Senator Barack Obama's parade of victories on Tuesday gives him an opening to make the case that Democratic voters have broken in his favor and that the party should coalesce around his candidacy."

More importantly, the AP delegate count now shows Obama firmly in the lead (even counting super-delegates) for the first time in the campaign. Andrea Mitchell, meanwhile, got off a good line, after revealing that Obama had grabbed a lot of white male voters from Clinton tonight: "This prove white men CAN jump."

Linda Caputo, the former Hillary press secretary, on CNN still makes the outrageous claim that she really "won" Michigan and Florida in a true fight. Wolf Blitzer four times pushes back that they were not real contests – Obama wasn't even on the ballot in Michigan – but she holds firm. This type of arrogance may cost Clinton votes in long run. Asked why Obama keeps sweeping caucus states, she replies, "He used to be a community organizer." Yeah, that's the ticket.

February 13

Is Obama Too Wimpy to Take On McCain?
Joseph Wilson, the former ambassador and husband of outed CIA employee Valerie Plame, lays into Obama and backs Clinton in a newspaper op-ed now also up at Huff Post. In doing so he recalls an episode I had forgotten, though you may disagree with his conclusion: "But will Mr. Obama fight? His brief time on the national scene gives little comfort. Consider a February 2006 exchange of letters with Mr. McCain on the subject of ethics reform.

"The wrathful Mr. McCain accused Mr. Obama of being 'disingenuous,' to which Mr. Obama meekly replied, 'The fact that you have now questioned my sincerity and my desire to put aside politics for the public interest is regrettable but does not in any way diminish my deep respect for you.' Then one of McCain's aides said of Obama, 'Obama wouldn't know the difference between an RPG and a bong.'

"Mr. McCain was insultingly dismissive but successful in intimidating his inexperienced colleague. Thus, in his one face-to-face encounter with Mr. McCain, Mr. Obama failed to stand his ground. What gives us confidence Mr. Obama will be stronger the next time he faces Mr. McCain, a seasoned political fighter with extensive national security credentials?"

February 14

Sweet Home, Barack Obama
Slate.com had some fun with Obama today. You remember "Bushifying." Now Slate has launched its "Obamaficator," a word generator which "Obamifies" words and gives definitions. There's "Obamaton" and dozens more. Here are a few samples:

– Barackismo: A strong or exaggerated sense of Obamliness
– Obamatose: in a deep slumber, dreaming of Obama

- Barackcupied: fixed on Barack Obama
- Obambination: the union of warring parties brought together by Obama
- Obamaly: A deviation from deep, unwavering love for Barack Obama
- Obamaraderie: Goodwill and lighthearted rapport at a campaign rally

February 19

Cheeseheads for Obama
Networks have called Wisconsin for Obama – he leads 58% to 41% with 99% of vote in – another landslide. Heavy independent vote once again proved the difference, with exit polls showing he barely carried Democrats. Big gender gap: He won white males by 2-1 while she easily carried white women.

The worst news for Clinton: After tonight Obama might lead by 150 in elected delegates. It now looks like, at best, she will only make slight gains today in Texas and Ohio – meaning that while the super-delegates could save her, they won't, due to popular pressure. NBC's Chuck Todd projects she would have to win over 60% of delegates in remaining races to gain the edge, which is virtually impossible.

February 20

Cindy McCain: A 'Formidable' Liability?
McCain won last night to wrap things up, blasted Obama, cited his lack of experience in foreign affairs, and said, "Thank you, Wisconsin, for bringing us to the point when even a superstitious naval aviator can claim with confidence and humility that I will be our party's nominee for President." Cindy McCain, the candidate's wife, generally satisfied to stand behind him silently, suddenly is in the headlines after slapping down Michelle Obama for her remark about not having so much pride in America until now – or something like that.

This caused Howard Fineman and Norah O'Donnell in MSNBC to rhapsodize last night about how this "formidable" (they agreed) woman will now be a tremendous asset to McCain. True? Well, for one thing, there is the matter of McCain cheating on his crippled first wife to fool around with wealthy Cindy, many years his junior. And he sure won't be able to go after Obama for his youthful drug use.

Here is an excerpt from a March 3, 2003, article in *The New York Times* by Melinda Henneberger: "[I]f the public had heard of her at all, it was probably as a result of the 1994 headlines about a federal investigation into her theft of painkillers from a medical charity she ran. Or because of the Keating Five savings and loan scandal a few years earlier, which she was drawn into as well. Today, drug-free since 1993, she looks back on that time in their lives as a moment that 'nearly destroyed both of us.'"....

"And she went through quite a bit. In 1991, her husband was mildly rebuked by the Senate Ethics Committee for exercising poor judgment in meeting with federal regulators who were investigating Charles Keating Jr., the owner of a failing savings and loan who was also a friend and donor. Mrs. McCain was involved in the matter because she had helped keep her husband's books and could not find receipts showing that they had reimbursed Mr. Keating for flying on his corporate jet to his vacation home in the Bahamas.

"It was under pressure of that scandal, and after back surgery, that she became addicted. And though her drug problem went on for a couple of years, her husband never noticed.

"In the end, it was Mrs. McCain's parents who became worried by her behavior and confronted her. More than a year later, when federal authorities began investigating reports that she had stolen drugs from the charity, the senator finally learned of his wife's addiction – just before her troubles, too, hit the front page."

'NY Times' Finally Unleashes Its McCain/Lobbyist Bombshell
It's been up on the *Times* site and all over MSNBC, if you haven't caught up with it yet. I had forgotten about the tale myself – back around Christmas that brief flap over a rumored (via Drudge) story that the paper had linking McCain, perhaps romantically, to a female lobbyist much younger than himself. It was then reported that McCain and the unnamed woman had hired fixer Bob Bennett to strong arm the *Times*. Whatever went down, the story never ran. Until tonight.

UPDATE: McCain campaign calls story a "hit and run smear campaign" – but while it says he has not violated the ethics of his job it does not specifically deny any romantic link....Also, it is amazing to see them claim, considering his steep involvement in the Keating scandal, that he has "never done favors for special interests or lobbyists." Will be interesting to see how Rush Limbaugh *et al* play this tomorrow: Who do they hate more, McCain or the *NYT*?

February 21

McCain denies 'NYT' claims, Weaver Confirms One Part
At a 9 a.m, presser today, with Cindy at his side in Toledo, John McCain refuted the *Times* story and said he was "disappointed" by it. He claimed that no one had come to him and tried to steer him away from the lobbyist, Vicki Iseman. He called her just a friend. "I intend to move on," McCain said. I bet he does.

Next move: *New York Times*. McCain's denial today that anyone came to him to warn him off the woman does not square with the *Times*' sources – so someone is telling a big lie.

Marc Ambinder at TheAtlantic.com reports an email from McCain associate Weaver who was quoted in *Times* story: "*The New York Times* knew about my meeting with Ms. Iseman and asked me about it and why it occurred. I informed the *Times*, in a written reply, that Ms. Iseman's comments about having strong ties to John's committee staff, personal staff and to him I felt were harmful and not true. And so I informed her and asked her to stop and desist. The moment I answered the inquiry from the *New York Times* I sent that answer also to Mark, Steve and Charlie. All of this happened in December. I've wanted John McCain to be president since I first approached him in 1997. I do so today. I love John McCain and I believe the country badly needs him."

Dough! – McCain Making Hay Off 'NYT' attack
In the proud tradition of candidates in both parties making the most (money) out of allegedly unfair attacks, both the McCain campaign and the RNC already have letters out fundraising around *The New York Times* blast.

In the wake of denials by McCain of certain claims, the paper's Executive Editor Bill Keller released this statement today: "On the substance, we think the story speaks for itself. On the timing, our policy is, we publish stories when they are ready. 'Ready' means the facts have been nailed down to our satisfaction, the subjects have all been given a full and fair chance to respond, and the reporting has been written up with all the proper context and caveats.

"This story was no exception. It was a long time in the works. It reached my desk late Tuesday afternoon. After a final edit and a routine check by our lawyers, we published it." Defenders of McCain have charged that the *Times* held the story and only released it once he had the GOP nod wrapped up. A McCain aide has claimed that the paper moved after it learned that the *New Republic* was about to release a story asserting that the paper was debating what to do with the story.

That Gabriel Sherman piece is now up at the *New Republic* site. He concludes: "The publication of the article capped three months of intense internal deliberations at the *Times* over whether to publish the negative piece and its most explosive charge about the affair. It pitted the reporters investigating the story, who believed they had nailed it, against executive editor Bill Keller, who believed they hadn't. It likely cost the paper one investigative reporter, who decided to leave in frustration. And the *Times* ended up publishing a piece in which the institutional tensions about just what the story should be are palpable."

February 25

Lowest Blow Yet in Campaign?
Who knows, but Drudge is featuring at top of his page (no siren) a photo of Obama in Muslim dress reportedly circulated by Clinton staffers with a week to go in the race. The picture comes from an official visit to Somalia in 2006, and is about as incriminating as George Bush holding hands with Saudi princes on his visits. Will Obama refer to "the silly season" again?

While Obama has won most primaries and is even doing okay in Texas (about a tie) and Ohio (just trailing by a bit), he has never surged far ahead in the national polls. Until now. For some reason – maybe Hillary saying she was so proud just to be sitting next to him at the last debate? – Obama has grabbed a startling 54%-38% lead in the *NYT/CBS* poll released tonight, and a Gallup poll (where Hillary led last week) has him up by 12%.

February 26

Bill Maher's Favorite Rightwinger Makes A Fool of Himself
It's always been hard to figure out what each sees in the other, but for some reason Bill Maher keeps inviting Rep. Jack Kingston of Georgia on his show and Kingston keeps coming back despite feigning outrage whenever Bill drops an "F-bomb." In his most recent appearance last week he repeated the myth about Obama refusing to put his hand over his heart and pledge to the flag in some "infamous" photo.

Last night he appeared on MSNBC with Dan Abrams and said that anyone who doesn't wear a flag pin all the time — namely Obama – should be considered unpatriotic. Abrams' eyes lit up as he noticed the Kingston was not wearing one either!

MARCH 2008

March 2

Live from New York, It's....Hillary Clinton?
Yes, she surprised the press by suddenly showing up in the Big Apple for *SNL* tonight. She shared billing with Wilco – who famously back Obama. They even have Obama stickers on their instrument cases....The Clinton appearance was somewhat labored, following yet another re-enactment of a debate with Obama. Hillary, live, had her trademark laugh mocked by Amy Poehler, and then she offered the usual, "Live from New York, it's etc." As the saying goes: might help, couldn't hurt.

Charges that the press has practically handed the Democratic nod to Obama on a platter by being unfair to Hillary have only grown this weekend, with the candidate herself re-enforcing the notion with that surprise visit to *SNL* – which had done as much to publicize the idea as anyone. But the Clintonistas are not laughing.

Anyway: I'm not convinced there is a great deal to the charge, at least if you look at the arc of the entire campaign over a few months. Someone can be "favored" by the media in a certain week, which may reverse the previous month (after complaints from the first victim), and so on. Until recent weeks, Clinton was widely declared the winner of one debate after another, with Obama turning in weaker showings. Was this "bias" or recognizing reality? Now it's said that he has improved greatly in the debates – can anyone really argue with this? If anything, the press has been pretty gentle in describing the extent of the thrashing Clinton received in most of the 11 straight primary/caucus defeats.

It would be odd if the media really have consciously bent over backward for Obama. They normally only do that for candidates who suck up to them – does the name John McCain ring a bell? Obama does not hang out with the press boys and girls which earns him no points in their book – though

I suppose it also cuts down on gaffes (which means he gets less "gotcha" coverage). Many in the media have dreamed about a "brokered convention" for decades – one leading pundit admitted as much on Olbermann's show recently – and so if anything they should have been trashing Obama the past month.

In any case, the critical media moment will come after Tuesday – if Hillary does well in Texas and Ohio. I suspect if that happens the media will happily portray her as The Comeback Kid 2008, if only to have something to cover through August. And already, the weekly Project for Excellence in Journalism survey reveals that coverage of Obama clearly turned more critical in recent days....

March 3

Dittoheads for Clinton
Jon Stewart was not sharp and she looked weary, though with a constant smile. Kicked off promisingly with Jon saying that the campaign was really about "judgment" – so what the hell was she doing on primary eve talking to him? She agreed it was "pathetic." But not much humor or any new insights followed. One really would have liked a little Colbertian touch there....

Final polls really do give her a good chance to win both Ohio and Texas. But horrible weather in the former, and a partial caucus system in the latter, complicates matters, as if they weren't complicated enough already. Enough already! One more twist: Rush Limbaugh is urging his dittoheads to vote for Hillary in the open Texas primary, which will certainly be the first and only time any of them pull the lever for her. With no real GOP race a lot could do that. If Obama loses in a close one will he blame it on that bum Rush?

March 4

A Hill of a Challenge
With polls closed everywhere at 9 p.m. – except for a few troubled places in Ohio (naturally) – John McCain was declared the winner of the Republican nomination, having won everywhere and the new delegates putting him over the top. He will receive President Bush's nod at the White House tomorrow.

On the Democratic side, Obama took Vermont but the other three races – in Texas, Ohio and Rhode Island – all went Clinton.

Even in the afterglow of a truly super Tuesday, the chief Clinton backers today are not laying out a plausible scenario for how they actually get enough delegates to win, except the ones (Terry McAuliffe and Ed Rendell) introducing the possibility of a re-vote in Michigan and Florida. If Hillary wins big there, then she has a shot, but the Clinton managers have resisted the idea, claiming, quite obnoxiously, that they already won in those states – even though they were "illegal" primaries from the party's view and Obama wasn't even on the ballot in Michigan.

Now Obama is on the spot. He can claim that Clinton had agreed to party rules, now wants to break them, so tough luck. But the party can shift course itself and say it's okay if the two states want to spend the money to vote again. Then Obama, if he still resists, looks like he has dissed the voters in those states, who would then take it out on him – running up the big margin she needs to win. Could happen. He may have to agree to a vote and a fair fight – which would make this a whole new ballgame, with The New Math suddenly not so one-sided in his favor.

Christopher Hitchens on MSNBC's "Morning Joe" made references to vampires and Obama's failure to "put a stake" through the Clinton candidacy – while she made the rounds of six top morning TV shows. Welcome to the funhouse for the next seven weeks.

Brian Williams on MSNBC made a couple of points about Hillary's comeback: a) the Clinton negative ads hurt Obama and he unwisely tried to refute her "red telephone" with a similar-looking one – people thought they were watching the anti-Obama ad b) SNL skit and aftermath was a factor indeed. Tina Fey new political kingmaker?

One disturbing nugget out of Ohio in MSNBC's exit polls. They asked if race played a role in their vote. Fully 1 in 5 said yes – and Clinton carried this crowd 57% to 43%.

James Fallows has a terrific post at his *Atlantic* blog estimating how far Hillary will go in scorching Obama (and helping McCain). Now Obama hints he will go just as negative.

March 6

No Stopping This Gal
Maybe Hillary should run as McCain's VP? That would solve the Democrats' problem, and give Rush Limbaugh a fit, besides. Here is Clinton today:

"I think that since we now know Sen. (John) McCain will be the nominee for the Republican Party, national security will be front and center in this election. We all know that. And I think it's imperative that each of us be able to demonstrate we can cross the commander-in-chief threshold," the New York senator told reporters crowded into an infant's bedroom-sized hotel conference room in Washington. "I believe that I've done that. Certainly, Sen. McCain has done that and you'll have to ask Sen. Obama with respect to his candidacy," she said.

Calling McCain, the presumptive GOP nominee a good friend and a "distinguished man with a great history of service to our country," Clinton said, "Both of us will be on that stage having crossed that threshold. That is a critical criterion for the next Democratic nominee to deal with."

March 7

Power Out: Interview Brings Down Top Obama Adviser
An off-the-cuff remark to the Scottish paper, *The Scotsman*, earlier this week has led to the surprising and swift exit of one of Barack Obama's top advisers today, Pulitzer Prize-winning author Samantha Power. The Harvard professor, who has been on leave this year to serve as a chief foreign affairs aide to Obama, has been sometimes called "his Condi."

Power had referred to Sen. Hillary Clinton, Obama's rival in the race for the White House, as a "monster," quickly called that "off-the-record," but too late, as the reporter insisted it was an on-the-record chat. She had told *The Scotsman*, after Obama's losses in primaries on Tuesday, that Clinton was stopping at nothing to try to win. "She is a monster, too – that is off the record – she is stooping to anything," Power said, trying to withdraw her remark.

She was in the United Kingdom to promote her new book on Sergio Vieira de Mello, the United Nations representative who died in a Baghdad bomb attack.

Today, the Clinton team called for Power's ouster. Power had apologized but that did not quell the uproar. Now she has resigned, stating: "With deep regret, I am resigning from my role as an advisor the Obama campaign effective today. Last Monday, I made inexcusable remarks that are at marked variance from my oft-stated admiration for Senator Clinton and from the spirit, tenor, and purpose of the Obama campaign. And I extend my deepest apologies to Senator Clinton, Senator Obama, and the remarkable team I have worked with over these long 14 months."

March 8

Fears About 'White Flight'
An AP story, picking up on some poll results, hints that a "white flight" from Obama may have already taken place in Ohio: "Some analysts think it's possible Obama's heavy black support is nudging some working-class white Democrats into Clinton's camp. If true, it could be an important factor in a contest that remains remarkably tight after a year of campaigning...

"Ronald Walters, a University of Maryland political scientist who tracks racial trends and is writing a book on Obama, thinks Obama's strong support from blacks made it easier for some whites in Ohio and Texas to vote for Clinton. 'There's some of that,' Walters said in an interview. He pointed to exit polls from Ohio, where 62 percent of all whites lack college degrees and many are anxious about their jobs in a weak economy. 'This is a racially sensitive group,' he said, referring specifically to whites who earn less than $50,000 a year and did not attend college. 'They are the quintessential Reagan Democrats,' he said."

March 9

Clarence Thomas for....Vice President?
I'm afraid I awoke a couple of commuters, and maybe caused someone else to spill his coffee, on the train to New York City this morning when I burst out in laughter reading the conclusion of the column by ever-reliable jokester Bill Kristol in *The New York Times*. He had already mentioned Joe Lieberman as a possible running mate for John McCain, and then moved on to the expected Gen. Petraeus and somewhat less predictable Gen. Odierno, the "heroes" of the surge and the coming "victory" in Iraq. But he concluded with a name I'd never seen floated before: U.S. Supreme Court Justice Clarence Thomas.

Here's the passage: "He could persuade the most impressive conservative in American public life, Clarence Thomas, to join the ticket." This, presumably, would be a plus, even a coup, in Kristolworld.

Well, we had a "Silent Cal" (Coolidge) as president so why not a "Silence Clarence" as Veep? As you may be aware, Thomas has shattered all high court records for lack of speaking or questioning as cases are brought before him. It's actually quite disturbing.

NPR reported two weeks ago, "It's been more than two years since Supreme Court Justice Clarence Thomas asked a question during arguments. The other eight justices regularly pepper attorneys with questions." More than 140 cases had come and gone without Thomas speaking. So the idea of a vice presidential debate between Thomas and a Democrat can only make you guffaw – and the networks worry about dead air. Imagine a Biden vs. Thomas debate! I would pay to watch that one.

Only a Kristol could conjure Thomas as a viable candidate for high office, or practically anything else. It's more like *The Onion* than *The Times*.

March 11

Gerry and the Pacemaker
On a day Barack Obama scored another primary win (in Mississippi), Geraldine Ferraro somehow has made worse her original comments to the fairly obscure *Daily Breeze* paper in California with an update today. You'll remember that she had said, "If Obama was a white man, he would not be in this position. And if he was a woman (of any color), he would not be in this position. He happens to be very lucky to be who he is. And the country is caught up in the concept."

After catching flak for that, Ferraro, a Clinton fundraiser and adviser, clarified today for the same paper: "Any time anybody does anything that in any way pulls this campaign down and says let's address reality and the problems we're facing in this world, you're accused of being racist, so you have to shut up. Racism works in two different directions. I really think they're attacking me because I'm white. How's that?" So now the Obamans want her canned and the Clintonistas say merely that they regret her remarks. At this rate, there will be no advisers left by June and Bob Shrum will be running both campaigns. At least then he would finally win one.

Now, if Obama can only avoid staying "in Mississippi a day too long," as Dylan warned. Meanwhile, Sinbad, the comedian, says Hillary is fibbing about their dangerous trip to Bosnia. What a year.

March 2008

March 14

The Wright Stuff: Obama Hits Pastor's Remarks
This won't be the last we hear of this, but here is Obama today, speaking to a Pittsburgh newspaper about the controversial video:

Q: I don't know if you've seen it, but it's all over the wire today, a statement that your pastor made in a sermon in 2003 that instead of singing "God Bless America," black people should sing a song essentially saying "God Damn America."

A: I haven't seen the line. This is a pastor who is on the brink of retirement who in the past has made some controversial statements. I profoundly disagree with some of these statements.

Q: What about this particular statement?

A: Obviously, I disagree with that. Here is what happens when you just cherry-pick statements from a guy who had a 40-year career as a pastor. There are times when people say things that are just wrong. But I think it's important to judge me on what I've said in the past and what I believe.

March 18

Rev. Hagee Confirms McCain Sought Endorsement
In an interview that will appear in this Sunday's *New York Times Magazine*, controversial televangelist Rev. John Hagee declares, "It's true that [John] McCain's campaign sought my endorsement." McCain has attempted to distance himself from some of Hagee's views, much as Barack Obama is doing in relation to Rev. Jeremiah Wright. But unlike McCain, Obama has not stood on stage with Wright and accepted his accolades this year.

Interviewed by Deborah Solomon, Hagee refused to discuss his statement that Hurricane Katrina was God's punishment for a gay rights parade in New Orleans, now calling it "so far off-base." He claimed, "Our church is not hard against the gay people. Our church teaches what the bible teaches, that it is not a righteous lifestyle. But of course we must love even sinners."

He also said that charges that he had bashed the Catholic Church ("false cult system," etc.) have been "grossly mischaracterized...I was referring to those Christians who ignore the Gospels." Asked what he thinks of Obama, he answered, "He is going to be difficult to beat, because the man is a master of communication. If he were in the ministry, he would make it in the major leagues overnight."

March 21

Bill Comes Due: Richardson backs Obama
It was no slam dunk, and came just hours after John Edwards failed to deliver on Leno. Obama's address on race in Philadelphia on Tuesday appeared to sway Bill Richardson, "who sent word to the senator that he was inspired and impressed by the speech," *The New York Times* reports. "Aides said the endorsement was locked down over the following two days."

Richardson: "I believe he is the kind of once-in-a-lifetime leader that can bring our nation together and restore America's moral leadership in the world."

March 30

When McCain Ripped Michael Moore
In the thousands of articles and blog postings about John McCain in recent weeks, I haven't seen anything about that notorious night in late-August 2004 when he attacked Michael Moore from the stage on opening night of the GOP convention in New York – causing a chorus of boos and finger pointing at the filmmaker, who soon left the hall. I remember watching it all, in amazement, on TV and then posting the first story about it on the *E&P* site (our Joe Strupp got the only word from Moore as he left the arena).

McCain was in the midst of a stout defense of the Iraq war when it happened. "Our choice wasn't between a benign status quo and the bloodshed of war," McCain said. "It was between war and a graver threat. Don't let anyone tell you otherwise. Not our critics abroad. Not our political opponents. And certainly not a disingenuous filmmaker who would have us believe that Saddam's Iraq was an oasis of peace, when in fact it was a place of indescribable cruelty, torture chambers, mass graves."

Moore, in the hall as a columnist for *USA Today*, doffed his trademark red cap and waved as the crowd offered prolonged boos, pointed at Moore and yelled, "Four more years!" and worse. Moore's movie, *Fahrenheit 9/11*, hadn't gone down well with them, obviously. McCain later claimed, with a straight face, referring to Moore, "I had no idea he was sitting there."

He had been repeatedly halted by security attempting to reach his reserved press seat in section #340 facing the side of the stage. Responding to the chants, he exclaimed, "Two more months!" He also said, "I can't believe they'd mention the film and help the box office."

Some Republicans nearby were not shy about sharing their views of Moore with reporters. A GOP consultant from Pennsylvania, David Welch, said, "He's a troublemaker. I think he's here to cause trouble." A short while later Moore exited, accompanied by heavy security, as boos reappeared. He told Strupp on the way out that he was not fleeing just because of the catcalls: He had to speak to a Planned Parenthood gathering at a theater uptown.

About this time, his first *USA Today* column appeared online, titled "The GOP Doesn't Reflect America." Moore congratulated the Republicans for being able to seize power while only representing one-third of the populace. "Our side is full of wimps who'd rather compromise than fight," he explained. "Not you guys."

March 31

A Penny For Your Thoughts – and 50 Cent for Obama

Now we know he has it wrapped up: Obama has gotten 50 Cent to come down off the Hill and switch to him. CNN reports: "Hillary Clinton appears to have lost a high-profile backer to rival Barak Obama. Rapper 50 Cent, who told *Time* last September he was supporting the New York senator's White House bid, now says he has decided to shift his allegiance to Obama. The multi-platinum star, born Curtis Jackson, told MTV that Obama's recent speech on race was the deciding factor for his decision. 'I heard Obama speak,' he said. 'He hit me with that he-just-got-done-watching-*Malcolm X*, and I swear to God, I'm like, Yo, Obama! I'm Obama to the end now, baby!'"

Hagel's Theory
Sen. Chuck Hagel – who has often been all talk and no action on Iraq – guested on *The Daily Show* tonight and as usual said all the right things about the war, especially for a GOPer. Interesting moment: He said he hadn't endorsed anyone for president, not even his "good friend" and fellow Viet vet John McCain. Is it possible he will sit it out or back a Dem? Or angle for the Veep slot with Obama or Clinton?

APRIL 2008

April 1

Letterman vs. McCain

Before welcoming his guest, David Letterman started with his putdowns of John McCain: "He looks like the guy at the hardware store who makes the keys. He looks like the guy who can't stop talking about how well his tomatoes are doing. He looks like the guy who goes into town for turpentine. He looks like the guy who always has wiry hair growing out of new places. He looks like the guy who points out the spots they missed at the car wash."

Then McCain walked out on stage. "Hi, Letterman," he said. "You think that stuff's pretty funny, don't you? Well, you look like a guy whose laptop would be seized by the authorities. You look like a guy caught smuggling reptiles in his pants....You look like the guy who the neighbors later say, 'He mostly kept to himself.' You look like the night manager of a creepy motel." And so on.

April 14

Bill Kristol Links Obama to – Karl Marx!

Bill Kristol's column in the Monday *New York Times* is always something to look forward to after a long weekend, as he continues to fill the political humor op-ed slot at the paper once filled so ably by Russell Baker. And, oh, those embarrassing corrections! Today he serves up an unintentionally hysterical classic, using Barack Obama's recent remarks (reported by Mayhill Fowler of Huffington Post) about "bitter" people clinging to religion in hard times to link the candidate to – are you ready for this? – Karl Marx.

After Marx, why not Lennon? The John Lennon who once proclaimed, "I don't believe in religion" and "I don't believe in Jesus." But by the end of the column, I stopped laughing when Kristol, whose writings and advocacy have so damaged "average" Americans, called Obama a fraudulent voice of the people because he is truly "disdainful of small-town America.... He's usually good at disguising this. But in San Francisco the mask slipped. And it's not so easy to get elected by a citizenry you patronize."

He concluded: "And what are the grounds for his supercilious disdain? If he were a war hero, if he had a career of remarkable civic achievement or public service – then he could perhaps be excused an unattractive but in a sense understandable hauteur. But what has Barack Obama accomplished that entitles him to look down on his fellow Americans?"

Now, let's take that paragraph, re-read it but substitute Bill Kristol for Barack Obama at the end. How does that hold up? Let's review Kristol as man-of-the-people, as "war hero" and his "remarkable" civic achievements, such as serving as leading the fight to scuttle health care reform under Clinton. Kristol claimed there was no health care crisis and wrote key memo urging Republicans to "kill," not try to amend, the Clinton plan. If the Clinton proposal passed, he warned, it would "revive ... the Democrats, as the generous protector of middle-class interests."

April 15

Lieberman Hints Obama May Be a 'Marxist'–After Hailing Him in 2006

Joe Lieberman, who is now hinting that Barack Obama may be a Marxist, happily trumpeted a key endorsement from Obama in his 2006 race for the U.S. Senate. Lieberman also thought enough of Obama at that point to serve as his "mentor" in the U.S. Senate.

As you may have heard, Lieberman was asked yesterday about Bill Kristol linking Obama to Marx – and we don't mean Groucho – in his *New York Times* column. On the Brian and Judge radio show, they asked if Obama was indeed a Marxist, Lieberman replied, "I must say, that's a good question... I will tell you that during this campaign, I've learned some things about him, about the kind of environment from which he came ideologically. And I wouldn't...I'd hesitate to say he's a Marxist, but he's got some positions that are far to the left of me and I think mainstream America."

Yet, just a little more than two years ago, Lieberman, facing a strong threat from antiwar candidate Ned Lamont in the Democratic primary, invited Obama to give a major speech in Connecticut endorsing him for re-election – which some liberals still hold against Obama. "I am absolutely certain Connecticut is going to have the good sense to send Joe Lieberman back to the U.S. Senate so he can continue to serve on our behalf," Obama proclaimed then.

An AP story in late March 2006 on the event noted that "Lieberman became Obama's mentor when Obama was sworn into the Senate in 2005. They stayed close at Thursday night's event, too, entering the room together and working the crowd in tandem." However, "scattered boos greeted Lieberman when he took the podium, and he had to stop three times during his remarks to shush the crowd so he could deliver key points."

So clearly Obama had stuck his neck way out for Lieberman. But Lieberman may still be smarting from Obama's decision, at the very end of the 2006 race, to endorse Lamont, who had won the primary, over Lieberman. The latter ran as a third party candidate (and won). Even so, liberals derided Obama for his very modest efforts on behalf of Lamont. Now Lieberman hints there may be something to this "Marxist" charge after all.

April 16

Springsteen, Political 'Boss,' Backs Obama

Bruce Springsteen has endorsed Barack Obama, at least partly in response to the current media obsession with the candidate's recent remarks about "bitter" average folk in Pennsylvania. Springsteen's move is not exactly a shock right now but it's another amazing step in an evolution I have watched closely since 1972, when I first met the fledgling rocker and co-wrote the first magazine article about him.

For the first few years that I knew him I swear I never heard a "political" sentiment escape his lips, and never saw him read a newspaper's opinion section. Now he has become a new kind of political "Boss." Move over, Boss Tweed..

Maybe he will write another op-ed piece that will be "born to run"— like his 2004 *New York Times* contribution titled "Chords of Change." He confessed at that time that he was a "dedicated" *Times* reader and Paul Krugman fan.

He also slammed the press in a 2004 *Rolling Stone* interview, declaring, "The press has let the country down. It's taken a very amoral stand, in that essential issues are often portrayed as simply one side says this and the other side says that....The job of the press is to tell the truth without fear or favor. We have to get back to that standard."

Springsteen started his political transformation back in the "anti-nuke" days of the late-1970s. Then, when *Born in the USA* hit, he spoke out and donated a fortune to Vietnam veterans groups, and from there, many other causes, while refusing to endorse candidates. This "political" – in the broadest sense – focus continued with public statements and more donations as he recorded his *Tom Joad* and *Seeger Sessions* CDs. Now he's singing "Barack in the USA."

It's true, he did ultimately endorse and perform for John Kerry in 2004 (while denouncing tax cuts for "well-to-do guitar players"). But backing Obama goes to the next level – picking a candidate in a primary race, and at a key moment. Springsteen, of course, is a rich man now (he's come a long way since that first piece for *Crawdaddy* in early 1973 that I helped write) but he retains credibility with the "working-class" kids and adults that Obama is trying so hard to reach.

Springsteen seems to be monitoring the over-the-top press coverage of the "bitter" controversy, noting "the exaggeration of certain of his comments and relationships. While these matters are worthy of some discussion, they have been ripped out of the context."

Obama, he writes, "has the depth, the reflectiveness, and the resilience to be our next President. He speaks to the America I've envisioned in my music for the past 35 years, a generous nation with a citizenry willing to tackle nuanced and complex problems, a country that's interested in its collective destiny and in the potential of its gathered spirit. After the terrible damage done over the past eight years, a great American reclamation project needs to be undertaken. I believe that Senator Obama is the best candidate to lead that project and to lead us into the 21st Century with a renewed sense of moral purpose and of ourselves as Americans."

You might say that Obama just collected one of America's true "super-delegates."

April 19

ABC's Clinton-Obama Debate – 'Shoddy' and 'Despicable'
In perhaps the most embarrassing performance by the media in a major presidential debate in years, ABC News hosts Charles Gibson and George Stephanopolous focused mainly on trivial issues as Hillary Clinton and Barack Obama faced off in Philadelphia on Wednesday night.

April 2008

Criticism of the network raged Thursday and Friday across news sites, blogs and in print. ABC News responded with a segment entitled "The Debate Over the Debate," but did not offer any self-criticism. Stephanopolous did say the order of the questions maybe could have been better.

Wars in Iraq and Afghanistan, the health care and mortgage crises, the overall state of the economy and dozens of other pressing issues had to wait until the midway point for their few moments in the sun as Obama was pressed to explain his recent "bitter" gaffe and relationship with Rev. Wright (seemingly a dead issue) and not wearing a flag pin while Clinton had to answer again for her Bosnia trip exaggerations.

Then it was back to Obama to defend his slim association with a former '60s radical – a question that came out of rightwing talk radio and Sean Hannity on TV, but delivered by former Bill Clinton aide Stephanopolous. This approach led to Obama's claim that Clinton's husband pardoned two other '60s radicals. And so on.

More time was spent on all of this than segments on getting out of Iraq and keeping people from losing their homes and other key issues. Gibson only got excited when he complained about anyone daring to raise taxes on his capital gains.

Yet neither candidate had the courage to ask the moderators to turn to those far more important issues. But some in the crowd did – booing Gibson near the end. Still, David Brooks' review at *The New York Times* concluded: "I thought the questions were excellent." He gave ABC an "A."

But Tom Shales of *The Washington Post* had an opposite view: "Charlie Gibson and George Stephanopoulos, turned in shoddy, despicable performances." Walter Shapiro, the former *USA Today* political writer, declared in Salon, "Broadcast to a prime-time network audience on ABC and devoid of a single policy question during its opening 50 minutes, the debate easily could have convinced the uninitiated that American politics has all the substance of a Beavis and Butt-Head marathon."

April 20

Flag This Item
Bob Schieffer today on *Face the Nation* takes up the new, raging, flag pin in lapel issue: "Finally, today, I watched the ABC debate the other night when

that question came up again about why Senator Obama doesn't wear a flag pin in his lapel. Since no one asked me, here is my thought on all that. I think it's a nice thing if people want to wear a flag on their lapel. But I believe it more important to keep the flag behind our lapel in our hearts. I feel the same way about wearing my religion on my sleeve. It just fits me better on the inside. When I go to see our local baseball team, I do wear my Washington Nationals baseball cap. But am I less a fan if I don't wear it to work?

"The truth is I have been known to wear a red, white and blue stars and stripes tie on the Fourth of July. But am I less patriotic when I trade it for my Santa Claus tie at Christmas? Patriotism is no more about signs or pins than religion is about reminding others how pious we think we are. No, the proof in these puddings is not the signs that we wear, but how we act. Wouldn't that also be a better way to judge our presidential candidates?"

Obama on 'Daily Show' Denies 'Slave' Rumor
Appearing on Comedy Central's *The Daily Show* Monday night on the eve of the Pennsylvania primary, Barack Obama denied a hot rumor – just started by host Jon Stewart – that he planned, if elected to the White House, to "enslave the white race." He quipped, "That is not our plan, Jon, but I think your paranoia might make you suitable as a debate moderator."

Obama, on a more serious note, said he had closed the gap in the state to "six to eight" points behind Hillary Clinton, setting himself up for a "defeat" if he does worse than that.

He also said Clinton's tough campaigning did him "a favor...She has put me through the paces." If she wins the nomination, he said, everything's "going to be old news" by the general election.

April 24

Excerpt from Rev. Wright Interview With Bill Moyers
It will air tomorrow night on PBS. This is the first major Wright interview since the Obama "controversy" broke last month.

April 2008

REVEREND WRIGHT: The persons who have heard the entire sermon understand the communication perfectly. When something is taken like a sound bite for a political purpose and put constantly over and over again, looped in the face of the public, that's not a failure to communicate. Those who are doing that are communicating exactly what they want to do, which is to paint me as somesort of fanatic or as the learned journalist from *The New York Times* called me, a "wackadoodle."

BILL MOYERS: What do you think they wanted to communicate?

WRIGHT: I think they wanted to communicate that I am unpatriotic, that I am un-American, that I am filled with hate speech, that I have a cult at Trinity United Church of Christ. And by the way, guess who goes to his church, hint, hint, hint? That's what they wanted to communicate.

They know nothing about the church. They know nothing about our prison ministry. They know nothing about our food ministry. They know nothing about our senior citizens home. They know nothing about all we try to do as a church and have tried to do, and still continue to do as a church that believes what Martin Marty said, that the two worlds have to be together. And that the gospel of Jesus Christ has to speak to those worlds, not only in terms of the preached message on a Sunday morning but in terms of the lived-out ministry throughout the week.

MOYERS: What did you think when you began to see those very brief sound bites circulating as they did?

WRIGHT: I felt it was unfair. I felt it was unjust. I felt it was untrue. I felt for those who were doing that, were doing it for some very devious reasons.

MOYERS: Here is a man who came to see you 20 years ago. Wanted to know about the neighborhood. Barack Obama was a skeptic when it came to religion. He sought you out because he knew you knew about the community. You led him to the faith.

You performed his wedding ceremony. You baptized his two children. You were, for 20 years, his spiritual counsel. He has said that. And, yet, he, in that speech at Philadelphia, had to say some hard things about you. How did those words...how did it go down with you when you heard Barack Obama say those things?

WRIGHT: It went down very simply. He's a politician, I'm a pastor. We speak to two different audiences. And he says what he has to say as a politician. I say what I have to say as a pastor. But they're two different worlds. I do what I do. He does what politicians do. So that what happened in Philadelphia where he had to respond to the sound bytes, he responded as a politician.

April 27

If It Ain't Brokered, Don't Fix It
Fans of Al Gore – and certain cable TV pundits only interested in a wild news event and ratings – have raised the scenario for months, but the idea has been widely mocked. Now, as the media turn on Obama, after turning on Clinton, and many lament that the mud will fly and anger rise for many more weeks, is the idea of a brokered convention really so implausible? See Bob Herbert's column in *The New York Times* on Saturday for the kind of pox-on-both-their houses that seems to be all the rage.

I'm not saying the brokered convention is now likely, or desirable – please, no hate mail – but if Hillary does very well from now until June, and the fight gets even nastier, try to imagine what the media atmosphere might be like after that. With Clinton already fostering an anti-Obama attitude, and Obama backers ready to resent the nomination being "stolen" by Hillary, it's likely that the media, and some Democratic pols, will be promoting the idea of a convention showdown.

While I'm far from ready to go to deeply into this now, or make any predictions, as a historian of American campaigns (with a couple of books on the subject to my credit), let me briefly recall the 1924 Democratic convention, when a compromise candidate indeed came out of nowhere and earned the nod – with disastrous results for the Democrats.

April 2008

This was the gathering that inspired the famous Will Rogers line, "I don't belong to any organized party, I'm a Democrat." In fact, Will (the top newspaper columnist and most beloved man in America) – who probably should have been president himself – had a lot of fun with it.

The convention was held in New York City from June 24 to... seemingly forever. Two powerful candidates headed the field : Gov. Al Smith of New York and William G. McAdoo, former Secretary of Treasury. There were some parallels to Obama and Clinton, with Smith deemed unelectable by many because he was a Catholic and McAdoo having a close familial relationship to a former president, as son-in-law of Woodrow Wilson.

They each had strong, very separate constituencies. McAdoo had the backing of Protestants, farmers, the vast majority of delegates from the South, Midwest and West. Smith, of course, was favored by Catholics, ethnics, liberals, those in big cities, especially in the Northeast. McAdoo's people favored Prohibition and refused to condemn the Ku Klux Klan; Smith's fans were against both.

Now here's a key difference: A nominee then had to gain two-thirds of the delegates to win the nod. If that were true today, a brokered convention would probably be inevitable. McAdoo got a majority on the first ballot, 431 votes, not close to the two-thirds needed, with Smith gaining 241. Will Rogers, who would have been my candidate, got one vote; Franklin D. Roosevelt earned two. With so much anger on both sides, neither candidate backed down, and the balloting went on, and on.

By the 100th ballot, Smith was in first place but Gov. John W. Davis, the obscure former congressman and "compromise" candidate, had now overtaken McAdoo in the number two slot. It was now July 9, more than two weeks into the affair – no wonder today's cable news gasbags are salivating – and Will Rogers was exclaiming that New York had invited the delegates to visit the city, but not move there permanently.

On the 103rd ballot, the delegates threw up their hands and nominated Davis.

Davis would be trounced by the seemingly weak Republican – a successor to the unpopular, disgraced, Warren G. Harding – "Silent Cal" Coolidge. But Davis did not have nearly the name value or accomplishments of an Al Gore or John Edwards or....you name it. So perhaps a compromise Democrat could still win this year.

Anyway: There's your history lesson. Now what? Hang on to your hats. But where is Will Rogers when we really need him? As he said, "Everything is changing. People are taking the comedians seriously and the politicians as a joke."

April 29

Obama and Bowling: When the Media Promoted 'Gutter Politics'
Now that Barack Obama seems to have his party's nomination for president locked up, he may no longer feel so bad about the media's recent obsession about his bowling skills. It's revealing, however, that ever since he famously rolled a couple of gutter balls in Pennsylvania (or was it Indiana?) he has been shooting hoops – with reporters and camera people on hand – every chance he gets.

Obama may be over it, but the whole "Bowling-gate" episode still bothers me.

Remember that op-ed by Elizabeth Edwards for *The New York Times* two days ago? It carried the title, "Bowling 1, Health Care 0." I had to look at it twice, thinking I was on the sports page. Surely it was a baseball score and should have read, "Bowling Green 1, Holy Cross 0?" But no, her piece probed a different sort of sport — a new brand of "gutter politics."

Edwards, the outspoken wife of Sen. John Edwards, criticized the media obsession with Obama's bowling form, and low score, during the previous two weeks. Even the supposedly lofty *Times* was not exempt. While cable news gasbags were the worst offenders, the *Times* had carried dozens of references to Bowling-gate in its news pages and blog entries. On the very Sunday the Edwards piece ran, there was Maureen Dowd, right alongside, referring to the "bowling debacle." She didn't mean the coverage, but Obama's performance.

A few days earlier, Dowd had to run an embarrassing correction after she alleged that Obama had improperly accepted the donation of bowling shoes from Sen. Bob Casey (D-Pa.), when it was the other way around. Now that's a "debacle."

Exploring the bowling crisis, Joe Scarborough at MSNBC had opined that Americans want a real macho man in the White House, perhaps forgetting his unceasing attacks on Bill Clinton's rather too-mannish behavior in office. Chris Matthews, also on MSNBC, suggested that Obama was "prissy."

In reply, all you need to ask is: Which president was the most avid bowler? And, of course, the answer is: Richard Nixon. He even paid $400 out of his own pocket to lease automatic pinsetters, and during Watergate went down to the basement to roll off some tension.

Actually, a search of the historical record finds that the White House bowling alley — sometimes two alleys — dates back to the Truman administration. But Truman (now known as a suitably tough guy) had no use for the sport. I've found only one photo of him bowling, which was published on the cover of *Kegler* magazine. Sure enough, he was wearing a tie, the button-downed look for which Obama earned much mocking.

Truman even wore a vest!

You won't find many references to bowling when examining the lives of other allegedly "manly" presidents, including JFK, LBJ (who couldn't even golf), Reagan, Poppy Bush. Who was the biggest bowling advocate near the top? Dan Quayle.

Nixon and Quayle. That is really something to aspire to.

In fact, the pair who might have done more bowling at the White House than anyone weren't even males. They were Lady Bird Johnson and Muriel Humphrey, who tried to bowl a few frames every week.

Of course, many presidents have golfed, but are you really going to tell me that this "sport" is more macho than driving the lane in basketball — which Obama happens to be good at? The Obama/Tiger Woods analogies only go so far, thank God. And as for bowling: Its popularity in the U.S. has been in a steep decline since the 1980s.

To get back to what's important, here's what Elizabeth Edwards wrote for the *Times*: "The vigorous press that was deemed an essential part of democracy at our country's inception is now consigned to smaller venues, to the Internet and, in the mainstream media, to occasional articles. I am not suggesting that every journalist for a mainstream media outlet is neglecting his or her duties to the public. And I know that serious newspapers and magazines run analytical articles, and public television broadcasts longer, more probing segments.

"But I am saying that every analysis that is shortened, every corner that is cut, moves us further away from the truth until what is left is the

Cliffs Notes of the news, or what I call strobe-light journalism, in which the outlines are accurate enough but we cannot really see the whole picture."

Edwards closed this way: "If voters want a vibrant, vigorous press, apparently we will have to demand it. Not by screaming out our windows as in the movie *Network*, but by talking calmly, repeatedly, constantly in the ears of those in whom we have entrusted this enormous responsibility. Do your job, so we can — as voters — do ours."

MAY 2008

<u>May 8</u>

Maureen Dowd Predicted Obama Over Hillary – Two Years Ago!
"It's only 2006," I wrote way back in March of that year over at *Editor & Publisher*, "and *New York Times* columnist Maureen Dowd has already written off Hillary Clinton in the 2008 presidential race." She had warned that Democrats "are racing like lemmings toward a race where, as one moaned, 'John McCain will dribble Hillary Clinton's head down the court like a basketball.'" But Mo yearned for Sen. Barack Obama of Illinois. At 44, Obama, she pointed out, was already a year older than John F. Kennedy when he became president.

"The weak and pathetic Democrats seem to move inexorably toward candidates who turn a lot of people off," she advised. "They should find someone captivating with an intensely American success story... and shape the campaign around that leader....The Democrats should not dismiss a politically less experienced but personally more charismatic prospect as 'an empty vessel.' Maybe an empty vessel can fill the room."

She added that it may be true "that Americans, as one Democrat told me, 'will never elect a guy as president who has a name like a Middle East terrorist.'" But the Democrats, she said, do not "stand for anything" and they have "no champion at a time when people are hungry for an exciting leader, when the party should be roaring and soaring against the Bushies' power-mad stumbles.

"They should groom an '08 star who can run on the pledge of doing what's right instead of only what's far right....Democrats think Senator Potential's experience does not match Senator Pothole's [but] Republicans won with Ronald Reagan and W. by taking guys with more likeability and sizzle than experience." Of course, as is her custom, Dowd turned on the snark for Obama shortly – repeatedly referring to him as Obambi – but at least she had it right at the start.

May 18

Two Top Columnists Question Obama's DNA
Liberal bloggers and commenters at *The Washington Post* op-ed section are rightly criticizing a column this week by syndicated scribe Kathleen Parker that questions Barack Obama's "deep-seated" Americanism. But she is only following the footsteps of Peggy Noonan of the *Wall Street Journal* who raised similar issues three weeks ago – and was praised by NBC's Brian Williams for a "Pulitzer"-worthy effort.

Noonan wrote then: "Hillary Clinton is not Barack Obama's problem. America is Mr. Obama's problem...[H]as he ever gotten misty-eyed over... the Wright Brothers and what kind of country allowed them to go off on their own and change everything? How about D-Day, or George Washington, or Henry Ford, or the losers and brigands who flocked to Sutter's Mill, who pushed their way west because there was gold in them thar hills?"

Henry Ford was a vicious anti-Semite, but no matter. For Noonan continued: "John McCain carries it in his bones. Mr. McCain learned it in school, in the Naval Academy, and, literally, at grandpa's knee....

"Mr. Obama? What does he think about all that history? Which is another way of saying: What does he think of America? That's why people talk about the flag pin absent from the lapel. They wonder if it means something. Not that the presence of the pin proves love of country – any cynic can wear a pin, and many cynics do. But what about Obama and America? Who would have taught him to love it, and what did he learn was lovable, and what does he think about it all?...

"[N]o one is questioning his patriotism, they're questioning its content, its fullness."

No one? And surely not Peggy Noonan. Obama, of course, has spoken about why he loves American often and at great length, if Noonan might have noticed if she was paying attention.

Now, Kathleen Parker, in contrast, borrowed the words of another to set forth her central premise. At least this time she didn't quote someone who suggested that certain liberals be taken out and shot, as she did in a column back in 2003.

She opened this week's column (she is published in dozens of papers) by quoting 24-year-old Josh Fry of West Virginia who said he backed John McCain over Barack Obama: "His feelings aren't racist, he explained. He would just be more comfortable with 'someone who is a full-blooded American as president.'"

We don't know Mr. Fry, but polls did show that an extraordinarily high number of voters in the recent Democratic primary in West Virginia did – privately – admit that race had an awful lot to do with their vote. But Parker assured us, again, that her own views had nothing to do with race: "Full-bloodedness is an old coin that's gaining currency in the new American realm. Meaning: Politics may no longer be so much about race and gender as about heritage, core values, and made-in-America. Just as we once and still have a cultural divide in this country, we now have a patriot divide. Who 'gets' America? And who doesn't?...It's about blood equity, heritage and commitment to hard-won American values. And roots.

"Some run deeper than others and therein lies the truth of Josh Fry's political sense. In a country that is rapidly changing demographically – and where new neighbors may have arrived last year, not last century – there is a very real sense that once-upon-a-time America is getting lost in the dash to diversity. We love to boast that we are a nation of immigrants – and we are. But there's a different sense of America among those who trace their bloodlines back through generations of sacrifice."

Parker, of course, ignores the fact that Obama, in fact, is half-white, is related (god help us) to Dick Cheney, and can trace his family back as far as McCain in America – to George Washington, even. And speaking of "generations of sacrifice": Obama's grandfather fought in World War II.

Those fine small-town Americans may not know any of that – and Parker sure doesn't remind them. "What they know," she relates, "is that their forefathers fought and died for an America that has worked pretty well for more than 200 years. What they sense is that their heritage is being swept under the carpet while multiculturalism becomes the new national narrative. And they fear what else might get lost in the remodeling of America."

Even Hillary Clinton has "figured it out," Parker writes. Her "own DNA is cobbled with many of the same values that rural and small-town Americans cling to. She understands viscerally what Obama has to study."

After noting other true American values such as easy gun ownership, Parker concludes, "Full-blooded Americans get this. Those who hope to lead the nation better get it soon." Of course, the only half-white and half-native Obama is not "full-blooded." Get it?

As for Parker's support for serve-your-country Americanism, few may remember her 2003 column that attacked Jessica Lynch, another West Virginian, and one who nearly lost her life for the U.S. in Iraq. "What the hell was Jessica Lynch doing in the U.S. Army?" Parker asked. "Regardless of what did or didn't happen over there, Lynch's book, movie and notoriety are not wasted, but offer a cautionary tale: A 5-foot-4-inch, 100-pound woman has no place in a war zone nor, arguably, in the military.

"The feminist argument that women can do anything men can do is so absurd that it seems unworthy of debate. That some women are as able as some men in some circumstances hardly constitutes a defense for 'girling' down our military – and putting men at greater risk – so that the Jessica Lynches can become kindergarten teachers." She closed by calling Lynch "a victim of the PC military career myth sold to young women through feminist propaganda."

May 20

Hillary Claims Sexism Worse than Racism in Campaign
In an article by *The Washington Post's* Lois Romano, Hillary Clinton briefly hit "sexism" in media coverage of her campaign as "deeply offensive to millions of women," but she went much further, as a transcript of the entire interview now makes clear.

Clinton criticized the "vitriol" from "misogynists" and said that the race factor was often discussed but not gender, adding "[E]very poll I've seen show more people would be reluctant to vote for a woman to vote for an African American, which rarely gets reported on either." She expressed amazement "that we would have a presidential campaign in which so much of what has occurred that has been very sexist would be just shrugged off."

She is fresh off a landslide win in West Virginia in which surveys revealed that race played a key factor, and that appears to be true, as well, in the results from Kentucky.

May 27

Liz Trotta on Obama 'Assassination'

Appearing on Fox News on Sunday, Lix Trotta, a former editor with the *Washington Times* and broadcast TV journalist, was asked by the host, Eric Shawn, about the latest Clinton controversy – Hillary's hint that she ought to say in the race because, you never know, something bad could happen to Obama, a la Bobby Kennedy in 1968.

Trotta, according to the widely-circulated video, replied, "And now we have what some are reading as a suggestion that somebody knock off Osama, uh Obama. Well, both, if we could." She laughed.

The host, Shawn, clearly understanding how far she had gone, quickly commented: "Talk about how you really feel."

Trotta offered a weak apology on Monday–and *The New York Times'* reaction on Tuesday? Bury it and make light of it. The *Times* carried nothing but a brief item on page A20 in its "The Caucus" column by Jim Rutenberg. The headline: "Same Joke, More Regret." But how much of a "joke" was it really, and how much regret?

A day after she had referred to Obama as "Osama" and quipped that maybe both of them should get bumped off, Trotta was given a chance to offer a "clarification," as Fox host Bill Hemmer put it. After talking for a couple of minutes about Hillary Clinton's own "backtracking" on her comment, Hemmer noted that "some people" were "criticizing you" for her Osama/Obama remark on Sunday.

Trotta said she felt bad, while also suggesting her remark was nothing particularly unusual or awful in this campaign year. She said, "Oh yes, I am so sorry about what happened yesterday and the lame attempt at humor. I fell all over myself, making it appear that I wished Barack Obama harm or any other candidate, for that matter, and I sincerely regret it and apologize to anybody I have offended. It is a very colorful political season"– she chuckled at this point–"and many of us are making mistakes and saying things we wish we had not said."

Hemmer replied: "Clarification noted."

JUNE 2008

June 4

Editorials Across Country Hail Obama Win

Editorials across the U.S. on the morning after largely hailed Barack Obama's final primary tally that cashed enough delegates to seemingly guarantee the nomination over Hillary Clinton. The *San Francisco Chronicle, Chicago Tribune* and many others hailed the historic victory, while the *St. Louis Post-Dispatch* had some fun comparing Clinton to Peter Pan urging followers to clap their hands and wish, and wish, for a miracle.

USA Today declared: "Never before has an African-American been a major-party candidate for the highest office in the land. As he declared himself the nominee, Obama left this landmark accomplishment unspoken. But history will record this moment as both a monumental political upset and a dramatic statement from a party that was just shaking off its segregationist wing when Obama was born some 46 years ago."

The New York Times has not yet weighed in, though Maureen Dowd wrote of Obama and Clinton: "He thought a little thing like winning would stop her?"

The *San Francisco Chronicle* observed: "The long wait is over. For the first time in its history, a nation that began by discounting the votes of African Americans will have a black man as a major party nominee...143 years after a civil war left more than 600,000 Americans dead and 44 years after the civil rights movement was embedded."

Roger Simon at *Politico* writes: "Barack Obama would like to remind you of something: He won and she didn't. It's about him now and not her. He has made history, and she is history."

June 5

Scarborough Predicted Hillary Would 'Grind Up' Obama
Maybe they should change the name of the show to Mourning Joe. On *The Daily Show* last night, Jon Stewart played a few clips of TV pundits dissing Barack Obama's chances vs. Hillary Clinton a year or so ago. One of them was Joe Scarborough, pooh-poohing Obama's chances. My search of the MSNBC site from that period uncovers much more, from December 22, 2006.

Say it ain't so, Joe! Here is one highlight.

SCARBOROUGH: Even before the final votes were tallied in the 2006 elections, politicians started lining up for the 2008 presidential sweepstakes. Without further ado, let me kill Hamlet in the first act and tell you how your favorite candidate will fare over the next 12 months.

Barack Obama: Forget the fact this guy's middle name is "Hussein." Forget the fact he has been in national politics for less than two years. Forget the fact that Hillary Clinton will raise more money than God in 2007. Forget all of that, the Washington press tells us, because Barack Obama is none other than the second coming of JFK.

Yeah, right.

Barack Hussein Obama is more Johnny Bravo than John Kennedy. The vest fits and the fans scream while DC's star-maker machinery shifts into overdrive.

Like Peter Brady's Bravo, Obama's shot at the top will be short lived. But since BHO is young enough, dynamic enough and (just) black enough to whip official Washington into a frenzy, expect this stupid story to stick around for a while. Soon enough though, this year's model will be shouting, "Please give a warm Chicago welcome to the next President of the United States, Hillary Clinton!"

Then he went on to his Hillary assessment:

Cheering for New York's junior senator excites Democratic activists about as much as rooting for General Electric. Regardless of their hand wringing, Hillary Inc. will grind up and spit out any Democratic challenger that gets in its way.

Ms. Clinton has completed six ruthlessly efficient years in the U.S. Senate and avoided even a whiff of scandal since Bubba moved to a separate zip code. But that doesn't mean the problematic ex-president won't be her campaign's chief asset. Time and again throughout the next few years, Bill Clinton will make the difference on fundraising, networking and strategy. And 2007 will show that any politico who dares to cross Team Clinton risks being crushed into dust.

Crushed into dust? Uh, not quite.

June 6

In Bill Clinton Story 'NYT' Draws the Line at 'Scumbag'

Apparently the great Grey Lady is still a bit modest. In its account of the Huffington Post scoop on Bill Clinton's tirade against Todd Purdum, *The New York Times* today quoted some of the ex-president's epithets, including "sleazy" and "slimy" but drew the line at "scumbag." Other leading news outlets were not so coy.

Clinton, of course, was responding to the quite negative profile about him written by Purdum for this month's *Vanity's Fair*. He apologized last night for some of his "inappropriate" language, captured by Huff Post's Mayhill Fowler. He probably would not have done that if he had not used the word "scumbag." But he realized that using that word made him look like a, well, "scumbag."

The *Times*' Michael Luo writes today: "According to the Huffington Post Web site, Mr. Clinton, as he worked the rope line at an event here, called Mr. Purdum 'sleazy,' 'slimy' and 'dishonest.' Speaking to a reporter for the Web site, Mr. Clinton said the article was part of a pattern of media bias against Mrs. Clinton and in favor of her rival for the Democratic nomination, Senator Barack Obama."

But Shailagh Murray and Anne Kornblut of *The Washington Post* went the full monty, explaining that Clinton "called Purdum 'sleazy' and a 'scumbag' in comments to a reporter for the Huffington Post, a liberal Web site, leading a spokesman for the candidate to issue an apology." *Newsday* also cited "scumbag."

The *Chicago Tribune's* popular The Swamp blog: "Reminded that Purdum is married to Clinton's former press secretary Dee Dee Myers, Clinton responded in part: 'That's all right – he's still a scumbag.'" The CNN

Web site: "Calling Purdum a 'scumbag,' Clinton said 'he's one of the guys that propagated all those lies about Whitewater for Kenneth Starr. He's just a dishonest guy – can't help it.'"

June 24

When 'Mad Men' in Media Took Control

This past winter it was good to see Upton Sinclair back in the news again amid the raves for the new film *There Will Be Blood*, very loosely based on his 1927 novel *Oil!* But Sinclair's most lasting contribution to modern media follies came seven years later, however, when the former socialist ran for governor of California as a Democrat (a tale I told in my 1992 book *The Campaign of the Century*). As another election showdown begins this summer, it is worth looking back at how the modern "media" campaign began.

On Aug. 28, 1934, Sinclair swept the Democratic primary for governor and all hell broke loose across the state, then across the continent. On the day after, the *Los Angeles Times,* under Harry Chandler, denounced Sinclair's "maggot-like horde" of supporters, and the Hearst press was no kinder. The movie studios threatened to move back east if Sinclair took office.

Sinclair, author of *The Jungle* and dozens of other muckraking books, led a grassroots "change" movement called EPIC (End Poverty in California). His friend H.L. Mencken explained in a column, "Upton Sinclair has been swallowing quack cures for all the sorrows of mankind since the turn of the century, is at it again in California, and on such a scale that the whole country is attracted by the spectacle." Will Rogers wrote much the same thing.

The prospect of a socialist governing the nation's most volatile state sparked nothing less than a revolution in American politics. With an assist from Hollywood — and leading newspapers — Sinclair's opponents virtually invented the modern media campaign. It marked a stunning advance in the art of public relations, "in which advertising men now believed they could sell or destroy political candidates as they sold one brand of soap and defamed its competitor," Arthur M. Schlesinger Jr. later observed.

The 1934 governor's race, in short, showed the candidates the way from the smoke-filled room to Madison Avenue, from the party boss to the "spin doctor." Freelance media experts, making unprecedented use of film, radio, newspapers, direct mail, opinion polls, and national fundraising, devised the most astonishing smear campaign ever. "Many American campaigns have been distinguished by dirty tactics," columnist Heywood Broun commented, "but I can think of none in which willful fraud has been so brazenly practiced."

The political innovation that produced the strongest impact was the manipulation of moving pictures. MGM's Louis B. Mayer and Irving Thalberg produced fake newsreels, using Hollywood actors. William Randolph Hearst helped distribute them. For the first time, the screen was used to demolish a candidate, a precursor of political attack ads on television. The first generation of "Hollywood liberals"—actors like Jimmy Cagney and Charlie Chaplin—protested in vain.

No institution dishonored itself quite like the California press. One anecdote that illustrates this: In October that year, *The New York Times'* star reporter Turner Catledge (later top editor of the paper) came to California. Naturally, he hooked up with the *Los Angeles Times'* political editor Kyle Palmer, who pretty much selected the state's chief executive every four years — hence his nickname, "The Little Governor."

Decades before the press combed through Barack Obama's books and Mike Huckabee's old sermons, the *L.A. Times* printed out-of-context excerpts from Sinclair's many books on its front page every single day. Palmer was also advising and even writing speeches for Sinclair's opponent. Over dinner, Catledge asked Palmer why the paper refused to be fair and balanced. "Turner, forget it," Palmer replied. "We don't go in for that kind of crap that you have back in New York, of being obliged to print both sides. We're going to beat this son of a bitch Sinclair any way we can. We're going to kill him."

And so they did. Sinclair's huge lead evaporated — especially after those fake newsreels hit the screen — and Gov. Frank Merriam won re-election. And today, "media politics" still dominates most election campaigns. This year, at least, "Web politics" is proving to be quite an adjunct or, even, a counterweight.

JULY 2008

July 3

'NYT' slaps Maureen Dowd for False 'Fist Bump' Tale

As we all know now, that story about Obama refusing to "fist bump" with a kid in Ohio turned out to be not only trivial but quite false. What you might not know is that one of those who helped spread it, Maureen Dowd, was slapped today with a prominent Correction box right on *The New York Times'* op-ed page.

It reads: "In describing an encounter between Barack Obama and a schoolboy in Zanesville, Ohio, Maureen Dowd's column on Wednesday used a campaign pool report. The report said that Mr. Obama had declined to bump fists with the boy. The campaign now says that the boy was trying to get Mr. Obama to autogrpah his hand, but the candidate declined, citing the possible reaction of the boy's mother."

Oddly, the *Times* has another piece on Fistbumpgate earlier in the first section, which mentions journos – but not Dowd – getting it all wrong. It only singles out the offenders as "a handful of blogs and on cable television." That item by Jeff Zeleny reprises a transcript of the Obama/boy chat, with the kid pressing him to the end for some kind of autograph, even after the candidate says, "See you."

Obama finally "signed his name in crayon on pictures they had been drawing." Zeleny concludes: "And that, folks, is the end of the tale of he fist bump that wasn't." Oh, if only a few other Obama myths would go away that fast.

July 10

'Nuts' Case: How Media Handled Jackson's 'Crude' Word

When a major political figure or celebrity utters a newsmaking, off-color, remark it is always interesting to observe how different news outlets handle the offending word or words. We monitored this recently when former President Bill Clinton called *Vanity Fair* writer Todd Purdum a bunch of names after the reporter had raked him over the coals in a major piece. Everyone in the media quoted the "sleazy" part of the Clinton quote but most skipped the "scumbag" reference.

So how did the media on Wednesday handle the now-infamous Rev. Jesse Jackson off-mike reference to Barack Obama while awaiting an appearance on "Fox and Friends" a few days ago?

The New York Times was coy: "Mr. Jackson made disparaging remarks, apparently including a crude reference to male genitalia, about how Mr. Obama was talking to black people." A later *Times* article cited a "vulgar reference." But CNN.com let it all hang out, so to speak, quoting Jackson: "See, Barack's been talking down to black people ... I want to cut his nuts off." Reuters quotes the Reverend, evermore: "I want to cut his nuts out."

The *New York Post* topped that, of course, putting it right in the headline: JESSE JACKSON SAYS HE WANTS TO CUT OBAMA'S 'NUTS OUT.'

Huh? "Off" or "out"? Bollocks! It's the sex pistol!

The *Los Angeles Times'* "Top of the Ticket" blog went with: "crude language." The AP first quoted Jackson mentioning the "regretfully crude" choice of words. Later in the day it got a little more specific, citing "a slang reference to his wanting to cut off Obama's testicles."

The *Washington Post's* "The Trail" blog really played it cool: "Whatever the Rev. Jesse Jackson Sr. said in a live microphone on Fox News, it was really, really bad...." But the *Chicago Tribune* eventually offered a more full report than nearly anyone: "'I want to cut his nuts out,' Jackson added, gesturing as if grabbing part of the male anatomy and then pulling."

July 14

Obama 'New Yorker' Cover: Satire or 'Dumb Stunt'?

Reaction today to the Barack/Michelle terrorist cover art in *The New Yorker* this week has been swift and wildly varying. Here is a cross-section:

Andrew Malcolm of the *Los Angeles Times*: "A lot of people won't get the joke. Or won't want to. And will use it for non-humorous purposes, which isn't the *New Yorker's* fault." The *Times* also put the cover in a new online gallery, "10 Magazine Covers That Shook the World!"

Eric Zorn, *Chicago Tribune*: "I take the editors at their word and await the upcoming cover in which they give the same ha-ha-isn't-it-silly? treatment to the rotten things people say about John McCain: Say a cartoon showing him looking about 150 years old and spouting demented non-sequiturs in the middle of a violent temper tantrum while, in the corner, his wife is passed out next to a bottle of pills. It's only satire, right?"

Ben Smith, Politico.com: "The risk to the right here is that a vote against Obama becomes seen as a vote not for those policy differences, or for John McCain, but for bigotry. That's a storyline the *New Yorker* was advancing."

James Poniewozik, *Time*'s Swampland: "Judging the cover as a cover is pretty easy by me: it's a pretty obvious and dumb stunt, the kind of subtle-as-a-brick cover the *New Yorker* has been doing now and then since the Tina Brown era, when it ran an Art Spiegelman cover of a Chasid kissing a black woman on a post-Crown Heights New York subway.

"The reader-reception call is tougher. There are ways of doing this kind of satire where, set in context, it would be applauded by many of the same people who are blasting it now. Say *The Colbert Report* or *The Daily Show* had done the same image, as part of a fictional 527 ad using actors to portray the Obamas. It'd be clear enough what sort of attitude the scene was spoofing, and how."

Andrew Sullivan, TheAtlantic.com: "[T]he notion that most Americans are incapable of seeing that [it is satire] strikes me as excessively paranoid and a little condescending."

Joel Achenbach at www.washingtonpost.com: "Here's a fundamental rule of humor: It must be funny to work. Another rule: 'Almost funny' is invariably just as bad, and often worse, than being extremely unfunny.

"I'm not even sure this cover is 'almost funny' – because it deals so heavy-handedly with such a sensitive topic. Osama on the wall, the flag burning, the Angela Davis wife – the natural response is to cringe rather than laugh. Of course, political cartooning by nature deals with caricatures and heavy-handed images, but usually they're leavened by some kind of quip, some verbal wink. In this case there's no punch line.

"The best response from the Obama camp would be to say, 'We recognize that it was meant as satire, but must confess that we didn't get a single chuckle out of it. Better luck next time.'"

July 16

"Anti-Christ Muslim" Email Still Circulating

With all the attention on this week's *New Yorker* cover, it should not be overlooked that one email that inspired it is still circulating, though long repudiated by the alleged author. A friend of mine received it this week from a close (rightwing) relative. It's cute that it cites Snopes as a source – since Snopes mocks it. I will reprint most of it here – and then the denial from the "author" and church (in Sun City, Florida). Here it is.

MAY WE ALL PRAY FOR WISDOM AND DISCERNMENT AND PRAY FOR EACH OTHER AS WE MAKE THIS DECISION OF A LIFETIME! OUR LIVES, CHILDREN AND GRANDCHILDREN'S LIVES WILL BE CHANGED FOREVER BECAUSE OF OUR CHOICE THIS ELECTION. MAY GOD BE WITH US ALL!

God help us if this man is elected!! But it is all stated in the Bible and it will happen sooner or later.

This is from Darlene Millican, wife of the pastor of Trinity Bapt. Church here in Sun City: "I have felt for sometime now that Obama is the one person that 'Frightens Me'. I believe the Bible has warned us that 'A man will come from the East that will be charismatic in nature and have proposed solutions for all our problems and his rhetoric will attract many supporters!'

"When will our pathetic Nation quit turning their back on God and understand that this man is 'A Muslim'… First, Last and always… and we are AT WAR with the Muslim Nation, whether our bleeding-heart, secular, Liberal friends believe it or not. This man fits every description from the Bible of the 'Anti-Christ'!

"I'm just glad to know that there are others that are frightened by this man! Who is Barack Obama? Very interesting and something that should be considered in your choice.

July 2008

"If you do not ever forward anything else, please forward this to all your contacts...this is very scary to think of what lies ahead of us here in our own United States...better heed this and pray about it and share it. snopes.com confirms this is factual. Check for yourself.

"Who is Barack Obama? Probable U. S. presidential candidate, Barack Hussein Obama was born in Honolulu, Hawaii, to Barack Hussein Obama, Sr., a black MUSLIM from Nyangoma-Kogel, Kenya and Ann Dunham, a white ATHEIST from Wichita, Kansas ....Obama takes great care to conceal the fact that he is a Muslim. He is quick to point out that, 'He was once a Muslim, but that he also attended Catholic school.' Obama's political handlers are attempting to make it appear that that he is not a radical.

"Barack Hussein Obama has joined the United Church of Christ in an attempt to downplay his Muslim background. ALSO, keep in mind that when he was sworn into office he DID NOT use the Holy Bible, but instead the Koran. Barack Hussein Obama will NOT recite the Pledge of Allegiance nor will he show any reverence for our flag. While others place their hands over their hearts, Obama turns his back to the flag and slouches. Do you want someone like this as your PRESIDENT?

"Let us all remain alert concerning Obama's expected presidential candidacy. The Muslims have said they plan on destroying the US from the inside out, what better way to start than at the highest level - through the President of the United States, one of their own! The Bible says 'He will come from among you!'

"Please forward to everyone you know. Would you want this man leading our country? NOT ME!!! WITHOUT GOD, WE ARE NOTHING!!!"

Ms. Millican has denied she wrote the email and her Trinity Baptist Church has just sent out the following: "It has been brought to our attention that an e-mail has been circulating from our pastor's wife, Darlene Millican about Barack Obama, with the subject line: 'Is He the Anti-Christ?' This is absolutely NOT TRUE!! Mrs. Millican has absolutely no idea how this horrible e-mail was started AND named her as the originator of such slander.... Darlene has spent her life teaching others to be and do their best for Christ . . . which includes not slandering others! We also have no idea how it would be sent out using the Church's e-mail."

July 18

Krugman: Obama Will Win – Then Media Will Crucify Him
Speaking at an early afternoon panel at the huge Netroots Nation confab in Austin, Texas, today, Paul Krugman of *The New York Times* predicted, with seeming confidence, an Obama victory in November – but added that "within three months of taking office, no, less than three months" the media would be out to get him, as much as they had at the high point of anti-Bill Clinton bashing.

Krugman was responding to a questioner who had stated that the media was "in the pocket" of the "government." Krugman pointed out that this was hardly the case when Clinton was in the White House and would be proven again when Obama took over. "Get ready for it," he warned.

He pointed out that this was not necessarily the case when a Republican came to power. In fact, much of his presentation was based on the lack of "symmetry" in how the media goes after Democrats and Republicans. Look at the most recent example of "outrage" over Nancy Pelosi saying that President Bush had totally failed, he said. Would the media, he asked, have batted an eye if a conservative had said the same of a Democratic president?

Krugman also said that there were relatively few prominent academic liberals such as himself because the liberal think tanks only get a fraction of the money that goes to the conservative ones. "There are more rightwing billionaires," he declared.

July 22

Austin Story on 'Netroots': Hit, Run, Error
It started innocently enough, over coffee in a hotel lobby, with me (as usual at that hour) huddled over a newspaper—in print, not on a laptop, unlike everyone else in the vicinity. A little more than a day later, the front-page

July 2008

article I was reading, and getting worked up about, would be pulled from the paper's Web site after a storm of protest. Now an editor's note in the Tuesday paper, more or less apologizing, has been published.

And I had at least a little something to do with it.

I was in Austin, Texas, this past weekend, after being invited to speak on a panel at the Netroots Nation annual convention of liberal-minded bloggers/activists. The subject was "War Pundits" and my colleagues on the panel included fellow authors Samantha Power and Mark Danner. In my brief remarks, I somehow managed to work in references to Austin icons Molly Ivins and Steve Earle, along with Bill Kristol and Sean Hannity.

About an hour before my panel, Al Gore showed up in the main ballroom – taking the microphone from Nancy Pelosi. Howard Dean and Wesley Clark had spoken earlier, with more than 2000 in attendance—including, reportedly, about 200 "MSM" reporters, C-SPAN and the like. Media coverage had been fairly positive (with the usual inaccuracies), probably because the attendees, and their friends, had proven instrumental in helping to hand Congress to the Democrats in 2006, then sparked wins in a few special elections, and seemed poised to repeat all that this November.

But frankly, when I bought the *Austin American-States*man at the Hilton's lobby coffee shop on Sunday morning, I was just looking to catch up on some national news and the baseball scores. Yet, staring me right in the face, just below the fold on the left side of the front page, was a report on the conference by one Patrick Beach, who was IDed as a "feature writer." That label often means trouble on the front page, and it certainly did here.

Beach described the gathering in stereotypes that better fit the aging Old Left of years ago than the much younger Netroots of today. I mean, how many of these bloggers have ever read much of Chomsky, as he suggested?

When Beach, at the start referred to the crowd as "marauding liberals" I knew it was not to be taken literally. But then we got this:

– The audience nearly staged a "faint-in" when Gore appeared (note use of '60s term).
– Pelosi is so far left her title should include "(D-Beijing)." This would come as a surprise to many in the crowd who have criticized her timidity – and posed hostile questions in the Q & A.

- The liberal blogosphere is "terribly self-confirming" – not like the mainstream media! In a contradiction, he then noted that at the conference they "critiqued themselves."
- Paul Krugman, as if to "galvanize stereotypes," wore Birkenstocks – but Beach throughout the article clearly needed no help in having his own stereotypes galvanized.
- It's shooting fish in a barrel "to paint liberals as overly intellectual types incapable of having fun unless reading Noam Chomsky counts, and its sure does for them." In fact, the convention was practically "party central," few attendees were "intellectuals," and only a tiny percentage, I would guess, are Chomsky lovers – again, an outmoded stereotype.
- Those who protested during the Pelosi/Gore "faint-in" were "shushed" as if they were at a Nanci Griffith concert. I certainly know who she is, but I can imagine most of these particular attendees reading this reference and asking, "Who???"
- One more reference to liberals don't wanna "have fun." And so on.

But it was the front-page placement that really irked me.

Well, I thought I would perform a public service and let some of the convention attendees know about all this – few are fans of dead-tree media – so I posted a summary at DailyKos (the popular blog that founded Netroots). The "Kossacks" as they are known could do what they wanted with it, if anything. Within a few minutes, so many people were reading and recommending my post that it shot to near the top of the DailyKos "diaries" for the day. It also got picked up at some other popular blogs.

Monday: I was back in New York and had turned the page on all this, until I got an email from Michael King, news editor at the *Austin Chronicle*, the long-running and successful alt-weekly. King informed me that the comments from Beach's article had been wiped and it was impossible to find the article on the paper's Web site, though it might still be there somewhere. Perhaps, he mused, "some editor finally looked at the piece and yanked it out of simple embarrassment."

Now a kind of apology from Editor Fred Zipp has appeared in the Tuesday edition. It follows in its entirety: "Readers expect front-page stories to speak directly and clearly about events and issues. Eliminating the possibility of misunderstanding from our work is a critical part of our daily newsroom routine. When we communicate in a way that could be misinterpreted, we fail to meet our standards.

"Our front-page story Sunday about the Netroots Nation convention included doses of irony and exaggeration. It made assertions (that House Speaker Nancy Pelosi might find herself at home politically in Beijing, for example) and characterizations ("marauding liberals" was one) meant to amuse. For many readers, we failed.

"In trying for a humorous take on the Netroots phenomenon without labeling it something other than a straightforward news story, we compromised our standards."

July 22

'Wall Street Got Drunk'

An ABC-TV outlet in Houston, and now the *Houston Chronicle*, have posted a video taken at a political fundraiser for Pete Olson, featuring George W. Bush last week – capturing some embarrassing/revealing moments after, he noted, he had asked cameras to be turned off.

The first moments from the July 18 event find him speaking almost incoherently in admitting, for once, that his friends in big business had screwed up: "There's no question about it. Wall Street got drunk—that's one of the reasons I asked you to turn off the TV cameras – it got drunk and now it's got a hangover. The question is how long will it sober up and not try to do all these fancy financial instruments."

Then, making light of the foreclosure crisis, he said: "And then we got a housing issue...not in Houston, and evidently not in Dallas, because Laura's over there trying to buy a house [great laughter]. I like Crawford but unfortunately after eight years of sacrifice, I am apparently no longer the decision maker."

No one is saying how ABC's Miya Shay got the video or how it emerged.

Here is some commentary:

David Gaffen at the *Wall Street Journal's* Marketbeat blog, headlines his post "Happy Hour in Washington," and notes: "What we are sure of is this: if Wall Street was drunk, who was the bartender handing out free drinks? Our thoughts at right." That image shows Alan Greenspan and President Bush.

Floyd Norris of the *New York Times* targeted the same pair on his blog: "A Federal Reserve chairman once said that the Fed's job was to take away the punch bowl when the party was getting good. Unfortunately, the Greenspan Fed and the Bush administration did all they could to keep the punch bowl full, fighting off efforts to regulate 'fancy financial instruments' or restrain the excessive leverage that will now lead to massive government bailouts to avert a financial disaster."

July 31

Michelle Obama: Political Spouse

For years, Connie Schultz has been one of my favorite local columnists, going back to her Pulitzer-winning days at Cleveland's *Plain Dealer*. She has since gone "national," via a syndicated column, two books, and the attention she received as the wife of Sherrod Brown, who won a surprising victory to the U.S. Senate from Ohio two years ago. In her column, however, she tends to downplay the latter angle, so it was a little surprising – but gratifying – to see her latest, where she reports on her interview with Michelle Obama, a fellow senatorial spouse, but with one key difference of course (well, more than one).

Schultz writes, from experience: "Anyone who has endured a high-stakes political race knows that campaigning requires a willingness to suffer a seemingly endless series of small humiliations. All that begging for campaign contributions, posing for photo-ops and talking about me, me, me as the press corps yawns.

"When you are the political spouse, who is still usually a wife, you also can feel reduced to a life of serial irrelevance."

Obama says she is especially intent on winning over Hillary voters: "The way I see it? There are a lot of people like me, like how I am about my husband, my candidate. They invested their hearts and souls into Hillary Clinton, and many of them did this for years. They have to figure out how they want to leverage their political power. I understand that. Politics is a patience game. You can't do this unless you have patience."

AUGUST 2008

August 7

McCain Will 'Play Rough' to Win

In the next issue of *Time* magazine, out tomorrow, reporter Michael Scherer reveals – though this is not exactly a shocker by now – that John McCain is ready to "play rough" to win in November. Scherer writes, "The new McCain is tight and focused. The candidate who once invited all comers onto the back of his bus now hangs a curtain on his campaign plane to prevent reporters from even catching a glimpse. Instead of charm and candor, he serves up fastballs. Instead of risk-taking, he seeks control. It's a whole new McCain ... Despite his backslapping reputation, McCain will play rough if he thinks it will help him win."

    A full-page illustration shows McCain throwing fastballs from a pitchers' mound. *Time*, keeping with the baseball theme, calls the new tactic "hardball" and "throwing heat." Scherer notes: "Gone are McCain's daily promises to conduct a 'respectful campaign.'" Now the McCain team has decided to "go for broke." Many may disagree, however, with Scherer's claim that McCain has kept the attacks so far "light and funny."

    Mark Salter, one of McCain's top, adds, "We were letting the press [get] in our heads ... [Now] we're going to say what the message is."

    The new *Time* poll finds Obama in front overall 46%-41% but with some startlingly wide specific edges for him: more likable by 65% to 20%, as candidate for change by 61% to 17%, and Obama beats McCain 48% to 35% on who understands voters' concerns best.

August 8

Obama's Promise to 'Win' in Afghanistan – Wise or Wrong?

That U.S. casualties had finally hit the 500 mark in Afghanistan drew wide press attention today, including coverage on the front page of *The New York Times*.

Every so often the media note that the ongoing American death toll in that country now eclipses the grim tally in Iraq. So the war in Afghanistan, long overlooked, is now getting more notice. Polls show that the American people are growing increasingly concerned, and pessimistic, about that conflict.

But does that mean the U.S., finally starting (perhaps) to dig out of Iraq, should now commit to another open-ended war, even for a good cause, not so far away?

Nearly everyone in the media, and on the political stage, say that this is the "good war." Liberals, including a certain senator named Obama, have long made political points on Iraq by stating that it was the wrong war in the wrong place at the wrong time - when we should have kept our eye on the ball in Afghanistan (and adjoining areas of Pakistan). Hell, I have made that argument myself, and it is not wrong.

We should have done that. And if we had, no doubt the situation in Afghanistan would be a lot better today, as would the overall "war on terror."

But we didn't, and now we are desperately trying to play catch up. So the overwhelming sentiment from American leaders, including Obama and many of his supporters, is: Take troops out of Iraq and move them (and maybe even more of them, as John McCain argues) right over to Afghanistan.

Obama has even said we must "win" there. But it's the same question we have faced in Iraq: What does he define as "winning"? How much are we willing to expend (in lives lost and money) at a time of a severe budget crunch and overstretched military? Shouldn't the native forces – and NATO – be doing more? And what about Pakistan? And so on. We've been fighting there even longer than in Iraq, if that seems possible. Now do want to jump out of a frying pan into that fire in an open-ended way?

Few voices in the mainstream media - and even in the liberal blogosphere – have tackled this subject, partly because of long arguing for the need to fight the "good war" as opposed to the "bad war." But now some very respected commentators – with impeccable pro-military credentials – are starting to sound off on the longterm dangers.

Joseph L. Galloway, the legendary war reporter – recently retired from Knight Ridder – has written a column for McClatchy Newspapers ringing an alarm about Afghanistan, based largely on a recent paper written by Gen. Barry McCaffrey for use at West Point.

Thomas Friedman in a recent *New York Times* column: "The main reason we are losing in Afghanistan is not because there are too few American soldiers, but because there are not enough Afghans ready to fight and die for the kind of government we want....Obama needs to ask himself honestly: 'Am I for sending more troops to Afghanistan because I really think we can win there, because I really think that that will bring an end to terrorism, or am I just doing it because to get elected in America, post-9/11, I have to be for winning some war?'"

Here is an excerpt from the Galloway column:

Gen. Barry McCaffrey, who retired from the U.S. Army with four stars and a chest full of combat medals including two Distinguished Service Crosses, says we can't shoot our way out of Afghanistan, and the two or three or more American combat brigades proposed by the two putative nominees for president are irrelevant...

The general says that despite the two presidential candidates' sound bites, a few more combat brigades from "our rapidly unraveling Army" won't make much difference in Afghanistan. Military means, he writes, won't be enough to counter terror created by resurgent Taliban forces; we can't win with a war of attrition; and the economic and political support from the international community is inadequate.

"This is a struggle for the hearts of the people, and good governance, and the creation of Afghan security forces," McCaffrey writes. He says the main theater of war is in frontier regions of Afghanistan and Pakistan, and the combatants are tribes, religious groups, criminals and drug lords. It'll take a quarter-century of nation-building, road and bridge building, the building of a better-trained and better-armed Afghan National Police and National Army and the eradication of a huge opium farming industry to achieve a good outcome in Afghanistan, McCaffrey wrote in his report to leaders at the U.S. Military Academy at West Point.

We can't afford to fail in Afghanistan, the general says, but he doesn't address the question of whether we can afford to succeed there, either.

August 13

James Fallows on Obama's 'Keyes' to Victory

A new *Atlantic* article by longtime contributor James Fallows reveals his thoughts after doing what no sane person would do (as he admits): viewing every single GOP and Democratic primary debate to date. The lengthy take reviews past Obama and McCain performances with an eye to predicting what will happen this fall. And it closes with an assessment of what a President Obama would be like as he puts "just words" into action.

Perhaps most pertinent for now is Fallows' view of the coming showdowns this autumn. He observes that Obama was surprisingly tentative in most of his debates so far, which is why he did not easily triumph over Hillary Clinton. He was much more relaxed and effective in taking on his 2004 opponent in the U.S. Senate race, Alan Keyes.

Fallows predicts, however, that McCain will truly look old and "is not a good debater, not even by comparison with George W. Bush" so he "will play the expectations game as hard as he can, knowing that's how the press will keep score." And: "Once he gets on the stage, McCain will try to remind Obama of Hillary Clinton – that is, of someone he must take seriously, someone who is willing to challenge him and even insult him to his face."

Obama "is vain about his idealism and 'nobility,' a staff member for one of Obama's Democratic opponents (not Clinton) told me on the phone. 'He is thin-skinned about having his motives and competence questioned, so that's what you do.' Grizzled pols like Hillary Clinton or her husband would laugh off such an attempt; Obama may still be innocent enough to be shaken by it. McCain made many dismissive references to Obama after Obama became the presumptive nominee. The easy next step is to do so while looking at him.

"For Obama the key is: look at John McCain, and see Alan Keyes."

August 15

Unlike 2004, Media Sinks 'Swiftboat' Book

Four years ago this month, I explored in a number of articles the belated or conflicted media response to the "swiftboating" of Sen. John Kerry, then the Democratic nominee for president. The mainstream press gave the

August 2008

charges – carried in ads, in books and articles, and in major TV appearances – a free ride for a spell, then a respectful airing mixed with critique, before in many cases finally attempting to shoot them down as overwhelmingly exaggerated or false. This delay, along with Kerry's own reluctance to face the matter squarely, quite possibly cost the Democrat the White House.

Now, this month, a bestselling anti-Obama book – by a co-author of the most prominent "swiftboat" anti-Kerry book in 2004 – has predictably been published (by Mary Matalin's imprint) and has gained immediate and wide attention in the mainstream. But this time, in many cases, the media response has been a "swift" kick to its credibility.

On Wednesday night, for example, when that author, Jerome Corsi, appeared with Larry King on CNN, he was forced to debate an antagonist, Media Matters' Paul Waldman – and, for much of the time, King himself. Waldman was even able to air some of Corsi's revolting Web comments in the years before he became famous as a swiftboater.

A *Washington Post* editorial for Friday's paper calls Corsi an "expert of misrepresentation," and adds, "footnoting to a discredited blog item does not constitute careful scholarship, and the bulk of Mr. Corsi's book has nothing to do with issues. He gets facts wrong... He makes offensive statements." Four years ago, the *Post* for too long offered a very "balanced" view of the anti-Kerry claims.

Mincing few words, *Post* columnist Eugene Robinson declares today, "Here come the goons, right on schedule." Corsi, he adds, "has crawled back out from under his rock to spew vicious lies about Barack Obama."

A *New York Times* blog item on Thursday connected Corsi to the "9/11 Truth" fringe, citing his questions about the official explanation of why the twin towers collapsed. Earlier this week, in a front-page article, the *Times* charged, "Several of the book's accusations, in fact, are unsubstantiated, misleading or inaccurate."

Among the other Corsi pieces this week one stands out. It appeared Thursday night via The Associated Press, written by one of its top political reporters, Nedra Pickler – a journalist the liberal blogosphere has frequently criticized. It covered the Obama campaign's release of a 40-page parsing of Corsi's *The Obama Nation* but, significantly (in the new "AP style"), Pickler added a huge dose of attitude as well. Adding to the Obama team's argument, Pickler observed on her own:

"The book is a compilation of all the innuendo and false rumors against Obama – that he was raised a Muslim, attended a radical, black church and secretly has a 'black rage' hidden beneath the surface. In fact, Obama is a Christian who attended Trinity United Church of Christ in Chicago.

"Corsi suggests, without a shred of proof, that Obama may be using drugs today. Obama has acknowledged using marijuana and cocaine as a teenager but says he quit when he went to college and hasn't used drugs since."

"He claims Obama received extensive Islamic religious education as a boy in Indonesia, education that was only offered to the truly faithful. Actually, Obama is a Christian and as a boy he attended both Catholic school and Indonesian public schools where some basic study of the Koran was offered."

"He accuses Obama of wanting to weaken the military even though Obama's campaign calls for adding 65,000 soldiers and 27,000 Marines."

"Corsi writes for World Net Daily, a conservative Web site whose lead headline Thursday was *Astonishing photo claims: Dead Bigfoot stored on ice*.

"In a series of Web posts several years ago, Corsi said Pope John Paul II was senile and unconcerned about sexual molestation of boys, referred to Islam 'a worthless, dangerous Satanic religion' and suggested Kerry was secretly Jewish."

August 18

Fans of Colbert and Stewart Get 'Real'
The results of the new Pew Survey on News Consumption (taken every two years and released this afternoon) suggest that viewers of the "fake news" programs *The Daily Show* and *The Colbert Report* are more knowledgeable about current events (as judged by three test questions) than watchers of "real" cable news shows hosted by Lou Dobbs, Bill O'Reilly and Larry King, among others – as well as average consumers of NBC, ABC, Fox News, CNN, C-SPAN (gasp) and daily newspapers.

The national average for answering the three questions was only 18%. But 34% of *The Colbert Report* fans got them right, with 30% of *The Daily Show* viewers doing so – even though the two Comedy Central shows draw younger audiences which generally scored less well on the "test" than older viewers/readers. The Pew Report observed: *"The Colbert Report* and *The*

Daily Show are notable for having relatively well-informed audiences that are younger than the national average."

Topping the knowledge list were *The New Yorker* and *The Atlantic* (48%), NPR (44%), MSNBC's Hardball (43%), and Fox's Hannity & Colmes at 42%.

While consumers of most news outlets scored poorly on the test, a separate question revealed that a vast majority believe they follow national news closely. Yet, somehow, only 53% were able to correctly identify which party now controls Congress. In another finding: no surprise, Democrats were found to favor CNN and MSNBC while Republicans strongly dig Fox.

Respondents were asked to identify which party now controls Congress, who is the current U.S. secretary of state and name the new prime minister of Great Britain.

August 19

Will Mechanic Again Get Scoop on Obama's Veep Pick?
Remember 2004? It's true, the *New York Post* got the most memorable scoop on John Kerry's pick for a running mate – Dick Gephardt – but an airline mechanic actually took the "true" honors. Will it happen again? The moral of this story: Keep an eye on all those aviation blogs!

The story, as it has been re-told in recent hours: A fellow named Bryan Smith, aka "aerosmith," posted the John Edwards 2004 nod on an aviation message board.

He had arrived at work on June 5, 2004, the day before Kerry formally announced that Edwards was his choice, in Pittsburgh. Smith told NPR that he was passing through a hangar at Pittsburgh airport to get to his work area at US Airways "when I was informed by, I am assuming, Mr. Kerry's people, that I should not peek in that hangar and that it was, in fact, closed for the day."

Naturally, every time he passed near or through the hangar that day, he took a glance. "Being a curious person, around 6 that evening, I peeked in and I saw they were putting John Edwards' name on the airplane," he said to NPR. "I wasn't the only one who knew this.....They concealed it rather quickly – they taped paper over the logos. I just happened to peek in at the right time before that occurred. I was just in transit."

A few hours later, at home, he "announced" the pick at an airline chat room, mentioning the "Edwards decals." The discussion at the site showed that "some people believed it and others didn't." He gave no thought to calling the media. Smith said he was a registered Democrat and would vote for "John and John."

So if the suspense is killing you: check out the hangars and mechanic sites.

August 23.

Biden Explains His 'Clean' Obama Comment – to Jon Stewart
Who can forget that day in January 2007 when Sen. Joseph Biden offered his infamous quip about "the first mainstream African-American who is articulate and bright and clean and a nice-looking guy." He was referring to the man who is now his new boss, Barack Obama. But by now, you have surely forgotten that this emerged on the very day Biden announced his race for president – and that he happened to appear that night on *The Daily Show* with Jon Stewart.

There he said (as I reported at the time) that he was simply trying to be "complimentary" toward Obama, but wasn't "artful" in doing so. He told Stewart that the "word that really got me in trouble" was calling Obama "clean....I should have said fresh. What I meant was he's got new ideas."

He said he had already called Obama, to which Stewart quipped, "I bet you did." Biden then said he also called former candidates Jesse Jackson and Al Sharpton, to which Stewart added: "And Michael Jordan?"

When Biden first appeared on stage, Stewart teased, "How's your day been?" Biden said, "It's a tough game," and crossed himself (he is Catholic). Stewart asked if wanted to talk about his comments that day and Biden replied, "No, I don't want to talk about it," but it was hard to tell if he was joking. In any case, he had no choice.

Stewart reminded him that just yesterday he had told the *Philadelphia Inquirer* that he had learned from previous campaigns to be careful, since "words matter." Stewart said, "And then you came out with this one," quoting the lines about Obama.

Biden said the whole day was a "reminder – 'welcome back to presidential politics.'" Stewart advised in a whisper, "When you are about to say one of those things, take a deep breath and count to 10."

August 25.

My Bloody First Democratic Convention – Chicago 1968

With the 2008 Democratic national convention about to begin in Denver, I can't help recalling the first DNC that I covered in 1968, exactly 40 years ago this week. Yes, it was the notorious gathering in Chicago, when the conflict turned bloody. I never made it inside the convention hall – but I did grab a front row seat for what "went down," as we used to say.

It culminated in the crushing of Sen. Eugene McCarthy's anti-Vietnam crusade inside the convention hall and the cracking of peacenik skulls by Mayor Richard Daley's police in the streets. Together, this doomed Hubert Humphrey to defeat in November at the hands of Richard Nixon.

I've been a political-campaign junkie all my life. At the age of 8, I paraded in front of my boyhood home in Niagara Falls, N.Y., waving an "I Like Ike" sign. In 1968 I got to cover my first presidential campaign when one of Sen. McCarthy's nephews came to town, before the state primary, and I interviewed him for the *Niagara Falls Gazette*, where I worked as a summer reporter during college. I had been chair of the McCarthy campaign at my college.

My mentor at the *Gazette* was a young, irreverent City Hall reporter named John Hanchette. He went on to become a Pulitzer Prize-winning national correspondent for Gannett News Service. Hanchette was in Chicago that week to cover party politics as a *Gazette* reporter and contributor to the Gannett News Service (GNS). I was to hang out with the young McCarthyites and the anti-war protesters. To get to Chicago I took my first ride on a jetliner.

To make a long story short: On the climactic night of Aug. 28, 1968, Hanchette and I ended up just floors apart in the same building: the Conrad Hilton Hotel in downtown Chicago. I was in McCarthy headquarters and Hanchette was in one of Gannett's makeshift newsrooms. Probably at about the same time, we pulled back the curtains and looked out our separate windows to see police savagely attacking protesters with nightsticks in the intersection directly below.

Like me, Hanchette headed for the streets. By that time, the peak violence had passed, but cops were still pushing reporters and other innocent bystanders through plate glass windows at the front of the hotel. I held back in the lobby, where someone had set off a stink bomb. Some Democrats started returning from the convention hall – after giving Humphrey the nomination even though McCarthy and Bobby Kennedy won most of the primaries (and you think Hillary has a beef?) – as protesters inside the Hilton chanted, "You killed the party! You killed the party!"

Finally, I screwed up my courage and crossed to Grant Park where the angry protest crowd gathered. And there I stayed all night, as the crowd and chants of "pig" directed at the cops increased. Many in the crowd wore bandages or had fresh blood on their faces. Phil Ochs arrived and sang, along with other notables, including some of the peacenik delegates. Cops lined the park – back up by jeeps with machines guns pointed at us.

When I returned to Niagara Falls that Friday, I wrote a column for that Sunday's paper. I described the eerie feeling of sitting in Grant Park, and thousands around me yelling at the soldiers and the media, "The whole world is watching!" – and knowing that, for once, it was true.

August 27

Repeat of 1968: Will Clintonites Cost Democrat the White House?
Judging by the hysterical media coverage of the DNC, one might assume that a legion of Hillary Clinton activists will fail to back, or even vote for, Barack Obama this fall. Some have even compared this to 1968, when many supporters of Eugene McCarthy and Robert F. Kennedy failed to embrace the Democratic candidate, Hubert Humphrey, allegedly dooming him to a narrow defeat in November.

As an expert on this matter, I'm here to testify this is all bunk.

First, and most importantly, there is no issue dividing the Obama and Clinton forces anything like the Vietnam War in '68. If Obama supported staying in Iraq for decades, and Clinton opposed it – or vice versa – then you might imagine something comparable. Nothing like this exists today.

Secondly, there is no question from the polls and the results of the primaries in 1968 that the U.S. public backed the antiwar McCarthy and RFK, who were denied the nomination. Clintonistas may be peeved about the outcome of the nomination process, but cannot point to her clear edge as the Democratic favorite.

Finally, Humphrey was basically the McCain candidate then – the "four more years" guy who had long supported the Vietnam war. Obama is hardly in that class. Humphrey was given more than two months to win over the peace crowd in '68 but made only tepid attempts. He had only himself to blame for his defeat. Obama may lose but if so it will be a lot more complex (race would have a lot to do with it) than any failure of Clinton activists to support him.

August 28

A 'Prickly' McCain Interview
As it did last week with the Democrats, *Time* magazine turns over much of its new issue – arriving tomorrow – to the Republican and their convention. It includes an amazing interview with a reluctant McCain, who *Time* brands right in its headline as "Prickly."

In a separate piece, Jay Carney and Michael Grunwald assert that McCain continues to consider himself a true man of "honor" but he and his aides "have convinced themselves that Obama is not honorable, that he does not love his country as much as himself. That makes it easier to justify doing whatever is necessary to defeat him – especially if it's done in the pursuit of honor." In fact, in the Q & A, McCain can't think of a single criticism of his campaign so far and refuses to answer when pressed. He also refuses to define what he means by "honor" when asked and refers interviewers Carney and Michael Scherer to his books. He claims some of his past quotes have been ripped "out of context."

They introduce the interview this way: "McCain at first seemed happy enough to do the interview. But his mood quickly soured. The McCain on display in the 24-minute interview was prickly, at times abrasive, and determined not to stray off message."

August 29

GOP Senator Admits She Knows Almost Nothing About Palin
Looking for a quick reaction, and likely endorsement, of John McCain's surprise pick today of Alaska Gov. Sarah Palin as his running mate this

morning, CNN turned to Sen. Kay Bailey Hutchison, the experienced Texan who was also on McCain's short list for the post. But, asked about Palin, all Hutchison could muster, just before the official announcement, was a few generalities about "spirit" and "enthusiasm," before admitting, "I don't know much about her."

CNN's John King then asked, well, what does it mean that such a longtime GOP leader such as yourself doesn't know much about her when McCain is hitting Obama on his lack of experience? Palin has served as governor of her state for less than two years. Hutchison repeated her earlier statements about "youth" and said flatly, "I don't know Sarah Palin," adding maybe that it was a "good thing" that she is fresh and not that well known.

Pressed again about why she would think that Palin was ready to be commander-in-chief, a charge leveled at Obama, Hutchison could only muster that, well, she was sure John McCain had sat down with her and was convinced of this. Early indications, however, suggest that he barely sat down with her at all.

CNN's John Roberts then said that what we do know is that she can eat a mooseburger, drive a snowmobile and fire a rifle. A few minutes later, CNN was reporting on an ethics probe of Palin in Alaska surrounding the state firing her brother-in-law, a state trooper involved in a "messy" divorce with her sister.

Meanwhile, Carl Cameron over at Fox was reporting that Palin is known as a big hockey fan and everyone knows that hockey fans are really "blue-collar." So this will allegedly help the ticket win Minnesota, Wisconsin, and so forth. Fox's Steve Doocy said that Palin was not so weak on foreign policy expertise. After all, he pointed out, her state is physically quite close to Russia.

Palin Comparison: Rove Had Mocked Obama Considering Kaine
Surely, the hypocrisy of John McCain charging Barack Obama with not being ready to be president will stand out in stark relief following his choice of Sarah Palin as his running mate. But there's also the little matter of GOP leaders previously mocking Obama for considering less-than-fully-experienced candidates for vice president.

Appearing on *Face the Nation* less than three weeks ago, Republican strategist Karl Rove singled out Virginia Governor Tim Kaine, who was on

Obama's short list. "With all due respect again to Governor Kaine, he's been a governor for three years, he's been able but undistinguished," Rove said. Note to Karl: Palin has been governor – of a much, much smaller state – for less than two years.

Rove also said: "I don't think people could really name a big, important thing that he's done. He was mayor of the 105th largest city in America." Of course, Palin was formerly mayor of a town that must be ranked about 15,000th biggest in America.

He added, "So if he were to pick Governor Kaine, it would be an intensely political choice where he said, 'You know what? I'm really not, first and foremost, concerned with – is this person capable of being president of the United States?'"

CBS summarized Rove's other statements as follows: "He expects presumptive Democratic nominee Barack Obama to choose a running mate based on political calculations, not the person's readiness for the job. 'I think he's going to make an intensely political choice, not a governing choice,' Rove said. 'He's going to view this through the prism of a candidate, not through the prism of president....He's not going to be thinking big and broad about the responsibilities of president."

Olbermann Hits AP Reporter Over Obama Speech

In an unusually heated attack on a veteran political reporter by a cable news host, MSNBC's Keith Olbermann laced into the Associated Press's Charles Babington an hour after Barack Obama had concluded his speech in Denver on Thursday night.

Nearly all of the top commentators and reporters on the three cable news networks had hailed Obama's speech as something new and powerful, and filled with specifics, and predicted it would have a positive effect on his chances vs. John McCain. This hallelujah chorus included conservatives such as Bill Kristol and Pat Buchanan and longtime Republican David Gergen, as well as Tom Brokaw and Brian Williams. Buchanan called it the best and most important political convention speech he had ever heard, going back 48 years.

So the liberal Olbermann was outraged that the AP's Babington had written, in his analysis of the speech, just off the wire, that Obama had tried nothing new and that his speech was lacking in specifics. He read the first few paragraphs on the air, lamented that it would be printed in hundreds of newspapers on Friday, and concluded, "It is analysis that strikes me as having borne no resemblance to the speech you and I just watched. None whatsoever. And for it to be distributed by the lone national news organization in terms of wire copy to newspapers around the country and Web sites is a remarkable failure of that news organization.

"Charles Babington, find a new line of work."

Olberman even criticized the reporter on his time-keeping, noting that the article said the speech was 35 minutes long when it was, he said, actually at least seven minutes longer than that. A few minutes later, the AP copy had been corrected to "44 minutes." And even as Babington was hitting Obama for a lack of specifics, AP was transmitting a second piece by another reporter, Jim Drinkard, that offered a detailed look at seven specific policy proposals in the speech.

Obama backers have criticized the coverage of their candidate by the AP's Washington Bureau Chief, Ron Fournier, and other AP reporters, for several months. Fournier has denied any slant but has said that he wants more analysis in stories.

2 Top Alaska Newspapers Question Palin's Fitness

Since yesterday's shocking arrival of Gov. Sarah Palin as John McCain's running mate we've been subjected to the usual cable news and print blathering about the pick from those who know little about her. But what about the journalists close to home – in Alaska – who know her best and have followed her career for years?

For the past 24 hours, the pages and Web sites of the two leading papers up there have raised all sorts of issues surrounding Palin, from her ethics problems to general lack of readiness for this giant step up. Right now the top story on the *Anchorage Daily News* Web site looks at new info in what it calls "troopergate" and opens: "Alaska's former commissioner of public safety says Gov. Sarah Palin, John McCain's pick to be vice president, personally talked to him on two occasions about a state trooper who was locked in a bitter custody battle with the governor's sister.

"In a phone conversation Friday night, Walt Monegan, who was Alaska's top cop until Palin fired him July 11, told the *Daily News* that the governor also had e-mailed him two or three times about her ex-brother-in-law, Trooper Mike Wooten, though the e-mails didn't mention Wooten by name. Monegan claims his refusal to fire Wooten was a major reason that Palin dismissed him. Wooten had been suspended for five days previously, based largely on complaints that Palin's family had initiated before Palin was governor."

A former reporter for the Anchorage daily, Gregg Erickson, in an online chat with the *Washington Post*, revealed that Palin's approval rating in the state was not the much-touted 80%, but 65% and sinking – and that among journalists who followed her it might be in the "teens." He added: "I have a hard time seeing how her qualifications stack up against the duties and responsibilities of being president.... I expect her to stick with simple truths. When asked about continued American troop presence in Iraq, she said she knows only one thing about that (I paraphrase): no one has attacked the American homeland since George Bush took the war to Iraq."

His paper found a number of leading Republican officeholders in the state who mocked Palin's qualifications. "She's not prepared to be governor. How can she be prepared to be vice president or president?" said Lyda Green, the president of the State Senate, a Republican from Palin's hometown of Wasilla. "Look at what she's done to this state. What would she do to the nation?"

Another top Republican, John Harris, the speaker of the House, when asked about her qualifications for veep, replied with this: "She's old enough. She's a U.S. citizen."

Dermot Cole, a columnist for the Fairbanks paper, observed that he thinks highly of Palin as a person but "in no way does her year-and-a-half as governor of Alaska qualify her to be vice president or president of the United States.

"One of the strange things Friday was that so many commentators and politicians did not know how to pronounce her name and had no clue about what she has actually done in Alaska....I may be proven wrong, but the decision announced by McCain strikes me as reckless. She is not prepared to be the next president should something happen to McCain."

And from the startling Saturday editorial in the *Daily News-Miner* in Fairbanks: "Sen. John McCain's selection of Gov. Sarah Palin as his vice presidential running mate was a stunning decision that should make Alaskans proud, even while we wonder about the actual merits of the choice.... Alaskans and Americans must ask, though, whether she should become vice president and, more importantly, be placed first in line to become president.

"In fact, as the governor herself acknowledged in her acceptance speech, she never set out to be involved in public affairs. She has never publicly demonstrated the kind of interest, much less expertise, in federal issues and foreign affairs that should mark a candidate for the second-highest office in the land. Republicans rightfully have criticized the Democratic nominee, Sen. Barack Obama, for his lack of experience, but Palin is a neophyte in comparison; how will Republicans reconcile the criticism of Obama with the obligatory cheering for Palin?

"Most people would acknowledge that, regardless of her charm and good intentions, Palin is not ready for the top job. McCain seems to have put his political interests ahead of the nation's when he created the possibility that she might fill it."

And from the editorial in the *Anchorage Daily News*: "It's stunning that someone with so little national and international experience might be heartbeat away from the presidency.

"Gov. Palin is a classic Alaska story. She is an example of the opportunity our state offers to those with talent, initiative and determination...McCain picked Palin despite a recent blemish on her ethically pure resume. While she was governor, members of her family and staff tried to get her ex-brother-in-law fired from the Alaska State Troopers. Her public safety commissioner would not do so; she forced him out, supposedly for other reasons. While she runs for vice-president, the Legislature has an investigator on the case.

"For all those advantages, Palin joins the ticket with one huge weakness: She's a total beginner on national and international issues. Gov. Palin will have to spend the next two months convincing Americans that she's ready to be a heartbeat away from the presidency."

August 31

On a Clear Day She Can See....Minsk?
When a Fox News morning host, Steve Doocy, testified to Sarah Palin's national security experience on Friday by saying that her state, Alaska, was close to Russia, it drew hoots across the media and blogosphere (and even, no doubt, from a few Fox viewers). This morning, on ABC in an interview with

George Stephanopoulos, Cindy McCain endorsed this very view. Asked about Palin's national security experience, Cindy could not come up with anything beyond the fact that, after all, her state is right next to Russia. "You know, the experience that she comes from is, what she has done in government – and remember that Alaska is the closest part of our continent to Russia."

She added that Palin has "way more experience than...." but Stephanopoulos cut her off before she could say, for example, "Barack Obama" or maybe "others give her credit for." Earlier in the interview, she said that Palin was "heavily experienced" in general, citing her going from the PTA to mayor to governor – and having a son headed for Iraq. She actually said that she started her political career at the PTA "like everybody else."

Meanwhile, Palin's mother-in-law, Faye Palin, told a New York *Daily News* reporter that she didn't agree with Sarah on everything and hadn't yet decided how she would vote. She added: "I'm not sure what she brings to the ticket other than she's a woman and a conservative. Well, she's a better speaker than McCain," Palin said with a laugh.

But this actually isn't as appalling as a phone interview Palin herself gave yesterday to a reporter back home, at the *Anchorage Daily News*. The reporter, Kyle Hopkins, asked, according to the transcript posted today, "Are you ready to be President Palin if necessary?"

"I am ... I am up to the task, of course, of focusing on the challenges that face America," she answered, and that was all she could say on her behalf on this question. Then she abruptly shifted to how her candidacy would help Alaska. "And I am very pleased with the situation that I am in, when, when you consider the situation now that Alaska will be in.

"And that is Alaska, and Alaskans will be allowed to contribute more to our great country and they'll be allowed to do that because I – if we're elected – will be in a position of opening the eyes of the country to what it is that Alaska is all about and what Alaska has to offer. So, I am happy to and very honored to be asked to do this. I know it's going to be great for Alaska."

Who said the woman was against earmarks? Actually, it seems like she sees herself as one big Alaska earmark.

The early returns are not good, with most in the media still stepping lightly around the issue of John McCain's hypocrisy in asserting, for months, that Barack Obama is "dangerously" inexperienced in facing international threats – and then appointing Palin as his running mate.

SEPTEMBER 2008

September 1

3 New Polls: Palin Pick Not Fooling Women

A new CNN/Opinion Research poll released today shows that he contest between Barack Obama and John McCain – after the twin "bounces" of the past few days – remains essentially tied, with Obama leading at 49% to 48%. But what's most intriguing are the results regarding McCain's choice for veep, who was expected to draw more women to the GOP ticket.

In fact, men seem to be more impressed with this move than women. Just now, this seems to be confirmed by a CBS poll, showing Obama with a 48% to 40% lead overall – but with a wide lead among women, at 50% to 36%, which has only widened. Only 13% of women said they might be more likely to vote for McCain because of Palin, with 11% saying they are now less likely.

CBS also reports: "Before the Democratic convention, McCain enjoyed a 12-point advantage with independent voters, but now Obama leads among this group 43 percent to 37 percent....The poll shows an increase in the number of Obama voters who are enthusiastic about him."

As for the CNN poll: "Women now appear slightly more likely to vote for Obama than they did a week ago, 53 percent now, compared to 50 percent," reports Keating Holland, CNN's director of polling. "But McCain picked up a couple of points among men. More important, McCain solidified his party's base with the Palin selection, dropping Obama's share of the Republican vote six points to just 5 percent now. The Palin selection did not help among women – that may come later – but it did appeal to Republican loyalists."

Men have a slightly more favorable opinion of Palin than women – 41 percent vs. 36 percent. "If McCain was hoping to boost his share of the women's vote, it didn't work," Holland said. And USA Today/Gallup has just released its post-Palin poll showing that Obama has widened his lead from four points to 50% - 43%.

Here is an excerpt from the CNN report: "Is Palin qualified to be president? Fifty percent say she is unqualified to assume the presidency if that becomes necessary; 45 percent say she's prepared for the White House. In recent history, the only running mate to earn less confidence from the public was Vice President Dan Quayle in 1992.

"Three quarters of all voters think McCain chose a female running mate specifically because he thought adding a woman to the Republican ticket would help him win in November."

September 2

The Dossier on Palin: 62 Pages of 'Oppo Research'
The McCain team may not have vetted Sarah Palin with boots on the ground in Alaska, but the Democrats sure did – two years ago when she ran for governor. The oppo-research, compiled in a 62-page document with countless summaries or direct quotes, largely from local newspapers, covers all of the important issues you would expect to see, from her views on abortion and abstinence to tangled oil pipeline questions.

But it also gets into some quirky, if revealing, areas as well, such as Palin founding a company called "Rouge Cru" – what she called a "classy" way to say redneck – in case her political career didn't work out a few years ago.

Politico.com obtained a copy and printed merely a handful of the hundreds of findings today. These included serious matters such as her use of the mayor's office in political campaigns. But it also posted a PDF of the entire document which, I'd wager, few have examined. I have now completed that task and present here some of the more outrageous, or surprising, revelations. They are posted here under their heading in the document. Note: *The Frontiersman* is the local weekly paper in Wasilla.

DEATH PENALTY
Asked about the death penalty, in extreme cases such as the murder of a child, Palin said, "My goodness, hang 'em up, yeah." [Anchorage Daily News, 8/18/06]

RELIGION
Palin wrote a Letter to the Editor saying only, "San Francisco judges forbidding our Pledge of Allegiance? They will take the phrase 'under God' away from me when my cold, dead lips can no longer utter those words. God bless America." [Juneau Empire, 6/30/02]

WALMART
Palin Presided Over a Wedding at a Walmart. He worked in the pets department. She was a cashier. A romance blossomed. And when it came time to say "I do," they chose – where else? – an aisle next to menswear. Sandwiched between racks of cotton pants and surrounded by "Back-to-School Specials" signs, Jake McCowan and Rosalyn Ryan exchanged vows last week at the place where they met, work and fell in love: the Wasilla Wal-Mart. A crowd of 200, including passengers from a tour bus and several dozen curious shoppers, watched the two employees tie the knot in an afternoon ceremony officiated by Wasilla Mayor Sarah Palin. "It was so sweet," said Palin, who fought back tears during the nuptials. "It was so Wasilla." [Anchorage Daily News, 8/28/99]

LEGAL
In 1993, Sarah Palin used a drift gillnet to harvest salmon from the Bristol Bay area without an annual permit. Palin plead guilty to the Criminal Negligence charge. Palin also had a case dismissed where she was charged with fishing without a photo ID. The case was filed 6/28/93 and was disposed 8/25/1993. The jurisdiction was the Third Judicial District-Dillingham. [Alaska Criminal History Records]

GAYS
Palin Said She Supported Ban on Gay Marriage and Denying Benefits to Gay Couples. "Palin said she's not out to judge anyone and has good friends who are gay, but that she supported the 1998 constitutional amendment [to ban gay marriage].....She said she doesn't know if people choose to be gay." [Anchorage Daily News, 8/6/06]

GENDER CARD
Stambaugh Sued for Gender Discrimination After Palin Said She Was Intimidated by His Size. After Palin fired Irl Stambaugh, the police chief, he sued the city

in part based on gender discrimination. The [Wasilla] Frontiersman wrote, "The gender discrimination issues stem from statements Palin allegedly made to others that she was intimidated by Stambaugh's size. He stands over 6-feet tall and weighs more than 200 pounds, which, the lawsuit said, is attributed to his gender." [Frontiersman, 2/26/97]

Palin Went to See Ivana Trump at Costco, Saying Alaska was So Desperate for "Any Semblance of Glamour and Culture." "Sarah Palin, a commercial fisherman from Wasilla, told her husband on Tuesday she was driving to Anchorage to shop at Costco. Instead, she headed straight for Ivana. And there, at J.C. Penney's cosmetic department, was Ivana, the former Mrs. Donald Trump, sitting at a table next to a photograph of herself. She wore a light-colored pantsuit and pink fingernail polish. Her blonde hair was coiffed in a bouffant French twist. 'We want to see Ivana,' said Palin, who admittedly smells like salmon for a large part of the summer, 'because we are so desperate in Alaska for any semblance of glamour and culture.'" [Anchorage Daily News, 4/3/96]

PERSONAL
Palin's Brother-In-Law Appeared on Reality Dating Show. Lt. Gov. candidate Sarah Palin thought it might help her campaign when brother-in-law Jack McCann showed up as a desirable catch on the new "reality" TV show, "Looking for Love: Bachelorettes in Alaska." That hope lasted until she actually saw an episode of the series, which turns out to be your basic meat market twitch & grin. "Oh Lord," she said. "My sisters and I watched it in horror." Jack, who is scheduled to appear again even though he crashed a mountain bike in the first episode, is pretty cute and has a sense of humor, Sarah reports. "He described his occupation . . . as an office environment consultant," she said. "He sells furniture." [Anchorage Daily News, 6/9/02]

Palin told The Associated Press that she and her husband, Todd, made a bet on whether Murkowski would run. If the governor says he'll enter the race, Palin has to get the Big Dipper tattooed on her ankle. If Murkowski says no, Todd gets a wedding ring inked on his finger. [Anchorage Daily News, 5/26/06]

September 2008

New York Tabs 'Out' Hockey Dad

When news emerged on Monday that Bristol Palin, 17, daughter of John McCain's running mate, was pregnant, all that was known about the father was that he was identified in her parents' statement as a certain "Levi." Since his hometown of Wasilla is awfully small – and the pregnancy was no secret locally – it probably didn't take a lot of digging to discover the dad's identity.

In any case, both New York City tabloids, the *Post* and the *Daily News*, have since IDed the father, along with presenting a photo of him (in a hockey shirt) and quotes from his My Space page. One of them might raise a few eyebrows: He declares that he is "in a relationship" but "I don't want kids."

He is Levi Johnston, and like the mother-to-be is about to enter his senior year at Wasilla High, according to the *Post*. The *Daily News* described him as a "superhunky bad-boy ice hockey player" and carried a photo of him on the ice. On his MySpace page, Johnston boasts, "I'm a fuckin' redneck" who likes to snowboard and ride dirt bikes. "But I live to play hockey. I like to go camping and hang out with the boys, do some fishing, shoot some shit and just fuckin' chillin' I guess….Ya fuck with me I'll kick [your] ass," he added.

September 3

Peggy Noonan's 'Live Mike' Disaster

Talk about flip flops! Peggy Noonan had an "open mile" problem at MSNBC today, in which Noonan referred to the "bullshit" narrative around Palin and was generally critical (off-camera) of McCain for making this pick. Well, here's some of what she wrote just this morning at the *Wall Street Journal's* online site:

"Because she jumbles up so many cultural categories, because she is a feminist not in the Yale Gender Studies sense but the How Do I Reload This Thang way, because she is a woman who in style, history, moxie and femininity is exactly like a normal American feminist and not an Abstract Theory feminist; because she wears makeup and heels and eats mooseburgers and is Alaska Tough, as Time magazine put it; because she is conservative, and pro-2nd Amendment and pro-life; and because conservatives can smell this sort of thing – who is really one of them and who is not – and will fight to the death for one of their beleaguered own; because of all of this she is a real and present danger to the American left, and to the Obama candidacy.

"She could become a transformative political presence."

And more: "I'll tell you how powerful Mrs. Palin already is: she reignited the culture wars just by showing up. She scrambled the battle lines, too. The crustiest old Republican men are shouting 'Sexism!' when she's slammed. Pro-woman Democrats are saying she must be a bad mother to be all ambitious with kids in the house...."

"I'm bumping into a lot of critics who do not buy the legitimacy of small town mayorship (Palin had two terms in Wasilla, Alaska, population 9,000 or so) and executive as opposed to legislative experience. But executives, even of small towns, run something. There are 262 cities in this country with a population of 100,000 or more. But there are close to a hundred thousand small towns with ten thousand people or less. 'You do the math,' the conservative pollster Kellyanne Conway told me. 'We are a nation of Wasillas, not Chicagos.'"

This is surely the New New Math. Stay tuned for the answer to this voting equation in November.

September 4

Cynthia Tucker vs. Bill O'Reilly
She's a Pulitzer-winning columnist and editorial page director at the *Atlanta Journal-Constitution*. He hosts a Fox News show, a syndicated column and a radio show. Now they are at war over teen pregnancy (you can guess what kicked that off), with O'Reilly calling her a "nut."

It started with Tucker in her Wednesday column writing: "For some reason, the pious social conservatives of the Republican Party did not denounce the 17-year-old daughter of Alaska Gov. Sarah Palin. Instead, they greeted the news of her pregnancy as evidence of the strong moral fiber of Palin and her husband, citing the fact that they have offered Bristol their comfort and support.

"For a minute there, I feared that right wingers would attack the young lady as evidence of the moral failings of a liberal, anything-goes culture, or as proof that her parents had failed to provide a Christian upbringing that eschews sex outside marriage. After all, that's what conservatives usually say when unmarried adolescent girls get pregnant.

"When Jamie Lynn Spears' pregnancy was revealed, for example, Bill O'Reilly went after her parents: 'On the pinhead front, 16-year-old Jamie Lynn Spears is pregnant. The sister of Britney says she is shocked. I bet. Now most teens are pinheads in some ways. But here the blame falls primarily on the parents of the girl, who obviously have little control over her or even over Britney Spears. Look at the way she behaves,' O'Reilly declared."

O'Reilly responded yesterday: "Now, the latest thing is that people like me don't condemn Palin's family but we condemn other people who, uh, gave birth out of wedlock. I've never condemned anybody who gave birth out of wedlock. Ever in my life. I don't make those kinds of determinations. What I do say and, this nut Cynthia Tucker in the *Atlanta Journal Constitution* makes a deal out of this, I said that Britney Spears and what's her sister's name who's pregnant, their parents were irresponsible - Jamie Lee - because they were running around unsupervised.

"Yeah, I said that and I believe it. It has nothing to do with the Palin situation, okay? So, I mean, it just, it really, it makes me angry."

September 5

Palin May NOT 'Meet the Press'?

Jay Carney of *Time* magazine appeared this morning on TV with a spokeswoman for the McCain campaign who seemed to say that Sarah Palin may steer clear of the press in the coming campaign. He opens his post at the mag's Swampland blog this way: "According to Nicole Wallace of the McCain campaign, the American people don't care whether Sarah Palin can answer specific questions about foreign and domestic policy. According to Wallace – in an appearance I did with her this morning on Joe Scarborough's show – the American people will learn all they need to know (and all they deserve to know) from Palin's scripted speeches and choreographed appearances on the campaign trail and in campaign ads....

"It's important to them to know if Palin can handle herself in an environment that isn't controlled and sanitized by campaign image makers and message mavens. Maybe she can, maybe she can't. As far as Wallace is concerned, it's none of their – or your – business." Wallace actually said, "who cares?"

Photo Research You Can Believe In?
Just bubbling up to the mainstream newspapers is one of the funniest – if revealing – incidents of the week. If you watched John McCain's speech on Thursday night at the RNC you probably noticed that strange big old building posted behind him at one point. It didn't really seem to fit what he was talking about, but what the heck. Well, a little research by the folks at Talking Points Memo revealed that it was a public school in California called Walter Reed. And the only plausible explanation was that a McCain photo person googled for famed Walter Reed *Medical Center* and grabbed this.

McCain campaign manager Rick Davis reportedly admitted the mistake at a *Vanity Fair* party and the campaign later denied it – but there's another problem. School officials are angry about being used as a prop (when McCain wants to undercut public schooling).

September 7

'Que Sarah, Sarah'
We're now into Day 9 of America's Media Held Hostage (i.e., denied any chance to interview or even chat with Sarah Palin). McCain campaign manager Rick Davis says Palin won't give any interviews until she feels "comfortable" giving one. This morning he added that she wouldn't give any "until the point in time when she'll be treated with respect and deference." Deference—got that?

Meanwhile, the media vetting, making up for the apparent lack of same from the GOP, will continue (with the Anchorage daily leading the pack) – or will the press be intimidated? Here's Clark Hoyt's take in this morning's *NYT* public editor column: "By choosing a running mate unknown to most of the nation, and doing so just before the Republican National Convention, John McCain made it inevitable that there would be a frantic media vetting. It turns out that Palin was for the Bridge to Nowhere before she was against it, that she sent e-mail complaining about a lack of disciplinary action against a state trooper who was going through a messy custody battle with her sister, and that she never made a decision as commander in chief of the Alaska National Guard, one of her qualifications cited by McCain.

"The drip-drip-drip of these stories seems like partisanship to Palin's partisans. But they fill out the picture of who she is, and they represent a free press doing its job, investigating a candidate who might one day be the leader of the Free World."

To Van Halen and Back
It started about 10 days ago when the press, asking "How do you pronounce it?", were told that "Palin" rhymes with "Van Halen." Then the Van Halen song "Right Now" was played at the Sarah Palin introduction ceremony. Then the band demanded that the McCain campaign stop playing their song at rallies.

Now *The New York Times* in its lenthy piece on Monday on Palin's baby #5 observes that, indeed, Trig Paxson Van Palin owes something to the band as well, as the Alaska governor when she was pregnant "joked about giving her child the middle name Van, since Van Palin would sound sort of like the hard rock band Van Halen." Apparently, the band does not return the love, joining the likes of Heart, Jackson Browne, Chuck Berry and others in demanding that McCain pull their tunes.

McCain: Larry David 'Yay,' Borat 'Boo'
Kate Phillips at *The New York Times* reports today that in an interview with the magazine *Marie Claire* done last month but yet to hit the stands, Senator John McCain reveals that he identifies with the character Kiefer Sutherland plays on *24*. In the interview McCain says that he has a lot in common with Jack Bauer who "escapes all the time." He says he does not believe in torture as Jack does on the series, however. McCain finds Borat "very, very coarse," likes *The Office* and *Curb Your Enthusiasm*, and defers to his wife on the domestic front.

September 10

Lipstick Traces
The *New York Post* declared it the BOAR WARS. Matt Drudge used HOLY SOW! But for Mark Silva of the *Chicago Tribune* it is more like SOW WHAT!

I refer, of course, to the fallout, faux and otherwise, from Barack Obama using the familiar political cliche "putting lipstick on a pig" to describe McCain policy, which the GOP and related media have turned into Obama directly calling Sarah Palin a "pig" because she used "lipstick" in her most quoted line from her recent convention speech. In fact, this is now leading the news coverage on TV and at many news and blog outlets.

The McCain campaign, besides hitting Obama with the now-discredited "lipstick pig" charge, released a video ad today featuring another mammal – a wolf – and the claim that the Democrats had airlifted a "mini-army" of 30 oppo-researchers into Alaska to dig up dirt on Sarah Palin. The source: the *Wall Street Journal's* conservative pundit John Fund. The Democrats have denied it, no evidence of this has turned up and Fund isn't talking.

David Hulen, a reporter for the *Anchorage Daily News* had some (pointed) fun with this today on the paper's politics blog. Here is an excerpt: "You'd think someone would have noticed the parachutes, but it is getting dark again at night....People connected with the McCain/Palin campaign tried over the weekend to feed the *ADN* a story that a group of Democrat operatives were in Anchorage plotting on how to dig up dirt on Palin. The information was pretty sketchy." He then asked readers to send along any signs of parachutes (or perhaps a landing by sea).

September 11

Things We Thought We'd Never See
David Perel, editor of the *National Enquirer*, has an op-ed in the *Wall Street Journal* today. It opens: "The private lives of the presidential candidates are off limits. Writing about people who do not hold elected office constitutes shameful scandal mongering. The families of the candidates should not be exploited for publicity. I know all of this to be true because Barack Obama said it. And so did John McCain."

It closes: "Inevitably the mainstream media, suffering from the corporate pressures of diminishing profits, will yield to new media and its populism. The two-newspaper city, once a staple of every metropolis, is already as rare as a grammatically correct sentence from George Bush.

"So with apologies to John Edwards, Sarah Palin and untold other Democrats and Republicans, the tabloid media gladly accepts its role of covering the scandals, relying on the American public to decide if that information is relevant to job performance."

Charlie Gibson's War
The New York Times today likened Gibson in his exclusive Sarah Plain interview to an old professor unhappily recognizing that his student does not deserve a passing grade. Meanwhile, Anne Kornblut at *The Washington Post* reports that Palin, in Alaska seeing her son off to war, took the long discredited route of linking Iraq to 9/11, telling an Iraq-bound brigade of soldiers that included her son that they would "defend the innocent from the enemies who planned and carried out and rejoiced in the death of thousands of Americans."

Kornblut points out: "The idea that Iraq shared responsibility with al-Qaeda for the attacks on the World Trade Center and the Pentagon, once promoted by Bush administration officials, has since been rejected even by the president himself. On any other day, Palin's statement would almost certainly have drawn a sharp rebuke from Democrats, but both parties had declared a halt to partisan activities to mark Thursday's (9/11) anniversary."

Let Biden Be Biden?
After keeping his mouth in check since the DNC, Joe Biden is returning to rare form with a number of verbal gaffes captured by the press in recent days, and recounted by the *NYT* today. Here is our favorite:

In Columbia, Mo., this week, Biden urged a paraplegic state official to stand up to be recognized. "Chuck, stand up, let the people see you," Biden shouted to State Senator Chuck Graham, before realizing, to his horror, that Graham uses a wheelchair.

"Oh, God love ya," Biden said. "What am I talking about?

September 13

Peggy Noonan: Obama Reeling
Peggy Noonan, the former Reagan speechwriter and longtime *WSJ* columnist, seems to have become Born Again. You remember her "open-mike" episode from a couple of weeks back on MSNBC when she privately derided GOP campaign tactics and the chances of McCain winning in November after the

Palin nomination. Now she says the race is "not over" but Obama is "in a bad place" and McCain is clearly winning.

That's amazing, considering that virtually every national poll has it at 50/50. But she knows this because "everyone" she knows tells her that. This confirms longheld suspicions that Noonan is so isolated and elitist that she doesn't know a single Democrat. And then there are those nasty sexist Democrats, "who don't really like women all that much," she reveals.

'Terror' DVD Getting Delivered to Millions This Weekend
A controversial DVD was home-delivered today with McClatchy papers in North Carolina, in Charlotte and Raleigh, and the *Miami Herald*, bringing the nationwide total to about 70 papers, with more coming tomorrow. An estimated 28 million copies have been sent out already, some by direct mail and in other periodicals. It seems to be only distributed in "swing" election states, and was made in 2005 by the New York-based Clarion Fund.

The documentary, *Obsession: Radical Islam's War Against the West*, showcases scenes of Muslim children being encouraged to become suicide bombers, interspersed with shots of Nazi rallies. 'The threat of Radical Islam is the most important issue facing us today," reads the sleeve of the DVD. "But it's a topic that neither the presidential candidates nor the media are discussing openly. It's our responsibility to ensure we can all make an informed vote in November."

It was shown on Fox News just before the 2006 mid-term elections, and conservative activist David Horowitz screened the film on campuses last year. An article at the group's site, www.radicalislam.org, all but endorsed McCain as the preferred candidate this past week, then was pulled down.

The New York Times distributed 145,000 copies last Sunday with papers in several leading markets – all in swing states. This included Denver, Philadelphia, and several areas in Florida, Ohio and elsewhere. A spokeswoman told *E&P* it did not violate its advertising/delivery standards.

An article at the site of the *Morning-Call* in Allentown, Pa. today reveals that it will be inserted in the Sunday paper there tomorrow. It continues: "A call to Clarion wasn't returned, but the nonprofit's spokesman, Gregory Ross, told the *Harrisburg Patriot-News* this week that 28 million copies of the DVD are being distributed nationwide throughout September. He said the intent is not to sway voters' opinions about the presidential candidates."

The New York Times spokeswoman told us: "We believe the broad principles of freedom of the press confer on us an obligation to keep our advertising columns as open as possible. Therefore our acceptance or rejection of an advertisement does not depend on whether it coincides with our editorial positions. In fact, there are many instances when we have published opinion advertisements that run counter to the stance we take on our own editorial pages." The publisher of the *News & Observer* in Raleigh, like the *Times*, defended distributing the DVD on free speech grounds.

September 16

Open the Door, Richard

John McCain once referred to the press as "my base." Now he has kicked some media off the Straight Talk Express while others are turning in their ticket. The latest former fan is columnist Richard Cohen of *The Washington Post*. He writes today, "I am one of the journalists accused over the years of being in the tank for McCain. Guilty." But now he uses words such as "debasement" and "farce" to refer to the candidate and rips the Palin pick.

"McCain has turned ugly," he observes. "His dishonesty would be unacceptable in any politician, but McCain has always set his own bar higher than most."

Sarah Palin: Not 'My Humps'

Our friends at the *Anchorage Daily News* resurrected today two fun candidate queries it published during the 2006 race for governor up there.

Asked to name her five favorite tunes, Sarah Palin got a little stuck after naming "Independence Day" by country artist Martina McBride: "Palin listed several other artists, but the songs are open to debate. One would have to be an old Van Halen number, she said, 'back when David Lee Roth sang.' Palin would also want to hear something from Hobo Jim – of 'I did, I did, I did the Iditarod trail' fame – plus a Kanye West tune and something from Black Eyed Peas. But not 'My Humps.'"

In a more general questionnaire reply, she revealed that 90% of primetime TV "irks me," her favorite coffee is "skinny white chocolate mocha" (a little yuppie "elite," huh?) which she drinks "all over town," her favorite movies are *Rudy, Miracle on Ice* and *Mr. Smith Goes to Washington*, and if she went to a costume party she would go as – Tina Fey.

Why Obama Won

September 17

A Wider Shade of Palin

It tries to stay ahead of the political curve, but this time *Saturday Night Live* was a bit behind the times. Its now-famous skit starring returnee Tina Fey as Sarah Palin closed with an especially cutting quip that came from Amy Poehler as Hillary. She advised journalists, clearly referring to the early swooning over Palin, to "grow a pair," and if they couldn't, they ought to borrow a pair from her.

But by then it was clear that, in the main, the mainstream media, for once, had cojones enough to go around.

One would like to think that the determination to vet a previously little-known vice-presidential candidate from an atypical, faraway state would have happened even if Palin and others in the McCain camp hadn't dissed the media at the Republican convention and in the days that followed. Forget the Red/Blue civil war: This was "black and white and Red all over." The McCain forces were saying "investigate, my friends, but we do not care what you find, and neither do the American people." It reminds me of Gary Hart daring the media to keep a watch on him for any marital infidelities and ....whoops.

It's long been said, "you can't lose by running against the media." Well, I guess we will soon find out about that one.

The early returns suggested, on the contrary, that baiting the media may have backfired for the GOP. McCain lost his comfortable lead over Obama gained during his "bump" from the Palin pick (before the media detective work began). Palin's favorable ratings in some polls had plunged more than 20 percentage points in that span. Numerous headlines stated something along the lines of "Palin Effect Wearing Thin." The lipstick was off the pit bull.

While the national media continued to focus on the folksy "hockey mom" — now, "grandmom" — angle, the tough-minded reports in the Alaska press exposed all sorts of ethical shortcomings or uneven performance in office. "Troopergate," Palin's misstatements about that "Bridge to Nowhere," and her (previous) embrace of earmarks had all drawn plenty of coverage back in her home state.

Pundits gave Palin high marks for her error-filled GOP convention speech — the bar had been set that low — but behind the scenes, editors and journalists across the lower 48 were devising plans and itineraries for sleuthing in and out of Alaska. Soon, reports started dribbling and then flowing out, and many of them weren't pretty.

Palin has remained popular among evangelicals and the core GOP faithful, but lost most of her standing with most of the others. And, just possibly, the press — along with leading blogs — deserved the lion's share of the credit (or blame, if you will). The voters, apparently, were eager to "keep up with the cojones."

The Hidden Cell-Phone Vote?

Carl Cannon, former White House correspondent with the *National Journal* (and still a contributor there) and now the D.C. bureau chief for *Reader's Digest*, just posted at his Loose Cannon blog an interesting take on polls – suggesting that Obama is actually still leading even if he appears to be in, at best, a dead heat. Why: "I believe they may be consistently under-representing voters aged 18-29—and, believe me, these young voters are living in Obama-land."

Why would pollsters make such a mistake? "A couple of reasons. The first, and easiest to understand, is that young people are difficult to survey because so many of them lack 'land line' telephones– and it's illegal to auto-dial to cell phones. Secondly, most pollsters—like political professionals and journalists of a certain age—are living in the past. They don't believe that voters in the 18-29 range will turn out in sufficient numbers."

September 18

But Will Sarah Smile?

We've had Hall and Oates' "Sara Smile" and Bob Dylan's ode to his wife "Sarah" but now for a new century here's an offering from Fairbanks musician – and TV anchor – Bob Miller, called "I'm a Sarah-ist." It's posted as a three-minute track at the *Anchorage Daily News* site. Quite well done, it claims the GOP was flailin'...bailin'...trailin'...until it named you know who. Miller kicks it off by saying he was going to record "Bridge Over Troubled Water" but Sarah "vetoed it."

September 21

AP Poll Reveals Troubling Racial Views Could Doom Obama
For almost a year, I have suggested that the media, and polls, were not accurately gauging the probable size of the white "race" vote vs. Obama. Now AP is out with a report on its own new poll that deserves a full read. Here is how it opens: "Deep-seated racial misgivings could cost Barack Obama the White House if the election is close, according to an AP-Yahoo News poll that found one-third of white Democrats harbor negative views toward blacks—many calling them 'lazy,' 'violent' or responsible for their own troubles.

"The poll, conducted with Stanford University, suggests that the percentage of voters who may turn away from Obama because of his race could easily be larger than the final difference between the candidates in 2004—about 2.5 percentage points."

September 22

But Is Palin Pro-Bono?
ABC News reports today that Sarah Palin will (finally) meet some foreign leaders at the United Nations on Tuesday and then "will be joined by Sen. John McCain for joint meetings on Wednesday with the presidents of Georgia and the Ukraine, as well as with the prime minister of India. The Republican running mate will also meet Wednesday with U2 lead singer Bono, who has been active in international humanitarian issues." The *Washington Post* observes that Bono's "work with the ONE Campaign has earned frequent plaudits from GOP presidential nominee John McCain on the campaign trail."

Foon Rhee at the *Boston Globe* puts it this way: "Sarah Palin has a busy dance card." Dancing with Bono? We'd love to see that. Which U2 song might be apt for this meeting? Two options: "Lady With the Spinning Head" and "Stranger in a Strange Land." Palin and Bono: They're one – but they're not the same.

McCain Camp Goes to War with 'NYT' – Keller Responds
It all began with a *New York Times* article today – not on the front page – that tied Rick Davis, John McCain's campaign manager to receiving nearly $2

million in payments in the past five years to run a firm defending Fannie May and Freddie Mac and others. It sparked a remarkable conference call with reporters in which Steve Schmidt, chief McCain strategist, hit back at the *Times*, charging that it is no longer even a journalistic operation but a propaganda organ for Obama.

That led Bill Keller, executive editor of the *Times*, to respond (in a note to *Politico*): "*The New York Times* is committed to covering the candidates fully, fairly and aggressively. It's our job to ask hard questions, fact-check their statements and their advertising, examine their programs, positions, biographies and advisors. Candidates and their campaign operatives are not always comfortable with that level of scrutiny, but it's what our readers expect and deserve."

Meanwhile, another *Politico* writer, Ben Smith, wrote a tough piece declaring that several facts put forth by the McCain team in the same conference call were false. This inspired a McCain aide to state that Smith, like the *Times*, was "in the tank" for Obama.

In a piece later in the day, *Politico* pointed out that McCain is an avid reader of the *Times* and "has enjoyed a very friendly relationship with the paper and many of its biggest stars – as recently as 24 hours before the Schmidt attack." Sam Stein at Huffington Post pointed out that Team McCain has cited the discredited *New York Times* in at least 60 emails in its rapid-response messages to the media: "For a party that rails against the *New York Times*, the Republicans sure depend on the Grey Lady to score political points."

Has McCain Lost His Will?

The conservative columnist George Will hit McCain pretty hard for his frantic response to the current financial crisis on ABC on Sunday, and on Tuesday opens his column with a quote from *Alice In Wonderland* (the queen crying, "Off with their heads"!) and closes with this: "It is arguable that, because of his inexperience, Obama is not ready for the presidency. It is arguable that McCain, because of his boiling moralism and bottomless reservoir of certitudes, is not suited to the presidency. Unreadiness can be corrected, although perhaps at great cost, by experience. Can a dismaying temperament be fixed?"

September 24

Why Did McCain Really Try to Call Off Debate?
By now you know that John McCain has said he will suspend his campaign schedule for a spell and asked Obama to delay Friday's big debate. He says it's because of the financial crisis. Pundits will no doubt weigh in with speculation on possible other motives.

First comment from reporter Ben Smith at *Politico*: "[I]n terms of the timing of this move: The only thing that's changed in the last 48 hours is the public polling." A new ABC/*Washington Post* poll happens to show Obama leading by 9%.

From an AP analysis: "Even as McCain said he was putting the good of the country ahead of politics, his surprise announcement was clearly political. It was an attempt to try to outmaneuver Obama on an issue in which he's trailing, the economy, as the Democrat gains in polls."

First reaction from one Obama team member is: The show must go on! The McCain campaign also announced that he was canceling today's planned appearance on the *Late Show with David Letterman*. More bad news for McCain: The guest replacing him on Letterman is...Keith Olbermann.

UPDATE– CNN reports: "McCain surrogate Sen. Lindsey Graham tells CNN the McCain campaign is proposing to the Presidential Debate Commission and the Obama camp that if there's no bailout deal by Friday, the first presidential debate should take the place of the VP debate, currently scheduled for next Thursday, October 2 in St. Louis." Well, that would be convenient...to get Palin off the stage. Palin exposed: The real crisis?

Just Palin Around: New Pakistani Prez Wants to Hug Her
The *L.A. Times'* politics blog reports this exchange between Sarah Palin and the new Pakistani president, Asif Ali Zardari (her meeting with Bono, alas, was called off):

ZARDARI: *"You are even more gorgeous than you are on the (inaudible)."*
PALIN: *"You are so nice. Thank you."*
ZARDARI: *"Now I know why the whole of America is crazy about you."*
PALIN: *"I'm supposed to pose again."*
ZARDARI: *"If he's insisting, I might hug."*

At that point, the pool reporter was escorted from the room.

September 25

Putin In Alaska Airspace?
Sarah Palin is mad at the media for mocking her for declaring, on multiple occasions, that being governor of a state near Russia gives her foreign policy credentials, or so she complains to Katie Couric. So, she repeats it again: "Well, it certainly does because our next door neighbors are foreign countries, they're in the state that I am the executive of." Huh? Also, something to do with Putin "rearing his head" and entering Alaska's "air space." Paging Norad! Soviet missile-in-chief overhead!

Obama: Sympathy for the Devils?
We always suspected it, but John McCormick on the *Tribune*'s "The Swamp" broke the news today: Asked in a quiet moment outside of his office yesterday by a *CQ* reporter whether he was a "Stones" or a "Beatles" guy, Obama replied: "Stones." For tonight's debate, still up in the air, Obama is still begging McCain, "Let's Spend the Night Together" but so far: no "Satisfaction." It should be pointed out, however, that Obama was only about five when the Beatles broke up and the Stones, alas, are still going, so it's an unfair choice, when you think about it. Me: I was always Dylan anyway.

September 26

Conservative Columnist Wants Palin to Drop Out
Conservative columnist and TV pundit Kathleen Parker has seen enough. In a surprising post at *National Review's* site, she calls for Sarah Palin to step aside for the good of the country (and benefit of her family). Parker, who has certainly criticized, even mocked, Obama in the past, writes: "No one hates saying that more than I do. Like so many women, I've been pulling for Palin, wishing her the best, hoping she will perform brilliantly. I've also noticed that I watch her interviews with the held breath of an anxious parent, my finger poised over the mute button in case it gets too painful. Unfortunately, it often does. My cringe reflex is exhausted.

"If B.S. were currency, Palin could bail out Wall Street herself. If Palin were a man, we'd all be guffawing, just as we do every time Joe Biden tickles the back of his throat with his toes. But because she's a woman — and the first ever on a Republican presidential ticket — we are reluctant to say what is painfully true.

"What to do? Only Palin can save McCain, her party, and the country she loves. She can bow out for personal reasons, perhaps because she wants to spend more time with her newborn. No one would criticize a mother who puts her family first. Do it for your country."

Debate #1 to... Obama?
Obama: Flag pin. McCain: No. So it went in the first great debate 2008. Mark Halperin at The Page gives Obama an A- and McCain a B-. CBS polled 500 undecided voters and found Obama won easily among them. Other network polls also gave it to Obama.

Rod Dreher, the "crunchy conservative" at Belief.net agrees. The MediaCurves focus group also gave it to Obama, including 23% of the Republicans. Most of the bloggers at the *National Review's* The Corner say McCain won easily. Andrew Sullivan, of course, does not agree. George Will says Obama benefits most.

NBC had Joe Biden on shortly after the debate. Brian Williams explained that a similar invitation was extended to Sarah Palin but she "declined." Rudy G. took her place. Even after picking Palin, McCain in the debate accused Obama of lacking the "knowledge and experience" to be president.

Stark moment in debate: McCain showed off a bracelet he was wearing given to him by the mother of dead Iraq soldier who asked him to make sure her son did not die in vain (so we should complete the mission). Obama then said he wore a similar bracelet but the mother in this case imparted a quite different message – don't let more mothers suffer this loss.

September 27

Why So Many Pundits Wrongly Scored the Debate 'Even'
It often happens that the pundit "scoring" of a presidential debate ends up quite at odds from the polls of viewers that soon follow. We've seen it again

September 2008

with last night's debate, which most pundits (on TV and in print) scored very or fairly even, with perhaps some recognition that Obama made small gains because he pretty much held his own on McCain's alleged foreign policy turf. Of course, as we now know, virtually every poll taken by the networks and outside sources gave Obama an edge – and not a small one. He easily swept surveys of undecideds, even carried a Fox focus group. At least in the polls, it was no contest.

We'll see if and how it affects the head-to-head match-up surveys in days ahead but for now we have to ask: Why did so many mainstream pundits blow it?

Of course, there is always the striving for "balance," the effects of pre-spinning, and in some cases their favoring of McCain from the outset. And, to be frank, McCain gave a pretty good account of himself. But many pundits threw out the window what they, and others, had said beforehand, about Obama needing to appear presidential and seem expert on international matters. When he did just that in the debate, they suddenly forgot the importance they had placed on it beforehand.

But here's the key to the viewer/pundit disparity. It took awhile for McCain to build up to it, but then he hammered it home near the end: Obama, he charged, lacked the "knowledge and experience" to be president. Pundits highlighted that and said it was the key to McCain gaining at least a tie. But I didn't hear a single person on TV point out: McCain just picked Sarah Palin for vice president! How, then, could he make such a charge against Obama?

My feeling is that the Couric interview might have done for McCain what the first Nixon-Kennedy debate did for Nixon in 1960 – as a true watershed moment. The American voters finally "got it" about Palin and so McCain's "best moment" against Obama either fell flat with many of them, or proved laughable. This was made all the more stark with Palin AWOL during the post-debate analysis – and Joe Biden all over the place.

But the pundits barely recognized this – and that's why they scored the debate fairly even, as viewers seem to have rated it a landslide for Obama. Subject for later: The many pundits who now have egg on their faces for their early hailing of Palin and/or predictions of how strongly she would help the ticket.

September 28

Tina Fey Nails – Shut? – The McCain Campaign
Sarah Palin's interview with Katie Couric was damaging enough. Now it's double-your-trouble time with Tina Fey's latest takeoff on *Saturday Night Live*. Most damaging: The well-publicized fact that many of the lines, and all of the sentiments, in her script were taken, improbably, right from the Couric transcript. So, for posterity, here is some of of it:

AMY POEHLER AS COURIC: "On foreign policy, I want to give you one more chance to explain your claim that you have foreign policy experience based on Alaska's proximity to Russia. What did you mean by that?"
TINA FEY AS PALIN: "Well, Alaska and Russia are only separated by a narrow maritime border. You got Alaska here, this right here is water, and this is Russia. So, we keep an eye on them."

COURIC: "And how do you do that exactly?"
PALIN: "Every morning, when Alaskans wake up, one of the first things they do, is look outside to see if there are any Russians hanging around. And if there are, you gotta go up to them and ask, 'What are you doing here?' and if they can't give you a good reason, it's our responsibility to say, you know, 'Shoo! Get back over there!'"

COURIC: "Senator McCain attempted to shut down his political campaign this week in order to deal with the economic crisis. What's your opinion of this potential 700 billion dollar bailout?"
PALIN: "Like every American I'm speaking with, we're ill about this. We're saying, 'Hey, why bail out Fanny and Freddie and not me?' But ultimately what the bailout does is, help those that are concerned about the healthcare reform that is needed to help shore up our economy to help...uh...it's gotta be all about job creation, too. Also, too, shoring up our economy and putting Fannie and Freddy back on the right track and so healthcare reform and reducing taxes and reining in spending...'cause Barack Obama, y'know...has got to accompany tax reductions and tax relief for Americans, also, having a dollar value meal at restaurants. That's gonna help. But one in five jobs being created today under the umbrella of job creation. That, you know...Also..."

COURIC: "What lessons have you learned from Iraq and how specifically, would you spread democracy abroad?"
PALIN: "Specifically, we would make every effort possible to spread democracy abroad to those who want it."

COURIC: "Yes, but specifically what would you do?"
PALIN: "We're gonna promote freedom. Usher in democratic values and ideals. And fight terror-loving terrorists."

COURIC: "But again, and not to belabor the point. One specific thing."
PALIN: "Katie, I'd like to use one of my lifelines."

COURIC: "I'm sorry?"
PALIN: "I want to phone a friend."

COURIC: "You don't have any lifelines."
PALIN: "Well in that case I'm gonna just have to get back to ya!"

'Stockton Record' Endorses Obama – First Dem It Has Backed Since FDR

As in 2004, *E&P* will be the place to look for a complete record of newspaper endorsements for president. Only a handful have arrived so far. Here's the latest: From the *Stockton Record* in California. In an explanatory note, the editors explain that Obama is the first Democrat for president the paper has endorsed in 72 years – since FDR ran for re-election in 1936.

In a troubling early indication for McCain, the *Record* notes: "While praiseworthy for putting the first woman on a major-party presidential ticket since Geraldine Ferraro in 1984, his selection of Palin as a running mate was appalling. The first-term governor is clearly not experienced enough to serve as vice president or president if required. Her lack of knowledge is being covered up by keeping her away from questioning reporters and doing interviews only with those considered friendly to her views."

The Late Paul Newman (and Me) and the '68 Race

In an age when Hollywood activism is a given – influential though often lampooned – it may be hard to imagine a time, not so long ago, when it was still rare and often required significant courage. You had to be there to understand the difference between then and now. One of the real groundbreakers was the late Paul Newman. As it happens, we both worked for Eugene McCarthy in 1968 and both of us ended up at the riotous Chicago convention in August 1968.

He was a McCarthy activist and a delegate from Connecticut; I had headed Students for McCarthy on my campus and then, as a newspaper reporter, covered the '68 convention – before taking to the streets to join the protesters.

Newman, like some others in the entertainment world, had been active in the civil rights movement earlier, but the numbers were not large and even fewer took part in political races – particularly when it involved actual campaigning. Newman, on the other hand, was a crusader for Eugene McCarthy and spoke at dozens of rallies and events – by one count, at least 15 in Indiana (a key battleground state in the primary season that year) alone. This was probably unprecedented.

Some credit him with, earlier, being largely responsible for McCarthy's strong showing in New Hampshire, which drove LBJ out of the race. The right-wing Manchester *Union-Leader* tweaked all this by running a photo of the actor with McCarthy and a caption, "Who's that guy with Newman?" Newman drew 2,000 at one rally there but said, "I didn't come here to help Gene McCarthy. I need McCarthy's help."

Newman was also filmed in political ads for the candidate, and emceed a telethon to raise money for McCarthy. In Indiana, he drew large crowds and told one assembly from the tail gate of a station wagon: "I am not a public speaker. I am not a politician. I'm not here because I'm an actor. I'm here because I've got six kids. I don't want it written on my gravestone, 'He was not part of his times.'" And he paved the way for many others in Hollywood to actively campaign for Robert F. Kennedy months after Newman had gone on the stump for McCarthy.

McCarthy, of course, would lose the nomination in Chicago after the bloody "police riot" in the streets and violence even inside the hall. There's a great photo out there of Newman angrily shouting on the convention floor – with fellow delegate Arthur Miller nearby.

The next day, I attended a McCarthy gathering where Newman appeared and protested the outcome of the race and the violence. Newman later told a *Time* reporter about "a month of serious drinking" before deciding on whether to support Humphrey that fall.

So Newman was kind of godfather to all the George Clooneys of today. And no one, before or since, ever dared to say he was not "part of his times."

September 29

Ohio Readers Upset About Racial Slur
Reaction to a story in Sunday's *Hamilton Journal-News* (Ohio) serves as a reminder that race is indeed a factor influencing some voters this election season. In his blog, columnist Dave Greber wrote that the news staff are "being bombarded" by response from readers, many of whom were "appalled" by a Middletown resident's racist comments against Sen. Obama. In the story, an 84-year-old white resident was quoted as saying, "black people aren't smart enough to rule the country. No one should vote for Obama." So far, dozens of readers have responded to the resident's comments, according to Greber.

September 30

Palin Invokes Her Journalism Degree!
In yet another interview with Katie Couric today, Sarah Palin was asked what newspapers and magazines she reads to keep up with events and inform her world view beyond Alaska. She would not name a single one, beyond "all of them," even when pressed. Wonder how the *Anchorage Daily News* feels about that?

Also, we all know that Sarah Palin ended up with a college degree in journalism (even if she had to go through five colleges to get it). But for the first time, probably, she mentioned it today in an interview, on the rightwing talk show hosted by Hugh Hewitt. She also referred to herself as "normal Joe Six-Pack American" and said it was time to have that type of Joe (not Biden) as vice president. The J-degree exchange:

HH: *Now Governor, the Gibson and the Couric interview struck many as sort of pop quizzes designed to embarrass you as opposed to interviews. Do you share that opinion?*

SP: Well, I have a degree in journalism also, so it surprises me that so much has changed since I received my education in journalistic ethics all those years ago. But I'm not going to pick a fight with those who buy ink by the barrelful. I'm going to take those shots and those pop quizzes and just say that's okay, those are good testing grounds. And they can continue on in that mode.

OCTOBER 2008

October 1

Conservative Pundit Who Dissed Palin Gets Whacked
Fascinating piece today by Kathleen Parker, the popular conservative syndicated columnist who had the nerve last week to question Sarah Palin's qualifications for the Veep spot in a lengthy posting at the *National Review* site. Now she reveals the attacks on her – from the right. By the way, in his interview with the *Des Moines Register* editorial board yesterday, John McCain dismissed assaults on Palin from conservatives as limited to those on the "cocktail" circuit in Washington, D.C.

Meanwhile, Sarah Palin has finally given a lengthy newspaper interview, but it was not with *The New York Times, Washington Post* or other large daily. Instead, it appears today in her hometown Wasilla, Alaska, weekly, *The Frontiersman*. And it was all via email. The paper ran the interview on its front page today with the intro: "The responses here were not edited and are preceded by the verbatim questions posed to her."

Asked, for example, to name any mistakes she had made as mayor of the town she only came up with underestimating her opponents. She also deflected any blame in the "troopergate" controversy, the book-banning charges and the allegations that she had something to do with rape victims having to pay for their own medical tests. "I'm not going to win over anyone in the media elite – I'm going to do my best for the American people," she said.

She also continued to say of the Bridge to Nowhere, "I cancelled the project," even though this has been challenged by various fact-checking organizations.

Amazingly, she suggests that her kids are the first candidate's offspring to have their privacy probed (another outright fib) – after bringing her pregnant teen daughter up on stage at the GOP convention and having her new baby passed around from arm to arm. Here are a few choice lines from her responses.

On the media: "Nothing really prepares you for hatred and made-up stories. But it's nothing like the hard times of a family that's lost a job, lost health insurance, or lost a son or daughter in battle. I would hope that the privacy of my children would be respected, as has been the tradition for the children of previous candidates."

On her town billing victims for rape kits: "The entire notion of making a victim of a crime pay for anything is crazy. I do not believe, nor have I ever believed, that rape victims should have to pay for an evidence-gathering test."

On the book banning: "As people there know, all questions posed to the library director were asked in a context of professionalism, regarding the library policy that was in place."

Yes, Newspaper Endorsements DO Matter

In the next few weeks, newspaper editorial boards (or, in some cases, merely the publisher or owner) will decide which candidate to endorse in the red-hot 2008 race for the White House. Well, many of them will, anyway. More and more papers are opting out of the endorsement process entirely, or concentrating just on local races where, the cliché holds, they "might actually make a difference."

Only a handful have declared so far, among them *The Seattle Times* (for Obama) and *New York Post* (for you know who). The latest: The *Canton Repository* in swing state Ohio (for Obama).

Stated or unstated, the common belief is that newspaper picks for president are meaningless; they influence no one, especially in an era when media approval ratings in polls rival the paltry numbers for lawyers. But actually, I beg to differ with those who say endorsements have no impact. Consider my amazingly accurate 11th hour predictions in 2004– based solely on newspaper editorials.

My magazine, *Editor & Publisher*, has a decades-long tradition of logging endorsements for president. I don't know how it was done in a timely fashion before the Internet Age – the mind boggles. We keep a running total of who led in the number of endorsements, as well as the audience size of the supporting papers. In 2004, it became a popular daily feature in the final weeks of the campaign, and in early November our final pre-election tally found Kerry edging Bush in endorsements by 213-205, but topping him rather easily in total circ, 20.8 million to 14.6 million. Since Bush won, barely, you might say "so much for newspapers swinging the election."

But hold on for a minute. I knew back then that endorsements in most states really did mean nothing, since the votes of their readers were barely being contested. The race actually would be decided in a dozen or more "toss-up" states, and in these tight contests, a newspaper endorsement – I believed – could be key, no matter how loudly others scoffed.

So, on election eve, I probed the endorsements in 15 battleground states and awarded electoral votes to one candidate or the other solely on that basis. When the votes were counted, I had accurately picked the winner in 14 of the states, from Hawaii to New Hampshire – including the one that would count most, Ohio. I had observed that Bush had earned the nod from *The Columbus Dispatch* (after much internal debate), got a no-decision from *The Plain Dealer* in Cleveland, and dominated in Cincinnati, Canton, and Youngstown. I had closed my awarding of Ohio with: "A slight nod to Bush, at least until the court cases begin." Ouch!

My only blunder: Florida. But I did note that if Bush won there, he would take the whole ball of wax. This is what happened.

So, did newspapers decide the election? A big maybe. But don't scoff as endorsements pile up – for Obama, I predict, given the trend in 2004 and some of the early indications.

October 2

GOP = Dog Food?

Coming in this Sunday's *New York Times Magazine*: A profile of a former "star in the Republican party," Rep. Tom Davis of Virginia. As the heading puts it: "Now, like dozens of his GOP colleagues, he's quitting Congress, fed up with his party, his president and the process."

In other words: "Tom Davis Gives Up," the *Times* reveals.

The article by Peter Baker fashions Davis as "moderate" who is outraged by super-partisanship and the "social conservatives" who have "hijacked" the party. Davis's favorite line about the GOP is, "if we were a dog food, they would take us off the shelf."

Mocking an average day of meaningless bills before Congress he quips, "tell them about the important work we're doing while Rome burns."

Baker (who met Davis 22 years ago) comments: "After 14 years in Congress, Tom Davis is giving up his place in the bucket brigade. Someone else will have to put out the fire. If anyone wants to try."

Davis calls the McCain-Palin ticket "a marriage of convenience. What are the negatives? What about her resume? I got through it in about 10 seconds. Does that hurt? He's the guy running on experience...And she's a heartbeat away." She does help with the "change" issue, he adds.

And aptly, in light of the start of the baseball playoffs, Davis, 59, cracks: "You know, the Cubs fans used to put the bags over their heads. That's what I feel when you say you're from Congress, because there are just so many things we're not doing."

The article points out that 26 Republicans are stepping down this year compared to only six Democrats. Many of he GOPers are moderates. "There's no question, we're a dying breed," says Rep. Jim Ramstad of Minn.

Davis on the current financial crisis: "Nobody keeps an eye on anything unless it hurts the other party."

October 3

Pundits Blow Debate Analysis (Again)
The funniest, and most revealing, moment in Howard Kurtz's lengthy debate wrapup at *The Washington Post* today comes about halfway through it. After hailing Palin's performance and quoting numerous mainstream pundits attesting to same, all to suggest that she succeeded in stopping the bleeding, Kurtz dryly posts the following *without* comment: "CNN's insta-poll: Biden, 51 to 36. CBS survey of uncommitted: Biden, 46 to 21."

Of course, he could have cited many other similar polls, and dove into the numbers that showed little if any movement for Palin in the key measure of faith that she is actually ready to be president. How about this one, from CBS: "On the question of the candidates' qualifications to assume the presidency, 87 percent of those polled said Biden is qualified and 42 percent said Palin is qualified."

I wrote last week on the same phenomenon after the McCain-Obama debate, which the vast majority of mainstream pundits declared "even" – but polls showed an easy win for Obama. And I posted several times earlier about

McCain's poll numbers dropping only partly because of the economy, but largely due to the Palin Effect wearing thin.

It's not just conservatives like Bill Kristol and David Brooks who have lowered the bar so radically that even a grasshopper could not limbo under it: See mainstream comments today by Adam Nagourney in *The New York Times* and Dan Balz in the *Washington Post*.

Yet the mainstream outlets wonder why so many have lost respect for their judgment. The voters, as revealed by the polls, are apparently not buying "aw shucks, wink, you betcha" as enough of a qualification for the presidency. Yet for many in the punditocracy that's just enough. Or as one put it, the story of the night was "The Wink."

David Brooks asks today, in his embarrassing column that hails Palin, "Where was this woman during her interview with Katie Couric?" Apparently average Americans, but not average pundits, know the difference between scripted, and genuine, answers. And, David: They expect more from a president than those feel-good qualities, after eight years of the man you trumpeted for the White House in 2000 over someone maybe a little more "elite," and a little smarter. So many voters in 2000 said they wanted to have a beer with Bush—and he had given up drinking. There's got to be a metaphor in there somewhere.

Bosniaks

Apparently several pundits on TV and print have hit Joe Biden for referring to Bosnian Muslims in the debate as "Bosniaks." Indeed, it does sound like a funny, flubby kind of term. Cokie Roberts even went so far as suggest that if Palin said it, the press would be all over her.

Let's hope not. Cokie and all the others are wrong. Bosniak is indeed another way, indeed the preferred way in some places, of describing Bosnian Muslims, as Josh Marshall at Talking Points Memo pointed out.

Meanwhile, various conservative pundits have distanced themselves from Sarah Palin but few if any have suggest that McCain may be toast. Syndicated columnist Charles Krauthammer does that today, based mainly on McCain's frantic fumbling of the financial crisis. Obama, he writes, was once cool, as in "hip," but now is cool as in "collected." Fatal problem for McCain?

Still with a hangover from the debate, Paul Krugman at his *NYT* blog posts this gem: "Sarah Palin finished her closing remarks by quoting Ronald Reagan: 'It was Ronald Reagan who said that freedom is always just one generation away from extinction. We don't pass it to our children in the bloodstream; we have to fight for it and protect it, and then hand it to them so that they shall do the same, or we're going to find ourselves spending our sunset years telling our children and our children's children about a time in America, back in the day, when men and women were free.'

"When did he say this? It was on a recording he made for Operation Coffeecup — a campaign organized by the American Medical Association to block the passage of Medicare. Doctors' wives were supposed to organize coffee klatches for patients, where they would play the Reagan recording, which declared that Medicare would lead us to totalitarianism."

Lowry: Under the Spell of Palin's 'Starbursts'

From editor Rich Lowry's take on the Palin/Biden debate at his *National Revie* site: "A very wise TV executive once told me that the key to TV is projecting through the screen. It's one of the keys to the success of, say, a Bill O'Reilly, who comes through the screen and grabs you by the throat. Palin too projects through the screen like crazy. I'm sure I'm not the only male in America who, when Palin dropped her first wink, sat up a little straighter on the couch and said, 'Hey, I think she just winked at me.' And her smile. By the end, when she clearly knew she was doing well, it was so sparkling it was almost mesmerizing. It sent little starbursts through the screen and ricocheting around the living rooms of America. This is a quality that can't be learned." Lowry was soon mocked across the liberal blogosphere, and elsewhere, for falling "hard" for Palin.

<u>October 4</u>

Palin: I Want My 'NYT'

Well, that's a switch. The sequence began with the *Times*' bizarre decision to place Obama's modest and aged connection with ex-radical Bill Ayres at the top of its front page today instead of inside. The McCain camp, and especially, Palin seized on it today, with Sarah claiming that this proved that Obama likes to "pal around" with terrorists and does not see America "the way we do." How does she know this? As the Russian ambassador said in

Dr. Strangelove, "I read it in *The New York Times*." And as Palin pointed out, "they are hardly ever wrong," except for the many, many times (in the view of the GOP) they certainly are.

October 5

Kristol Not Clear
Three nights after the big debate, Bill Kristol and his GOP colleagues remain delusional. Nothing new in that, but for once this is a very good thing.

You might understand Republicans immediately claiming victory for Sarah Palin in last Thursday's debate. That's what the spin room is for, and what else do they have to hope for? So: Why not. Good try, and all that.

In the following days, however, sane partisans, Fox News pundits and GOP operatives, you would think, would sober up when all of the post-debate polls found that not only had Palin lost, in the minds of viewers/voters, she had lost badly. Yet still they kept pushing the line that she had produced, maybe, a game-changer.

That's fine for argument's sake: Again, what's to lose? This: Carried away by their enthused (and why not?) base, top GOP pundits and strategists have gone on to advise Team McCain, Let Sarah be Sarah! She did so great in the debate, unleash her! Give her more rope! Hell, turn it into a Palin/McCain ticket, as Stephen Colbert advised weeks ago.

That's where it gets humorous for us, and dangerous for the GOP: Team McCain seems to be taking that advice.

Yet, it gets even more insane. Bill Kristol, besides goading Palin into going even more negative, ends his column today with: "Hockey Mom knows best." This in the face of all the evidence that virtually from the end of her post-convention bounce (which was purely base- and media-driven), her ticket has lost points in national and most state polls almost by the day – seemingly by the hour in some cases. Palin's favorable ratings have sunk like a stone, with no Arctic ice underneath.

Of course, Kristol is the same "fella" (as Palin might say) who proposed Clarence Thomas for the McCain veep spot, calling him "the most impressive conservative in American public life." You betcha!

Now there are new polls just out tonight, showing an ever-widening margin for Obama in CNN and NBC surveys, and almost unfathomable leads in states like Virginia and Minnesota. Palin is in Florida today. Watch for Obama to get a five-point bounce there tomorrow.

In other words, the public has disliked her more and more the more and more she is being Palin. The more they see and hear, the less they like. Yet the call goes forth: Give the voters more of her! Starbursts to the rescue!

To which I say to Kristol and the others, in the immortal words of former hero George W. Bush: Bring her on! Que Sarah, Sarah.

Running On the Barack Streets
As you must have heard by now, Bruce Springsteen is singing for Barack Obama this weekend, drawing a massive crowd (aimed at voter registration) in Philly yesterday, on to Ohio and Michigan, with a NYC concert with Billy Joel coming up shortly. This political activity is not exactly a shock right now, especially since he also sang for Kerry in 2004.

Now he has become a new kind of political "Boss"– and ready to play a key role in the weeks ahead. As he declared in conclusion in Philly: "So now is the time to stand with Barack Obama and Joe Biden, roll up our sleeves, and come on up for the rising."

It's clear that he offered his endorsement last spring at least partly in response to the then-current media obsession with the "bitter" controversy. Obama, he now asserts, "has the depth, the reflectiveness, and the resilience to be our next President. He speaks to the America I've envisioned in my music for the past 35 years, a generous nation with a citizenry willing to tackle nuanced and complex problems, a country that's interested in its collective destiny and in the potential of its gathered spirit. After the terrible damage done over the past eight years, a great American reclamation project needs to be undertaken. I believe that Senator Obama is the best candidate to lead that project and to lead us into the 21st Century with a renewed sense of moral purpose and of ourselves as Americans."

Yesterday, flipping around the cable news channels, just about the only counterweight to all the Palin/Ayers slams at Obama was footage of the Boss singing in his beloved Philly. I'm sure Obama's team would take the Sarah/Bruce comparison every day of the week.

Palin, verbatim, in her latest Fox News interview, with Carl Cameron, which was meant to clear up some "misunderstandings" in the Katie Couric sessions: "As we send our young men and women overseas in a war zone to fight for democracy and freedoms, including freedom of the press, we've really got to have a mutually beneficial relationship here with those fighting the freedom of the press, and then the press, though not taking advantage and exploiting a situation, perhaps they would want to capture and abuse the privilege. We just want truth, we want fairness, we want balance."

Two Top Papers Go After McCain
Two subjects relating to John McCain pretty much off-limits until recently receive major treatment in two leading papers today. The *L.A. Times* looks at his pre-POW military record and finds three air crashes and a lot of recklessness. Paul Farhi in *The Washington Post* probes the breakup of McCain's first marriage and what it meant to his career. Here's the opening: "In early 1980, John McCain was a man in transition – and in a hurry.

"Nine months earlier, at a cocktail reception in Hawaii, he met a glamorous young heiress named Cindy Lou Hensley and, by all accounts, fell instantly in love. McCain spent months flying from Washington to Arizona pursuing this new relationship. Soon, the 43-year-old naval attache and his 25-year-old sweetheart were engaged.

"There was only one complication: McCain was still married." The article goes on to reveal that McCain told Larry King in 2002 that he was divorced at that time. And in his 2002 memoir he stated that he was separated from wife, which also was not true, according to legal documents.

October 6

"Kill Him!"
The New York Times bears part of the blame for kicking this off with its frontpaging of its nothing-really-new Bill Ayers story on Saturday. Today John McCain at a rally asked rhetorically, "Who is the REAL Barack Obama?" Someone in the audience shouted, "Terrorist!" McCain looked a little startled (should he have been, given his attacks of the past two days?), his wife smiled a little, many in the crowd signaled approval. Then McCain said – and it's actually unintentionally funny – that when someone asks that question "all you get is another barrage of insults." The *NYT* report on the speech did not mention this episode at all.

Meanwhile, Dana Milbank of the *Washington Post* reported from a Palin rally that when she mentioned the Obama/Ayers link someone shouted: "Kill him!" Unclear which bad guy, Obama or Ayers, was supposed to die.

And, natch, there is an Ayers movie project that may get more attention now. "Only in America" they should call it.

October 7

Palin Crowd Turns on Journos
We noted yesterday a Tampa reporter's claim that journos were being kept from mingling with attendees at a Palin rally in Florida because some negative things had been printed in the past. At the same rally, the *Washington Post's* Dana Milbank experienced something much more disturbing: "Palin's routine attacks on the media have begun to spill into ugliness. In Clearwater, arriving reporters were greeted with shouts and taunts by the crowd of about 3,000. Palin then went on to blame Katie Couric's questions for her 'less-than-successful interview with kinda mainstream media.' At that, Palin supporters turned on reporters in the press area, waving thunder sticks and shouting abuse. Others hurled obscenities at a camera crew. One Palin supporter shouted a racial epithet at an African American sound man for a network and told him, 'Sit down, boy.'"

Another Flabby Debate
Karen Tumulty at *Time* faults everyone for tonight's listless McCain-Obama showdown, from moderator to candidates. Top Drudge headline is simply: BORING. James Fallows finds McCain's "that one" crack (while pointing to Obama) likely damaging. Michael Gerson: McCain won but life is "unfair" so he is getting blamed for everything going bad in the country. Fellow conservative Stephen Hayes: McCain good, Obama unfortunately great. First scientific poll result, from CNN: Obama wins 54% - 30%. Second result from CBS of uncommitted voters: Obama wins 39% to 27%, with 35% calling it a draw.

My view: It was kind of a disgrace. We've come to lower our expectations for real debates in the "debate" process, but this one was a terrible disappointment.

Who picked the questions from among the – we were told – six million sent in online plus the dozens from the people in the hall? The first half was fine but then why air the same foreign policy questions raised two weeks ago – knowing they were certain to draw the very same, almost word-for-word responses? After kicking off the debate by saying we were in the worst economic crisis in 80 years?

The transcript for the last half hour could have been typed up in advance. Remember, this was supposed to be the "domestic policy" debate. Yet there we were once again talking about raids on Pakistan and defending Israel. Tom Brokaw and the debate organizers (and whoever picked the final questions) let down the American public.

Brokaw kept complaining that the candidates were not staying within their time limits – and then did nothing to stop them beyond pleading with them to, maybe, keep an eye on the flashing lights, pretty please, huh? And his "follow up" questions were weak. I thought I'd never say this but – maybe they should let the blogosphere handle the next one.

7-11 Role: The Only Poll that Matters?

You've heard of "quickie" polls, but what about Kwik-E-Mart polls? *USA Today* is following every week how 7-11 stores are forecasting the election by asking visitors to fill up their coffee in red or blue cups labeled with the names of you know who. 7-11 claims this method has accurately predicted the last two races for the White House. So far Obama is in the cups, but does it matter a hill of beans? He's leading McCain 58% to 42%, with the latter taking only New Hampshire, Idaho and West Virginia so far. But there are lot of morning cup o' joes to go.

Does Michelle Say, 'Bring It On Home to Me'?

The possible future First Lady tonight made her first appearance on *The Daily Show*, which did not produce a lot of yucks. Jon did introduce her, in scary tones, as a longtime "associate" of Barack Obama. (He refrained from accusing her husband of fathering two black babies.) Funniest bit may have been Jon showing her husband perched cooly on his stool during the debate and comparing the look to a '60s "album cover." Well, yes, Sam Cooke (a plausible Obama model) did write and sing one of the greatest songs of that era or any other, "Change Is Gonna Come."

Meanwhile, Fox News is obsessed with the allegedly "mortifying" cover of this week's *Newsweek* issue. It's Sarah Palin, so why are they upset? Well, it was supposedly not retouched – and seems to show (in one anchor's eyes) a hint of a moustache! One angry guest actually calls it, without irony, a "slap in the face."

<u>October 9</u>

The Dishonesty of David Brooks
Love her or hate her, you have to admit, at least Sarah Palin tells us what she really feels. In contrast, David Brooks' dishonesty is frightening.

Last Friday for *The New York Times*, following the vice-presidential debate, Brooks wrote of Palin, "She established debating parity with Joe Biden ... By the end of the debate, most Republicans were not crouching behind the couch, but standing on it. The race has not been transformed, but few could have expected as vibrant and tactically clever a performance as the one Sarah Palin turned in Thursday night."

Forget, for the moment, this epic lapse of judgment – every poll showed that viewers actually gave Biden an easy win. Flash forward three days later. Interviewed at a New York City event unveiling the new design for *The Atlantic*, Brooks suddenly admitted, speaking of Palin, that she was "not even close" to being ready to be vice president.

He also declared her a "fatal cancer" on the same party whose members, he'd just revealed, were standing on that couch after the debate. Shouldn't he have warned them?

It may or may not surprise you to learn that Brooks has not *written* a word declaring Palin unfit or why the selection of someone "not even close" to be being qualified for vice president by a 72-year-old cancer survivor might disqualify John McCain from Brooks' consideration for his support.

Perhaps Brooks didn't think anyone was taking notes on Monday – let alone shooting video of his damaging assessment. But his blast at Palin had been buzzed about since Monday.

Now, it's true that Brooks in his Friday post-debate column did paint Palin as a bit of a rube who owed her purported success in the debate not to intellect (he has praised Obama on this count) but for appealing to all the "folks" out there – and running not only against Washington but the entire East Coast. But nowhere in that column, or anywhere in print, has he shared with readers what appear to be his true feelings: that she is simply not qualified for the veep office, let alone the one above it.

He hinted at this in a Sept. 16 column, which lamented her lack of "experience," but it closed with a knock on the "smug condescension that has so marked the reaction to the Palin nomination in the first place."

Even worse, what does it betray about his honesty and credibility – and those of other conservative pundits who have mocked Palin but refused to rule out McCain for president because of his monumental lack of wisdom and integrity in picking her (the most important political decision he has ever made)? Brooks in his Monday talk underlined this when he commented, "The more I follow politicians, the more I think experience matters, the ability to have a template of things in your mind that you can refer to on the spot, because believe me, once in office there's no time to think or make decisions."

On Sept. 25, Brooks had revealed in his column that he was disappointed in the McCain campaign so far – but did not mention the Palin pick once. His complaint: McCain "has no central argument." Still he hailed the candidate as a "good judge of character," adding, "He is, above all – and this is completely impossible to convey in the midst of a campaign – a serious man prone to serious things."

Andrew Sullivan at his *Atlantic* blog had it right when he commented that Brooks "does not apparently draw the obvious conclusion from this. The only non-negotiable criterion for the vice-presidency is an ability at a moment's notice to become the president, if the worst happens. Palin fails by that criterion.

"So McCain's first presidential level decision was not just a poor one. It was a disqualifying one. This was pass/fail. McCain failed. If you do not believe that Palin is qualified for the job McCain selected her for, then there are only two conclusions: either you cannot support McCain or you do not believe the presidency of the United States is a serious job. So which one is it, David? You have four weeks to let us know." Actually, now, a little less than that.

Who needs Mark Shields? Maybe Brooks should debate *himself* on PBS this week. Yet many of Brooks' colleagues on the right have had no trouble frankly labeling Palin unqualified. The list includes everyone from

David Frum to Christopher Buckley. Some have cited this in stating they can no longer support McCain.

Just today, Matthew Dowd, the key Bush strategist in 2004, jumped on the anti-Palin bandwagon, stating flatly that she is not at all qualified for higher office, and suggested that McCain, no doubt, will regret the Palin pick after the results in November arrive. Myself, I am tempted to label the Brooks-Palin team "Brooks and Dumb." Or is that Brooks and Kristol?

(Update: Brooks never did come clean in print before the election.)

'Time' Probes Race Issue
Coming tomorrow from *Time* magazine, we've learned, is a cover package that largely focuses on the "race" issue in the race to the White House.

Peter Beinart writes, "In the past, Republicans often used race to make their opponents seem anti-white. In 2008, with their incessant talk about who loves their country and who doesn't, McCain and Palin are doing something different: they're using race to make Obama seem anti-American... Today many of America's racial challenges come from without, as Third World immigration transforms the nation and U.S. workers and leaders struggle to come to terms with China and India, the emerging, nonwhite superpowers. If Martin Luther King Jr. symbolized that earlier transition, Barack Obama may have inadvertently come to symbolize this one. How he fares on Nov. 4 will be a sign of America's willingness to embrace the realities of a new age."

Here are some key poll findings:

- 38% said they know someone likely to vote for Obama because of his race; 44% said they know someone who is less likely to vote for Obama because of his race
- 64% of whites say Obama isn't white or black — he's a little bit of both; 71% of blacks agree
- 55% say Obama's election would help to heal America's racial history and division

'SNL' Mocks the Debate – As Questioner Speaks Out
The *SNL* special tonight was pretty funny with its debate bit, and right on, as its Brokaw character opened by saying that he had sifted through thousands of questions submitted before settling on the eight weakest

ones. Bill Murray got to ask a question – about whether the two candidates would promise to make sure that his beloved Cubbies stop losing in the playoffs.

Also tonight: Remember that young black guy who asked a question in the debate about the bailout and McCain went over and told him that, of course, he probably had never heard of Fannie and Freddie until recently. Now that guy has put up a lengthy post at Facebook, revealing that he certainly did know (he is going for an advanced degree) and get this – the whole "undecided voter" concept for the town hall was bogus, at least in his case. He had informed the vetters quite clearly that he was strongly leaning to Obama.

<u>October 10</u>

Ayers Is Human
Surprising letter to editor in *NYT* today by the man who prosecuted the Weathermen in the 1970s expressing outrage over linking Obama to Bill Ayers, adding, "Although I dearly wanted to obtain convictions against all the Weathermen, including Bill Ayers, I am very pleased to learn that he has become a responsible citizen." And he gets in this dig at the paper: "I do take issue with the statement in your news article that the Weathermen indictment was dismissed because of 'prosecutorial misconduct.' It was dismissed because of illegal activities, including wiretaps, break-ins and mail interceptions, initiated by John N. Mitchell, attorney general at that time, and W. Mark Felt, an F.B.I. assistant director."

Felt, of course (you may have already forgotten) was also known as a guy called "Deep Throat."

German Engineering?
Articles today in top newspapers and from Joe Klein at *Time* and elsewhere note the rising anger, threats of violence and racism stirred up at McCain-Palin rallies, and some of it directed at the media. It was enough to inspire some concerns in a McCain team conference call Thursday but not enough to try to halt it. The very sober David Gergen on CNN last night expressed real concern, especially in a time of economic crisis for so many, sparking desperation and desire to lash out.

But later in the day, after a few attendees raised bigoted statements in a town hall, McCain finally tried to stop it. He dared to call Obama a decent family man (and was booed for his efforts). He took the microphone from one woman who accused Obama of being an "Arab," telling her no, he is not, he is "decent" – as if Arabs or Muslims cannot fit that description.

He even assured the crowd that they should not fear "danger" if Obama becomes president. All the while his campaign was running ads aimed at Obama titled "Dangerous."

Bill Buckley's Son Voting for Obama

"Sorry, Dad, I'm Voting for Obama," runs the hed over a posting by the noted humorist/author Christopher Buckley over at Tina Brown's new site, The Beast. It opens: "Let me be the latest conservative/libertarian/whatever to leap onto the Barack Obama bandwagon. It's a good thing my dear old mum and pup are no longer alive. They'd cut off my allowance.

"Or would they? But let's get that part out of the way. The only reason my vote would be of any interest to anyone is that my last name happens to be Buckley—a name I inherited. So in the event anyone notices or cares, the headline will be: 'William F. Buckley's Son Says He Is Pro-Obama.' I know, I know: It lacks the throw-weight of 'Ron Reagan Jr. to Address Democratic Convention,' but it'll have to do."

Troopergate Report: She 'Abused Power'

The *Anchorage Daily News* camped out all day in the hall – and blogged – as the state's legislative committee read and then voted on the release of the much-awaited "Troopergate" report involving Gov. Sarah Palin. In the end, the committee voted 12-0, with all Republicans joining in, to release it. *The New York Times* noted that the report "was commissioned and released by a bipartisan state legislative panel made up of 10 Republicans and 4 Democrats." The McCain campaign had released its own review yesterday absolving his running mate of any wrongdoing whatsoever.

Now the official report is out and The Associated Press opens with: "Sarah Palin unlawfully abused her power as governor by trying to have her former brother-in-law fired as a state trooper, the chief investigator of an Alaska legislative panel concluded Friday. The politically charged inquiry imperiled her reputation as a reformer on John McCain's Republican ticket.

"Investigator Stephen Branchflower, in a report by a bipartisan panel that investigated the matter, found Palin in violation of a state ethics law that prohibits public officials from using their office for personal gain."

One key finding: Palin used claims involving personal threats to her family as "cover" for what was really a vindictive action against the trooper for personal reasons. Here are the first two findings from the report:

–Finding Number One

For the reasons explained in section IV of this report, I find that Governor Sarah Palin abused her power by violating Alaska Statute 39.52.110(a) of the Alaska Executive Branch Ethics Act. ....The legislature reaffirms that each public officer holds office as a public trust, and any effort to benefit a personal or financial interest through official action is a violation of that trust.

–Finding Number Two

I find that, although Walt Monegan's refusal to fire Trooper Michael Wooten was not the sole reason he was fired by Governor Sarah Palin, it was likely a contributing factor to his termination as Commissioner of Public Safety. In spite of that, Governor Palin's firing of Commissioner Monegan was a proper and lawful exercise of her constitutional and statutory authority to hire and fire executive branch department heads.

October 11

Hockey Mom Booed at – Hockey Game

You never know where you are going to find a political scoop, but Lynn Zinser at her *New York Times* hockey blog "Slapshot" posted first that Sarah Palin, in her much-ballyhooed appearance dropping the puck at the Philadelphia Flyers' opener, was greeted by "resounding (almost deafening) boos from the Flyers crowd."

Fox Sports observed more kindly on its site, "The crowd reacted with a mixture of cheers and boos at her appearance." AP also detected a "mixture" of cheers and boos, but videos quickly posted on YouTube suggested a more negative response.

Palin brought two of her daughters along. Apparently they are skipping school all month. (Perhaps Palin should call herself a "hooky Mom" instead.) She quipped beforehand that dressing her youngest in a Flyers' jersey might prevent the boos and catcalls. No chance, and it also raised the ire of some commentators that she had, once again, "used" her children.

Of course, getting booed in Philadelphia sports arenas is nothing new. As the story goes, the fans there even booed Santa Claus on one occasion. But Zinser's post had a lot more in mind: "I would object to this sideshow whichever political party it involved. Having vice presidential candidate Sarah Palin drop the ceremonial first puck at the Flyers' opener Saturday night was problematic not because it was Palin — Flyers owner Ed Snider's decision under the flimsy excuse of 'honoring' hockey moms — but because it is injecting politics in a place it should not be."

More: "The biggest problem: when Palin came onto the Wachovia Center ice Saturday night — greeted by resounding (almost deafening) boos from the Flyers crowd — the two hockey players who had no choice but to appear with her in that photo-op were turned into props in a political campaign. If Rangers center Scott Gomez or Flyers center Mike Richards wanted to make some sort of political statement, that would be fine, but in this case, they were thrust into a situation not of their choosing. Snider put them there with his ill-advised mixing of politics and sports.

"The level of discomfort has been palpable for the Rangers' two Alaska natives, Gomez and Brandon Dubinsky, as they have been asked questions about Palin and the election in recent weeks. Dubinsky, a 22-year-old who has shied away from nothing since he broke in with the Rangers last year, looks petrified when the topic gets brought up. I think both would rather play goalie in a shootout than weigh in on the presidential election."

October 13

Kurtz: The Horror, The Horror, Facing the Boys on the Bus
Howie Kurtz asks in *Washington Post* (after he went out on the road for awhile): Has the Web and the digital age doomed the "boys on the bus"? Here is the lede: "The reporters waded gingerly into two-inch-deep mud and settled behind scratched wooden tables as Barack Obama was being introduced

to more than 10,000 screaming fans at the state fairgrounds here. Before the Democratic nominee took the podium, the text of his speech arrived by BlackBerry. The address was carried by CNN, Fox and MSNBC. While he was still delivering his applause lines, an Atlantic blogger posted excerpts. And despite the huge foot-stomping crowd that could barely be glimpsed from the media tent, most reporters remained hunched over their laptops.

"Does the campaign trail still matter much in an age of digital warfare? Or is it now a mere sideshow, meant to provide the media with pretty pictures of colorful crowds while the guts of the contest unfold elsewhere? And if so, are the boys (and girls) on the bus spinning their wheels? 'Anything interesting that happens on the road is going to be eaten up before you can get to it,' says Slate correspondent John Dickerson. 'By the time you see the papers, you feel like you know it all.'

"On the road, some of the nation's top print journalists morph into bloggers who post paragraphs on each mini-development, giving them a more stenographic role that leaves less time for actual reporting, or even thinking. Obama advisers have concluded that newspaper and magazine stories no longer have the same resonance but that a brief item by, say, *Politico* bloggers can spread like wildfire."

Circular Firing Squad

Bill Kristol has virtually doomed the McCain campaign with bad advice, going back at least as far as touting Sarah Palin for veep long before her selection (he had earlier mentioned Clarence Thomas for this post), and continuing in this vein by urging the name-calling campaign that has apparently flopped. Naturally, in today's column, he blamed it all on McCain (for actually taking his advice?), and suggested that he should "fire his campaign" and "start over."

Now, asked to respond, McCain campaign spokeswoman Nancy Pfotenhauer said on Fox News: "Well, you know Bill is entitled to his perspective. And I used to work for Bill. And I can tell you personally sometimes he's brilliant and sometimes he's not. And this is one where it's the latter category. You know, I think unfortunately he has bought into the Obama campaign's party line." Actually, you might think he has been on the Obama payroll for months.

Obama Blasted for Playing T-Ball During Vietnam War!
This from *The Onion* but, sadly, you could imagine coming from almost any real news outlet: "At a press conference on Monday, members of the Vietnam Veterans Alliance blasted Democratic nominee Barack Obama for his failure to serve in the Southeast Asian war that ended 33 years ago, alleging that during the conflict the candidate frequently engaged in games of T-ball. 'While our boys were dying in Vietnam, Barack Obama was running around a little league field, laughing and having fun without a care in the world,' VVA spokesman James Lowry said. 'John McCain left his wife and three children behind and fought bravely, but I guess Sen. Obama decided that practicing cursive and learning how to ride a bike was just more important than defending his country in her hour of need. I bet he wasn't even able to point out Vietnam on a map.'"

October 14

Anchorage Paper: Palin's Defense on Troopergate An 'Embarrassment'
The *Anchorage Daily News*' angry editorial today was topped with the headline: "Palin vindicated? Governor offers Orwellian spin." It opens: "Sarah Palin's reaction to the Legislature's Troopergate report is an embarrassment to Alaskans and the nation.

"She claims the report 'vindicates' her. She said that the investigation found 'no unlawful or unethical activity on my part.'

"Her response is either astoundingly ignorant or downright Orwellian." An excerpt: "In plain English, she did something 'unlawful.' She broke the state ethics law. Perhaps Gov. Palin has been too busy to actually read the Troopergate report. Perhaps she is relying on briefings from McCain campaign spinmeisters. That's the charitable interpretation. Because if she had actually read it, she couldn't claim 'vindication' with a straight face."

Campbell Brown to Media: Stop the Anti-Muslim Bias
We've been waiting months, if not years, for this but finally a top TV pundit has declared: So what if a candidate for office – or anyone in America, for that matter – *is* a Muslim? Why is that a "disqualifier"?

Campbell Brown, the increasingly outspoken CNN primetime host, was apparently ticked off by John McCain's much-lauded response to a woman at one of his rallies last week who had informed him that Obama is an "Arab." McCain said, no, Obama is a "decent" follow. Brown said last night, "So what if Obama was Arab or Muslim? So what if John McCain was Arab or Muslim? Would it matter? When did that become a disqualifier for higher office in our country? When did Arab and Muslim become dirty words? The equivalent of dishonorable or radical?

"I feel like I am stating the obvious here, but apparently it needs to be said: There is a difference between radical Muslims who support jihad against America and Muslims who want to practice their religion freely and have normal lives like anyone else. There are more than 1.2 million Arab-Americans and about 7 million Muslim-Americans, former Cabinet secretaries, members of Congress, successful business people, normal average Americans from all walks of life.

"And the media is complicit here, too. We've all been too quick to accept the idea that calling someone Muslim is a slur.... We can't tolerate this ignorance – in the media and on the campaign trail."

October 15

Most Ignored Subject by the Press
In my view it is the new trend in "early voting." That is, many more states are allowing, even encouraging, people to vote way before election day, and citizens are taking them up on the offer in amazing numbers. This will lead to more votes cast and probably more from younger people, who really like this method. This year, it also really hurts McCain, with the early voting starting in most places last week just as his poll numbers started crumbling. He may very well rally by election day – but by then millions of votes will have been cast.

Debate and Switch: Meet Joe the Plumber
Four and out? A sweep for the Democrats? I expected to sit down tonight and write the same script from the past three encounters: The Democrat easily wins on points and demeanor, pundits call it a draw anyway, polls mock the pundits by showing an easy win for the Dem. Ho-hum.

But this one at Hofstra was a little different, perhaps because of the seating arrangement, McCain's growing desperation, or a more pushy moderator. It was like Muhammad Ali vs. Sonny Liston – the glider vs. the puncher – but without the knockout of Liston.

The big winner: Joe the Plumber.

Joe, can I be your agent? The book and movie deals will be arriving within hours. Forget Joe Six-Pack: We have a new American icon, who may not need a designated driver on the way home from the soccer game.

And by the way, the average annual pay for a plumber in the U.S. is around $45,000, well within Obama's tax-cut plan. Does Joe the Plumber really have $250,000 to buy that business? Or is he just Joe Blow?

The two candidates invoked and evoked Joe the Plumber, even addressed him directly. Obama seemed to be more concerned about speaking to him than remembering why Sarah Palin was a joke as a veep candidate. Handed a golden opportunity to confront this – he wasn't asked at first if she was qualified, just to say why his veep choice was better – he simply danced around it. Meanwhile, he let McCain sock Biden, and for that matter, punch all night without much more than a jab in return.

It was rope-a-dope but without the Ali flurry that destroyed George Foreman. Still, because of his answers on abortion and the Supreme Court choices, and some of the economic and medical issues, he managed to come out okay, possibly even on top. Ali did win many fights on many an off-night.

But forget the instant polls after the debate. The only view anyone will now care about belongs to.... Joe the Plumber. Hey Joe, where ya gonna go? A nation turns its lonely eyes to you.

UPDATE: Thankfully, AP has reached Joe and he still isn't saying who he will vote for. "It's pretty surreal, man, my name being mentioned in a presidential campaign," he said. One report indicates that he has always been a McCain supporter. Interviewed by Katie Couric this morning he compared Obama to...Sammy Davis Jr. Whoops, another McCain vetting failure? Did he learn anything the last time?

Fictitious 'Washington Post' Report Exposed!
In recent months, conservatives have been caught red-faced spreading smears about Barack Obama via emails and blogs and Web sites, their sources eventually unmasked as tainted or Not Real People. It happened again this

week when they went bonkers over an alleged African wire service account of a fake quote from Michelle Obama. Now here's another example, but this one involves a *Washington Post* reporter named Dale Lindsdorf.

Of course, there is no Dale Lindsdorf at the *Post* (or seemingly anywhere) but when did that get in the way of a good smear? Even a giveaway line where Obama endorses an old Coke commercial song as our new national anthem did not deter the 'wingers from believing it.

For at least two weeks the "Lindsdorf" account of an Obama appearance on "Meet the Press" on Sept. 7 has been rocketing around the world and back again via email and the Internet, sometimes showing up at reputable sites – such as the *Post* itself – in their Comments sections. Someone even brought it up today in an online chat with *Post* reporter Ann Kornblut at the paper's site. She said she knew of no Lindsdorf but would check on it (hey, put Bob Woodward on the case).

The charge is the old familiar tale of Obama not believing in honoring the flag, and hating America, with the new twist that he said this on "Meet the Press" a month ago (somehow the world missed this) and that it has been confirmed by the aforementioned Dale Lindsdorf. Thankfully, it was debunked today on the Snopes.com site, which traced it back to a satiric entry at an obscure site that was taken seriously and spread widely.

The giveaway should have been Obama saying he wanted to junk our "bellicose" national anthem, the "Star-Spangled Banner," and replace it with the more peaceful "I'd Like to Teach the World to Sing" – adding that if that was our anthem "then I might salute it."

He supposedly then added, "It's my intention, if elected, to disarm America to the level of acceptance to our Middle East Brethren." And: "My wife disrespects the Flag for many personal reasons. Together she and I have attended several flag burning ceremonies in the past, many years ago."

October 16

'Joe the Plumber' Springs a Leak

The noted blogger Andrew Sullivan with a funny, if true, line today about Joe the (Not Quite) Plumber: He has now had more press conferences than

Sarah Palin. But like Palin, as we noted previously, "Joe" had not exactly been vetted before appearing on the national stage last night. Today it has already emerged that he is not an "undecided" voter but a registered Republican, once belonged to the Natural Law Party and opposes Social Security. AP has a new story that reveals he doesn't even have a plumbing license, owes back taxes – and his real first name is not Joe or Joseph but Samuel. Surely more to come but really, after this afternoon, who cares?

October 18

Palin (In the Flesh) on 'SNL'
She had surprisingly little to do in the opening segment – and she took a lot of heat, especially on her some-parts-of-USA-not-patriotic statement. And the whole set up reminded people that she has not, in fact, had a press conference during the entire campaign (unlike Joe the Plumber). Tina Fey even did another beauty pageant riff. I wonder if this was what Palin bargained for? I expected her to turn the tables and portray Fey as her *30 Rock* character. Instead all she got to do was hear Alec Baldwin call her "hotter in person" and yell "live from New York."

Later in the show she endured a rap number on "Weekend Update," also making fun of her, featuring Amy Poehler and a Todd Palin lookalike. Palin just kind of sat there and danced in her seat as they gunned down a moose and some such. Fortunately for her, it was hard to hear many of the acerbic lyrics. Is getting points for being a good sport enough at this stage? That she is in on the joke that she is a…joke?

Ocober 20

Semi-Colin or Exclamation Point?
Colin Powell, as rumored, came out for Obama on *Meet the Press*, although he again failed to express real regret over his role in taking the nation to war in Iraq in 2003. He did speak movingly about the issue raised by Campbell Brown earlier: The so-what-if-Obama-was-a-Muslim angle. In any case, Rush Limbaugh, George Will, and some other conservatives have quickly called race the main factor in the Powell endorsement. Limbaugh asks, name another white liberal he has ever endorsed.

October 2008

Obama Widens Lead in Newspaper Endorsements
Barack Obama's smashing lead over John McCain in newspaper endorsements could prove significant – especially since the deluge began four days ago, just as Obama began to sink in most polls. Will they help him rebound? By our count over at *Editor & Publisher* he leads by a better than 3 to 1 margin (103 to 32 at last count). In contrast, when we did our final count in 2004, John Kerry barely edged George Bush, 213-205.

What's startling is the list of large papers that have backed Obama. It's a who's who of the dominant papers in nearly every giant metro: Boston, New York, both papers in Chicago, Cleveland, Philly, Pittsburgh, Washington D.C., San Francisco, Sacramento, St. Louis, Atlanta, both papers in L.A., Detroit, both papers in Seattle, Portland, Miami, Orlando, Raleigh, Buffalo and more. McCain's only clear wins are in Columbus and San Diego, and he barely manages a split in Texas, of all places. It's a veritable landslide.

But even more revealing, Obama has an even wider lead in those that have switched sides. That flipflop number is now close to 25, with McCain only picking up one paper from the Kerry side in 2004 (the *Daily Press* in Newport News, Va.). The list of switches to Obama includes such GOP stalwarts as the *Chicago Tribune* (never has endorsed a Democrat in its long history), *Houston Chronicle* and *Austin American-Statesman*, plus the *Denver Post*, *New York Daily News* and a host of others. Two other large papers that did not endorse at all in 2004, the *L.A. Times* and *Plain Dealer* in Cleveland, also backed Obama. And the list goes on and on. True, many Obama papers are in safe blue states but many others are in the red zone.

What's Up, Docs?
Dr. Lawrence Altman at *The New York Times* reports on health issues surrounding all of the candidates, including Joe Biden's aneuryism history, and notes that little has emerged from Obama (a single page), who has a smoking problem. But nothing at all has come from Sarah Palin and she declined to respond to any requests from the *Times* for anything. The section on McCain's cancer includes the following: "If Mr. McCain's 2000 left-temple melanoma was a metastasis, as the Armed Forces pathologists' report suggested, it would be classified as Stage III. The reclassification would change his statistical odds for survival at 10 years from about 60 percent to 36 percent, according to a published study."

October 20

Bearing a Hate Crime
What next, after cries of "Kill him!" at campaign rallies? *The Asheville (N.C.) Citizen Times* reports, "A dead bear was found dumped this morning on the Western Carolina University campus, draped with a pair of Obama campaign signs, university police said." Maintenance workers at 7:45 a.m. found a 75-pound bear cub dumped at the roundabout at the entrance to campus, said Tom Johnson, chief of university police.

"It looked like it had been shot in the head as best we can tell. A couple of Obama campaign signs had been stapled together and stuck over its head," Johnson said. University police called in state Wildlife Resources officials to remove the body and help in the investigation. "This is certainly unacceptable," Johnson said, according to the paper. "Someone was wanting to draw attention to the election.

"If we find out who they are, we'll make sure Western Carolina University deplores the inappropriate behavior that led to this troubling incident," said Leila Tvedt, associate vice chancellor "We cannot speculate on the motives of the people involved, nor who those people might be. Campus police are cooperating with authorities to investigate this matter."

October 21

Lobster Overcooked by 'Post'
Pretty funny – and revealing: The *New York Post* has retracted a Page Six item on Michelle Obama livin' it up in tough times with a lobster dinner at the Waldorf in NYC. As the paper now admits, she wasn't even in NYC on that date. But too late for Rush Limbaugh and others on the right who cited the story to prove the Obamas' hypocrisy. It is hard to charge "anti-Americanism" in regard to lobster – what is more American? – but certainly it is "elite" in price and smacks of liberal New England.. Too bad it was a lie.

October 22

Palin Runs Dry in Polls
It may yet turn out differently, but at this stage in the campaign for the White House it appears that if John McCain loses in November the turning

point, in my view, will not be the financial crisis hitting in late September but his choice of Sarah Palin as his veep in late August. Now two new national polls show that voters cite that choice as the main reason they have turned from McCain.

Indeed, his slippage in the polls began in September after his convention bounce, and before the financial crisis truly hit, as media vetting on Palin began and she ventured out for her first TV interview. But here is another measure: the brutal criticism of that pick in newspaper editorial endorsements of his opponent – from GOP-leaning papers that endorsed George W. Bush.

Many of them cited his Palin pick as a key reason for switching sides this time around. As the *Chicago Tribune*, which backed a Democrat for president for the first time in its history, frankly declared, "McCain failed in his most important executive decision." Yet McCain said today, referring to Palin, "I think she is the most qualified of any that has run recently for vice president."

Here is a gallery of some of these comments, all from Bush-backing papers in 2004.

ASBURY PARK (N.J.) PRESS
"If McCain, who is 72 and has a history of cancer, should die in the presidency, he would be succeeded by Sarah Palin, whose selection as the vice presidential candidate calls McCain's judgment into serious question. She is not qualified to lead a nation facing its toughest challenges in decades."

SALT LAKE TRIBUNE
"Then, out of nowhere, and without proper vetting, the impetuous McCain picked Alaska Gov. Sarah Palin as his running mate. She quickly proved grievously underequipped to step into the presidency should McCain, at 72 and with a history of health problems, die in office. More than any single factor, McCain's bad judgment in choosing the inarticulate, insular and ethically challenged Palin disqualifies him for the presidency."

HOUSTON CHRONICLE
"Perhaps the worst mistake McCain made in his campaign for the White House was the choice of the inexperienced and inflammatory Palin as his vice-presidential running mate. Had he selected a moderate, experienced

Republican lawmaker such as Texas Sen. Kay Bailey Hutchison with a strong appeal to independents, the *Chronicle's* choice for an endorsement would have been far more difficult."

STOCKTON (Ca.) RECORD
"If elected, at 72, [McCain] would be the oldest incoming president in U.S. history. He's in good health now, we're told, although he has withheld most of his medical records. That means Gov. Sarah Palin could very well become president. And that brings us to McCain's most troubling trait: his judgment. While praiseworthy for putting the first woman on a major-party presidential ticket since Geraldine Ferraro in 1984, his selection of Palin as a running mate was appalling."

<u>October 23</u>

Barack to the 'Roots'

Peter Daou was an influential early political blogger back in the day, then went on to run the online outreach operation for Hillary Clinton. He has come to back Obama – and pays tribute to his netroots "roots" in a new piece up at Huffington Post. Here is an excerpt that looks ahead to an Obama victory on election day in November:

"In that seminal moment, much will be celebrated. And much forgotten. One thing that shouldn't be overlooked is the tortured path to that day and the ragtag group of activists who, from the fear of knowing that America had taken a terrible turn at the dawn of a millennium, embraced a new medium and labored tirelessly, thanklessly, defending the Constitution and the rule of law.

"Day after day, they congregated on Websites, blogs, message boards and any other online forum they could find to write, debate, argue and resist a radical administration and a lockstep Republican Party. Mocked and feared, dismissed as 'angry' and treated with disdain, they fought their opponents, fought their own party, fought the media, fought one another, all to a single end, the defense of inviolable American ideals against a brazen onslaught from a shameful and shameless administration.

"When we look back at the eight years beginning with a grim night in 2000 when George W. Bush was declared the victor over Al Gore, we should give credit to those who held tough when Bush was at the height of his swagger; we should honor the 'ten percenters' who took pride in opposing Bush when his approval rating was near 90%, the media fawning over him.... No one knew if blogs would become quaint artifacts. Many hoped they would. Blogging was about speaking up for America's guiding principles, liberty, justice, equality, opportunity, democracy."

Newspaper Endorsements Since 1940 Show Wide GOP Edge

E&P, citing tradition, has been counting and listing all of the editorial page endorsements for president again this year. But what about in years past? Have Democrats usually earned the nod from so-called "liberal" press? Or is Obama just an especially good candidate – or McCain a poor one – this year, in the eyes of most newspapers?

We have noted previously that in our 2004 count, John Kerry barely edged George Bush 213-205. But what about before then?

Well, in 2000 we found when we asked papers about their endorsements we found 137 saying they had backed Bush and only 99 naming Gore. In 1996, by our count, Bob Dole topped Bill Clinton in this area by 122-80, among the editorials identified.

And before then? An October 26, 1996, article by Jodi B. Cohen summarized E&P findings going back to 1940. We're not sure exactly how E&P got the word on these endorsements in the days before e-mail, fax, and the Web – Pony Express? But here is that accounting, which shows an extremely wide GOP edge going way back, with even JFK and FDR taking it on the chin. A Democrat did not earn the most editorial votes until Johnson edged Goldwater in 1964 and then not again until Clinton recorded a very narrow "win" in 1992.

1940: Willkie (R) over Roosevelt (D) 813-289.
1944: Dewey (R) over Roosevelt (D) 796-291,
1948: Dewey (R) over Truman (D) 771-182,
1952: Eisenhower (R) over Stevenson (D) 933-202
1956: Eisenhower (R) over Stevenson (D) 740-189
1960: Nixon (R) over Kennedy (D) 731-208
1964: Johnson (D) over Goldwater (R) 440-359
1968: Nixon (R) over Humphrey (D) 634-146

1972: Nixon (R) over McGovern (D) 753-56
1976: Ford (R) over Carter (D) 411-80
1980: Reagan (R) over Carter(D) 443-126
1984: Reagan (R) over Mondale (D) 381-62
1988: Bush (R) over Dukakis (D) 195-51
1992: Clinton (D) over Bush (R) 149-125

Scott McClellan Endorses Obama
Scott McClellan, President Bush's former chief spokesman, says he is backing Barack Obama for president. McClellan made the endorsement during a taping of comedian D.L. Hughley's new show premiering on CNN this weekend. McClellan, who earlier this year wrote that tell-all book critical of the White House – and media – surrounding the Iraq war, said he wanted to support the candidate who has the best chance for changing the way Washington works and getting things done. He's the second former Bush administration figure this week to publicly back Obama, following former Secretary of State Colin Powell.

October 24

'Hot' Toddy
Sarah Palin will still have a good job if she loses in November but what about her husband? Caribaya rum is supposedly looking out for his interests, offering him a job as its celebrity spokesman/billboard "hottie," at least according to a press release sent by its NYC publicity office today.

It kicks off with, "VP CANDIDATE SARAH PALIN'S HUSBAND IS THE HOTTEST THING TO HIT POLITICS: NEW YORK-BASED RUM COMPANY WANTS TO MAKE ALASKA'S FIRST MAN, AMERICA'S NEXT SUPERMODEL WITH BILLBOARD AD CAMPAIGN." It follows with an open letter to "Todd" purportedly from CEO Martin Silver.

Tongue-in-cheek or not, here is the first part of the text: "I would like to take this opportunity to express my congratulations on being the nation's 'newest hottie.' We at Caribaya Rums are searching for a product supermodel to be placed on billboards and ads across the nation.

"We would like to make an offer to you about representing our rum products. We at Caribaya Rums think that you would become a sex symbol to the millions of women that enjoy our product, as well as become the new face in the advertising world. Even though you live in the land of cold, we are sure that you would melt the tons of hearts that see this ad.

"Celebrities and politicians provide the best exposure for product sales. Look what former U.S. Senate Majority Leader Bob Dole did for Viagra. If your wife moves to Washington, you might be looking for a new job. Our ads appear on the back of every New York City bus. Since our product comes from the tropical islands, our Madison Avenue team feels that a possible ad can have you revealing your bare chest, dressed in Hawaiian boxer shorts, surrounded by our rum."

King's View of Campaign Coverage

John King, chief CNN political correspondent, in an interview with South Carolina ETV taped Wednesday, admitted that some criticism of the media's handling of election coverage is legitimate, that Sarah Palin has been treated differently and that some of his colleagues are indeed "out of touch." The interview airs on *The Big Picture*, Oct. 30 at 7:30 p.m. *E&P* has been sent highlights.

"We did invest our thinking too much at the beginning, in the Clinton juggernaut," he said. "Of course, Senator Clinton was going to win—the Clinton name is the gold standard in Democratic politics. Of course she's going to win. And so, when people say now we haven't spent enough time looking at Barack Obama's background, a lot of that was because people were looking at Senator Clinton early on as the frontrunner, and thinking 'Well, this guy, he's going to mount a good race, but he can't possibly beat her.' And then he does, and we're on into the general election.

"I think there's some very legitimate criticism that we did not treat all of the candidates in the Democratic race—particularly the top two or three—equally, because of the Clinton obsession in the national media. It is a very fair point. We need to learn that lesson."

Has Sarah Palin been treated much differently by the press than her counterparts? King said, "Part of that may be legitimate. Part of that may be how the McCain campaign put her out there. We whine too much sometimes. If the McCain campaign doesn't want to make Sarah Palin available for interviews, OK, just say they won't make her available for interviews. We don't have to jump up and down and scream and cry about that...In today's democracy, if she is doing talk radio, if she is going to town halls, if she is out campaigning, we should make note of it…it is not our job to whine or complain…

"If (people) think that's important, if a voter thinks it's important that she's not doing the Sunday shows, then the voter will make their decision based on that. Other voters will think, 'So what? Why do I want to listen to you? I want to see her in a town hall. I want to see her giving a speech.' So, we need to observe, not object so much…." In other words: Don't do your journalistic duty.

And is Palin right about the media being elitist? King: "I say this all the time, and many in my business disagree with me, but one of the things I love about what I do is I travel. And there are a lot of people who sit—they're wonderful people—they're well-intentioned, don't get me wrong, but they sit in New York or Washington—and they don't come to South Carolina or North Carolina or Ohio or any other swing state out here and actually talk to human beings….

"And so their attitudes are influenced by the fact that they live in Washington or New York and they don't travel enough. And the criticism is that makes them elitist. I would just say sometimes there are some people who are very influential in our business who are somewhat out of touch."

'Mutilation' of McCain Worker in Pittsburgh a Hoax

It had drawn wide local and national – even political attention, with some of the candidates for president/vice president weighing in or even calling – but now the story has fallen apart. Police in Pittsburgh have declared it all a hoax and are pressing charges against the McCain worker, Ashley Todd, at the center of the episode.

She has confessed – and now blames the media for falling for it and turning it into a political story.

It started yesterday afternoon with Matt Drudge screaming at the top of his popular site in red type – but no siren – that a Pittsburgh campaign worker for McCain (paid by a Republican group), age 20, had been viciously attacked and the letter "B" carved into her face, presumably by a Barack Obama fan, who had allegedly seen a McCain bumper sticker on her car. Her name, it soon emerged, was Ashley Todd and she had come to Pittsburgh from College Station, Texas, to help out.

Quickly it started to appear overblown (Drudge downgraded it to smaller, black type) as the police noted that it seemed to be part of a robbery ($60) and the woman did not seek medical attention. But later press reports revealed she would visit a hospital, Sarah Palin and maybe John McCain had called her and the Obama camp had condemned the attack.

Still later, however, conservative columnist Michelle Malkin, and some others, grew skeptical. For one thing, the "B" was carved a little too lightly and perfectly – and backward, as if done using a mirror. Smoking Gun probed her too-pat "Twitter" tweets and Gawker looked at her MySpace page.

Then police said that evidence from the ATM that she reportedly visited did not match her account. And then she changed her story, admitting that her assailant did not see a McCain bumper sticker, and adding to here account a sexual assault – and losing consciousness.

John Moody, executive vice president at Fox News, commented on his blog that "this incident could become a watershed event in the 11 days before the election. If Ms. Todd's allegations are proven accurate, some voters may revisit their support for Senator Obama, not because they are racists (with due respect to Rep. John Murtha), but because they suddenly feel they do not know enough about the Democratic nominee. If the incident turns out to be a hoax, Senator McCain's quest for the presidency is over, forever linked to race-baiting."

Now the Pittsburgh TV station KDKA reports: "Police sources tell KDKA that a campaign worker has now confessed to making up a story that a mugger attacked her and cut the letter 'B' in her face after seeing her McCain bumper sticker.

"This afternoon, a Pittsburgh police commander told KDKA Investigator Marty Griffin that Todd confessed to making up the story. The commander added that Todd will face charges; but police have not commented on what those charges will be."

It's bad enough that Jonathan Martin, *Poltico*'s McCain camp-follower, reported the alleged "mutilation" of the McCain worker yesterday as fact. Today he admits that it turned out to be a hoax but opens his account with: "Seems like McCain just can't catch a break." Ponder that line for a moment.

Meanwhile, Greg Sargent at Talking Points Memo has linked a McCain spokesman to pushing the story, in saying flatly that the carving of the "B" definitely happened and that, no doubt, the "B" stood for "Barack."

No further comment about the end of the McCain campaign from Fox's John Moody.

October 25

Frum Here to Eternity
Amazing quote from Sen. Joe Lieberman today to reporters back home in Connecticut as he continued to defend Sarah Palin: "Thank God she's not going to have to be president from Day One. McCain's going to be alive and well." And added: "Let's hope she never has to be ready because we hope McCain is elected and live out his term."

Topping that, an amazing piece in the *Washington Post* by David Frum, the former "axis of evil" Bush speechwriter and GOP stalwart who has been critical of the McCain campaign and now lowers the boom, calling for conservative funders to stop giving him any money and focus instead on the Senate so that his party does not suffer truly epic losses: "McCain's awful campaign is having awful consequences down the ballot. I spoke a little while ago to a senior Republican House member. 'There is not a safe Republican seat in the country,' he warned. 'I don't mean that we're going to lose all of them. But we could lose any of them.'" Like others, Frum now sees the Palin pick as truly disastrous and warns that a Democratic landslide could lead to, gasp, a takeover of our political culture by MSNBC and liberal bloggers! Meanwhile, Bill Kristol at the *Weekly Standard* still prays for a McCain win, as it would lead to the "dejection of the mainstream media."

Alaska's Biggest Paper Endorses...Obama
The Anchorage Daily News, has endorsed Barack Obama for president, despite – or at least partly because of – its state governor's presence on the opposing ticket. While praising Palin's energy, the paper's editorial adds, "Yet despite her formidable gifts, few who have worked closely with the governor would argue she is truly ready to assume command of the most important, powerful nation on earth. To step in and juggle the demands of an economic meltdown,

two deadly wars and a deteriorating climate crisis would stretch the governor beyond her range. Like picking Sen. McCain for president, putting her one 72-year-old heartbeat from the leadership of the free world is just too risky at this time....

"Gov. Palin's nomination clearly alters the landscape for Alaskans as we survey this race for the presidency – but it does not overwhelm all other judgment. The election, after all is said and done, is not about Sarah Palin, and our sober view is that her running mate, Sen. John McCain, is the wrong choice for president at this critical time for our nation."

The paper has drawn national attention with many hard-hitting probes of the governor's background and tenures in elected office.

It was just one of many joining in the Obama landslide of endorsements this weekend. It's now a rout, with Obama leading 194-82. More than 35 papers have now switched from Bush to Obama. The latest major papers to flip: The *Providence Journal* and *The Fort Worth Star-Telegram* deep in the red heart of Texas. That, amazingly, gives Obama three of the five major papers in that state.

McCain held on to his home state *Arizona Republic* and papers in Richmond and Cincinnati. This really reveals how far McCain has fallen: *The Indianapolis Star*, proudly GOP-leaning, which backed Bush the last time, decided not to endorse anyone this time around. It just couldn't bring itself to push the lever for this Republican.

The *Times-Picayune* in New Orleans, which also sat out 2004, endorsed Obama today. After the White House's handling of Katrina, it's no wonder, but not so long ago, eight years in fact, it had endorsed George W. Bush. Look what that got them.

October 27

Another Assassination Plot: Get Used to It?
As with the meth-heads who hoped to assassinated Obama at the Democratic convention in Denver, this probably wouldn't have gotten very far, but still, from the AP: "Federal agents have broken up a plot by two neo-Nazi skinheads to assassinate Democratic presidential candidate Barack Obama and shoot or decapitate 102 black people, the Bureau of Alcohol, Tobacco Firearms and Explosives said Monday.

"In court records unsealed Monday in U.S. District Court in Jackson, Tenn., federal agents said they disrupted plans to rob a gun store and target a predominantly African-American high school in a murder spree that was to begin in Tennessee. Agents said the skinheads did not identify the school by name.

"Jim Cavanaugh, special agent in charge of ATF's Nashville field office, said the two men planned to shoot 88 black people and decapitate another 14. The numbers 88 and 14 are symbolic in the white supremacist community."

October 28

Palin Called a 'Diva' and 'Whack'—And That's From the McCain Team
David Frum at his *National Review* diary takes on the *Washington Times'* Tony Blankley and Rush Limbaugh on their prescriptions for a conservative comeback in years ahead: "When Rush and Blankley tell us the blueprint is there, if only we would follow it, they are telling us something that is not true. They are offering flattering illusions when we need truth. They are leading us to disaster - and beyond disaster, to irrelevance."

Meanwhile, Mike Allen at *Politico* says a McCain aide has anonymously one-upped yesterday's claim, from that campaign, that Palin is a "diva" and "going rogue" by saying she is "whack." Jon Stewart did a funny segment on this last night, which ended with Palin on the cover of *Rogue* magazine. No wonder each member of the team may want to blame the other: the *Anchorage Daily News* features a finding from a new Pew survey that Palin is now a huge "drag" on the ticket with 49% now viewing her unfavorably and only 44 favorably.

October 29

McCain Campaign Targets Palestinian 'Pal'
You'd think that since polls show that the McCain focus on Obama's associations (Bill Ayers etc.) have only hurt him that the GOP and conservative bloggers would look elsewhere in the final week. But no, the current #1 issue seems to be that Obama attended a book party for a respected pro-Palestinian

professor in Chicago several years ago. This has been known since the *L.A. Times* "exposed" it in April but now it has turned into an attack on the media as McCain backers have demanded that the *Times* release a video of that distant event. A McCain spokesman accused the paper of "suppressing" the evidence.

Finally the paper responded today, explaining that it could not do it as it was shown the video by a source on condition that it not be released.

Palin in a speech today said that the *L.A. Times* should get a Pulitzer for "kowtowing." And McCain in a radio interview in Florida said: "The *Los Angeles Times* refuses to make that videotape public. I'm not in the business of talking about media bias [oh, no?] but what if there was a tape with John McCain with a neo-Nazi outfit being held by some media outlet? I think the treatment of the issue would be slightly different." It would probably even be different if someone had a tape of Obama with a – or in a – neo-Nazi outfit.

Obama's Honky Half
The candidate appeared with Jon Stewart tonight. Obama cracked that no matter what he does, yes, there will be some Sean Hannity fans who won't want to go out for a beer with him. One funny bit: After Obama questioned the "Bradley Effect" – that a lot of white supporters won't be able to pull the lever for him – Stewart speculated that, on Election Day, Obama's own white half might suddenly decide in the voting booth: "I can't do this."

"It's a problem," Obama quipped. "I've been going through therapy to make sure I vote properly on the 4th."

Speaking of prejudice: We've noted in this space previously that deep red Texas has become pink this year, at least in terms of newspaper endorsements. But now comes word that despite (because of?) this, a major poll in the state finds that 23% of its citizens still believe that Obama is, in fact, a Muslim.

October 30

A Thrilla from Wasilla
It's not exactly a shock that *The Frontiersman*, the weekly in Wasilla, Alaska, would endorse John McCain this week – unlike many other papers in the state it has found little to criticize in hometown fave Sarah Palin – but

the tone is a little surprising, especially with so much national focus on the small town. Here's a sample: "Aside from domestic agendas, we're a nation at war. America needs as its Commander-in-Chief a warrior, not a wimp."

The paper also blamed the Democrats for the current financial crisis–for allegedly passing laws that allowed all those bad loans. Oddly, it had very little to say about how Palin helps the ticket and if she is ready to serve as commander-in-chief. Even they couldn't work up the nerve for that.

The paper has button for a "Reader's Poll" next to the link for the editorial on its home page – but no poll appears. One imagines that the early results may not have been too favorable.

Gunned Down

A Montana executive of a rifle company that bears his name, Dan Cooper, lost his job because he told *USA Today* that he supports Obama for president. *USA Today* reporter Ken Dilanian wrote about executives such as Cooper who are "sold on Obama." The story also revealed the $3,300 contribution that gunsmith Cooper made to the Obama campaign, and wrote that he had switched from Republican to Democrat for this election "because of the war and because the Republican party has moved so far to the right in recent years."

Within 24 hours, gun owners, bloggers and open letters went viral on the Internet, threatening to boycott the company's products – many claiming (without much evidence) that Obama will try to restrict their right to bear arms. Cooper Firearms sent out a press release Thursday stating that the company does not share the political views of Dan Cooper and that his views may affect (infect?) the employees and shareholders of Cooper Firearms, and asked for Cooper's resignation. Even Montana Gov. Brian Schweitzer weighed in from his pro-gun state on the backlash against Cooper, telling *USA Today* that "it's silly season." Well, not so silly for now out-of-work Cooper.

Kristol Cracks

Appearing once again on *The Daily Show*, Bill Kristol, Jon Stewart's favorite whipping boy ("Bill Kristol, aren't you ever right?"), tonight defended the McCain-Palin ticket, at one point informing Jon that he was getting his news from suspect sources. "You're reading *The New York Times* too much," Kristol declared.

"Bill, you *work* for *The New York Times*," Stewart pointed out.

Otherwise, Kristol confidently predicted a McCain win. Stewart got him to say that Obama was not a radical and would, in fact, be a "conventional president" who would disappoint the left. Jon then asked, So why are you and McCain calling him a dangerous radical if you don't mean it? In a bit of a news flash, Stewart confessed that he would have voted for McCain over Gore in 2000 – but he doesn't recognize that McCain today.

October 31

Dylan Speaks: McCain Team Blowing 'Idiot Wind'
It's always been one of my favorite mid-period Dylan songs (from *Blood on the Tracks*, for you youngsters), so it was good to see it getting thrust into the final days of the election campaign. I speak of "Idiot Wind" from the mid-1970s. It opens, "Someone's got it in for me/They're planting stories in the press/Whoever it is I wish they'd cut it out quick/But when they will I can only guess."

The *Washington Post*, preparing a lacerating editorial attack against John McCain for his dirty campaign tactics, asked the latest GOP bogeyman, the Palestinian professor/scholar (and Obama acquaintance) Rashid Khalidi, what he thinks of the current uproar. He wrote back briefly, "I will stick to my policy of letting this idiot wind blow over." The *Post* then put "Idiot Wind" right in its headline.

Indeed, when the dust settles, so to speak, next week, perhaps the phrase "Idiot Wind" will endure as the lasting depiction of the McCain-Palin campaign. We don't need a Weatherman, such as Bill Ayers, to know which way the wind blows. Obama is now bringing it all Barack home.

The refrain of Dylan's "Idiot Wind" captures the tone of the McCain-Palin campaign perfectly:

Idiot wind, blowing like a circle around my skull,
From the Grand Coulee Dam to the Capitol.
Idiot wind, blowing every time you move your teeth,
You're an idiot, babe.
It's a wonder that you still know how to breathe.

Why Obama Won

And then there's this:

You hurt the ones that I love best and cover up the truth with lies.
One day you'll be in the ditch, flies buzzin around your eyes,
Blood on your saddle.

And:

I noticed at the ceremony, your corrupt ways had finally made you blind
I can't remember your face anymore, your mouth has changed,
Your eyes don't look into mine.

And finally:

I've been double-crossed now
for the very last time
and now I'm finally free

And so will we —in another five days.

NOVEMBER 2008

November 1

Palin Gets Punk'd
This seemed like a viral joke but since the Palin campaign has now confirmed, it must be true: One member of the Quebec radio team, the "Masked Avengers," which specializes in prank calls to celebrities, somehow got Sarah Palin on the line, in a pre-arranged hookup, and kept her there, one of them pretending to be Nicholas Sarkozy, for several minutes – even as "Sarkozy" told her he wanted to go hunting with her in a helicopter (but without Cheney) to "kill animals" and affirmed that his wife, Carla Bruni, was "hot in bed." Palin told the French leader that she and her running mate "loved" him and admitted that she might want to become president herself one day.

He courteously asked if Joe the Plumber was her husband. Palin hardly batted an eye until told, at the end, that she had been "pranked." Even then she patiently asked what station they were calling from before an aide finally got her to yield the phone. The Obama campaign promptly announced that it carefully screens all calls before handing the phone over to their candidate.

Indeed, things seemed to be getting nuttier as Election Day approaches. From Gail Collins at *The New York Times* today: "Our two-year presidential campaign now ends with a month-long vote, followed by weeks of litigation over provisional ballots. After that, the new president is sworn in and given 100 days to accomplish his legislative agenda, after which everyone will start plotting for 2012."

One still has to marvel over the factoid we reported yesterday: A major poll in Texas finding that 23% there still believe Obama is a Muslim. And that's in a state where three of the five biggest papers have, improbably, endorsed Obama. Meanwhile, McCain tries to stir the crowds with claims that "socialist" Obama wants to redistribute wealth. *Politico* notes that McCain, quite revealingly, has ditched his favored "town hall" format for appearances for the past two weeks, afraid of more embarrassing/racist statements from the crowds.

McCain, Cindy, Palin Do 'SNL'
If you can't lick 'em, join 'em? A wild opening for *SNL* tonight. The real McCain appeared with a fake Palin (Tina Fey) to do a QVC infomercial hawking items such as "Joe" action figures (Plumber, Six-Pack, Biden) and sharp knives (displayed by the real Cindy McCain) that "cut through pork." Fey then went "rogue," walking off to the side to sell a few "Palin 2012" t-shirts.

Is this really supposed to help the GOP campaign? To have your running mate—already something of a punch line – mocked with you smiling nearby? It's the stuff of celebrity roasts – but they are always backward looking, and affectionate, not unfriendly and in the midst of battle.

After host Ben Affleck did a long and savage Keith Olbermann segment, McCain returned for Weekend Update to weigh closing campaign strategies such as pulling the "reverse maverick" or playing "Sad Grandpa." Is he throwing in the towel? After he exited, Seth Meyers noted that Daylight Savings Time was arriving tonight but McCain had just denounced it as "redistributing sunlight." Now *that's* funny.

<u>November 2</u>

The Dean Lists
Take it with two large grains of salt, folks, but: A *Washington Post* analysis today finds Obama with nearly 300 electoral votes wrapped up (270 needed for election), and Democrats poised to make big gains in the House and Senate. The *Post* counted 159 polls in the past six weeks with not a single one showing McCain ahead.

David Broder's centrist assessments and predictions at the *Post* during the 2008 campaign have often proven wrong but he is still "The Dean" of political reporters so when he declares that this year's race is the greatest he has ever covered – including 1960, which he thought would never be topped – it's worth a read. But one thing: Broder hits Obama for rejecting McCain's call for a series of town hall debates. Yet McCain's worst debate of the fall, everyone agrees, was the one in the town hall format.

November 2008

Springsteen: The Real Working-Class Hero

Normally it would just be funny, if Joe the Plumber (or JTP, as press insiders have dubbed him) was just another sudden celeb shooting off his mouth and getting ludicrous airtime, even if it is mainly just Fox. But the man has appeared at numerous rallies at McCain's side. McCain has called him his "mentor," an "American hero," and promises to bring him to Washington if elected. So Joe's appearance on Fox today, in which he suggested Obama was disloyal to his country, really showed how far the campaign – and the mainstream media – have fallen.

Later, an audience of over 80,000 Obama supporters in Cleveland turned out despite the threat of rain to hear a real friend to the working class, Bruce Springsteen, play an acoustic "Youngstown," "This Land is Your Land" and "The Rising," among other tunes. He said to the audience while encouraging them to vote Obama on Tuesday, "I spent 35 years writing ... about what it means to be an American. The nation needs someone with Senator Obama's understanding, his temperedness, his deliberativeness, his maturity, his pragmatism, his toughness and his faith." He went on to say, "But most of all it needs us, it needs you, it needs me ... because all a nation has that keeps it together is the social contract between its people."

At the same time, Hank Williams, Jr., at a Palin rally, said as he was about to sing the National Anthem – "you know, that song that, uh, Mr. Obama's not real crazy about." Palin then failed to correct him. She should have quoted the tune by Hank's daddy, "You're Gonna Change Or I'm Gonna Leave." Instead she simply defended his First Amendment rights. Hank also sang a song that referred to Palin as quite a "dish."

November 3

Brothers, Pull Up Your Pants

ABC News reports that in an interview with MTV, Obama called local laws against sagging pants a "waste of time." But while he does not favor legal prohibitions on low-riders, he said "brothers should pull up their pants."

Obama: "Here is my attitude. I think people passing a law against people wearing sagging pants is a waste of time. We should be focused on creating jobs, improving our schools, health care, dealing with the war in

Iraq, and anybody, any public official, that is worrying about sagging pants probably needs to spend some time focusing on real problems out there.

"Having said that, brothers should pull up their pants. You are walking by your mother, your grandmother, your underwear is showing. What's wrong with that? Come on. There are some issues that we face, that you don't have to pass a law, but that doesn't mean folks can't have some sense and some respect for other people and, you know, some people might not want to see your underwear – I'm one of them."

It's All Over But the Counting? Why Obama Won #1

Yes, at least one in four votes has already been cast, but the election is certainly still in doubt. That isn't stopping many from venturing to explain why Obama has done so well (i.e. essentially won, already).

David Carr and Brian Stelter, media writers for *The New York Times*, observed today, "The Republicans have made a habit of running against the media in elections past. This year, the mainstream media found itself at times running against both parties. Perhaps drawing on Mr. Obama's background as a community organizer, his campaign decided early on to build a social network that would flank, and in some cases outflank, traditional news media.

"With a Facebook group that had 2.3 million adherents and a huge push on YouTube – last week alone, the campaign uploaded 70 videos, many of them tailored to battleground states – the campaign used peer-to-peer communication to build a juggernaut that did not depend on the whims and choices of the media's collective brain trust...."

Yes, Tina Fey's Palin parodies were carried on mainstream TV—but were viewed more often online (50 million times at least). "The idea that something can be seen more online than on TV, and arguably have more influence that way, is a tipping point," Andrew Heyward, the former CBS News chief, said. YouTube videos mentioning either Obama or McCain have been viewed 2.3 billion times, according to TubeMogul. A Pew Research Center survey conducted in October found that 39 percent of registered voters had watched campaign videos online.

The *Times* reporters concluded: "Given the profound change in the media landscape in just four years, in 2012, voters will be following the election through news sites that have not been invented on platforms that cannot be anticipated." Said Mark Jurkowitz of the Project for Excellence in

Journalism: "There was a palpable hunger for information and data about this election that has nothing to do with media. *Nobody* reports, *you* decide."

Cheney's Hometown Paper Comes Out for Obama
For the past six weeks, we have chronicled the landslide in newspaper endorsements for Barack Obama, now about 250 to 110. Now comes another sign of defeat: This morning, Dick Cheney's hometown paper in Wyoming, the *Casper Star-Tribune*, switched to Obama. Just this past Saturday, Cheney campaigned in Casper for three local Republicans and John McCain. A video of his McCain endorsement was then distributed by the campaign – the *Obama* campaign.

But McCain did pick up some otherworldly support today. Appearing at a final campaign rally in UFO-mad Roswell, N.M., McCain gleefully shouted, "I am pleased to announce I have received the alien endorsement!" And we thought he was *against* illegal aliens.

My Predictions for the Battleground States
Everyone's making predictions on Tuesday's election with, as usual, the key "swing" or "battleground" or "tossup" states getting the most attention. Experts, or just plain gasbags, can juggle all sorts of information, from reports on the ground to one of seemingly 500 polls. But at *Editor & Publisher* we do it a little differently on election eve: We predict the winner in key states purely on the basis on newspaper endorsements in that state.

As I've noted before, in 2004, I did the same thing – and picked 14 of the 15 tight races correctly, as well as the overall Bush win. So, with perhaps undue confidence, allow me to take the plunge once again. Using this strict measure, I predict Obama will take 11 out of 13 battlegrounds, losing in West Virginia and in Virginia (where, actually, I expect him to win, see below). Here is a rundown, in no particular order. Again, my picks are based *purely* on newspaper endorsements – both the number and the size/influence of the papers in each candidate's column.

PENNSYLVANIA
Forget McCain "narrowing the gap." He lost both big Philly dailies and split in Pittsburgh–gaining the lesser paper there. Obama has taken the smaller dailies by 2-1 with the papers in York, Easton and Erie, among others, switching from Bush. Winner: Obama.

OHIO

In 2004, Bush won because he nailed Columbus – and Cleveland sat it out. This year, Columbus remains in the GOP column but the *Plain Dealer* went for Obama. The Cincy paper again went Republican. But once again, Obama takes the smaller papers 2-1, with about half dozen switching over from Bush. The Akron, Toledo, Dayton, Canton and Youngstown papers give this state to Obama.

WEST VIRGINIA

Papers fully back McCain.

NORTH CAROLINA

We have to give Obama an upset here since he has in the bag all of the leading papers. A loss here would be embarrassing for...me. Obama takes it.

COLORADO

We correctly gave this to Bush in 2004 largely because he won the Denver papers. This time around, the *Post* backed Obama and the *Rocky* managed to endorse no one. Obama does well elsewhere here, too, with some Bush flip-floppers. Obama again.

FLORIDA

Will I blow this one again? Well, I will stick my neck out and give it to Obama, since, like Kerry in 2004, he dominates the editorial picks.

INDIANA

With the *Indy Star* begging off the GOP candidate and remaining neutral, the state leans to the Big O.

IOWA

Easy Obama win.

MISSOURI

I have to give this to Obama, too, as he held the likely papers and picked up a Bush switcher in Joplin.

NEVADA
The candidates split the two Vegas papers but Obama got Reno, so give this to him, too.

NEW HAMPSHIRE
Pretty much a toss up, but Obama leads by 5 dailies to 3 in our most recent count, so he can have that one, too.

NEW MEXICO
Ditto.

VIRGINIA
Well, I am probably going to take it on the chin here. The endorsements, big and small, in the state proper definitely favor McCain. However, I have my cop-out ready. The paper that has the highest distribution in what Sarah Palin suggested was the not-real-America part of the state (in the north) is *The Washington Post*, which backed Obama. So we'll see if it kicks the butt of the dailies in Richmond and elsewhere.

November 4

Midnight Express
In the traditional midnight voting in Dixville Notch, the tiny New Hampshire hamlet, Barack Obama won a surprise landslide by 15 to 6. The Obama supporters in the room let out a whoop, since the GOP candidate usually wins easily and Bush beat Kerry 19-7 after also trouncing Gore in 2000. Bush's father topped Dukakis 34-3 and Reagan trounced Mondale 29-1. Voters in the town of 75 gather at midnight on Election Day and the polls close one minute later. They've been doing this since 1960.

Even Before Polls Open: Why Obama Won #2
Anxious to get to the post-election analysis, *The New York Times'* presents this morning, at the top of its front page: "The '08 Campaign: A Sea Change for Politics As We Know It." Adam Nagourney opens, "The 2008 race for the White House that comes to an end on Tuesday fundamentally upended the way presidential campaigns are fought in this country, a legacy that has almost

been lost with all the attention being paid to the battle between Senators John McCain and Barack Obama.

"It has rewritten the rules on how to reach voters, raise money, organize supporters, manage the news media, track and mold public opinion, and wage — and withstand — political attacks, including many carried by blogs that did not exist four years ago."

Nagourney concludes: "The changes go beyond what Mr. Obama did and reflect a cultural shift in voters, producing an audience that is at once better informed, more skeptical and, from reading blogs, sometimes trafficking in rumors or suspect information. As a result, this new electorate tends to be more questioning of what it is told by campaigns and often uses the Web to do its own fact-checking."

Daytime Soap Opera
Bill the Bomber, the main focus of the McCain campaign for much of the closing drive, was spotted this morning showing up to vote about the same time and same place when the Obamas turned out. This proves everything alleged about the terror link. No doubt Bill Ayers was there to advise Barack who to vote for.

A pool report related: "Bill Ayers showed up with his wife to cast his vote. *Newsweek*'s Richard Wolffe first noticed Ayers. Your pooler confirmed his identity after yelling out 'Mr. Ayers, who did you vote for?' He turned around but did not answer. An official from the Chicago elections board told your pooler sternly not to yell at the polling station."

For another good laugh go to the Fox News home page. It highlights voting problems, which is fine, but the top two examples right now: A photo of people voting at one site in deep-blue state Vermont where someone might be able to look over their shoulders – and two "Black Panthers" intimidating voters in Philly....surely affiliated with Acorn.

Meanwhile, in a brighter note over at the *San Antonio (Texas) Express-News*, a 92-year-old woman wasn't going to let a stroke keep her from casting her vote. Betty Owen hasn't been able to walk since she suffered a stroke four years ago. Since her daughter failed to arrange for her mother to vote by absentee ballot, she made up for it at the last minute by arranging an ambulance to transport Owen from her retirement home to her polling location for free, according to the article.

"I couldn't find mom's voter registration card," the daughter told the *Express-News*. "I didn't know you didn't need it for an absentee ballot. And then I found it yesterday." In the polling location's parking lot, an election judge and support worker climbed into the ambulance with an electronic voting machine. Owen, dressed in her Sunday best, cast her vote – a straight Democratic ballot this year, according to the *Express-News*.

Primetime Thriller
In a bizarre moment on CNN, Wolf Blitzer brought to "The Situation Room" a hologram of one of his reporters at Grant Park in Chicago. She stood there and talked like she was in the room, with the requisite jokes about "beaming up Scotty" and the like. Wolf was so excited I thought he was going to try to have sex with her freaky image right then and there.

Over at Fox, they're pretty gloomy before most of votes have even come in. The private exit polls must be even worse than tidbits that have emerged. Going down with the ship – which he helped McCain board – Bill Kristol is still defending the Palin pick, calling her a net plus for the candidate, despite every bit of evidence in the exit polls showing otherwise. For example: by 60% to 38% voters said she was not qualified to be president. Kristol's next loss: His *New York Times* column?

One recalls that Kristol, on Dec. 17, 2006, also on Fox confidently declared: "If [Hillary Clinton] gets a race against John Edwards and Barack Obama, she's going to be the nominee. Gore is the only threat to her ... Barack Obama is not going to beat Hillary Clinton in a single democratic primary. I'll predict that right now."

Back to tonight: Another classic moment at Fox sure to boost YouTube views found Karl Rove at the set's main board, pointing to Ohio and saying McCain must have it to win – then interrupted by Brit Hume who informed him, sadly, that guess what, they have just called Ohio for Obama, sealing the deal. So at end of his eight years of work for the White House (including his days at Fox), Rove has managed to leave his president with the lowest approval rating for any president ever and a likely landslide loss for his party. Heckuva job, Rovie.

Sweet Home, All Obama
The networks reported Obama's triumph at the strike of 11 p.m. (EST) when California's polls closed, and the world, it seemed, went wild. But like announcers

Why Obama Won

at the close of some major sporting events, the MSNBC gang remained silent and just let the images do the talking for the next five minutes, as cameras showed cheering crowds in Chicago, in Harlem, at colleges, at Ebenezer Baptist Church in Atlanta, and elsewhere. For once they shut up and let viewers really experience an historic and moving moment. Words would not suffice anyway. In the crowd in Chicago: Oprah and Jesse Jackson (not together), weeping.

Out in Arizona, McCain delivered a dignified concession speech with one jarring note: Twice he had to silence the boos and catcalls from his crowd when he mentioned Obama's name. Hey folks, he could have said: Better get used to it.

When Obama came out to meet the Chicago crowd of 200,000 exactly one hour later, he acted subdued (overwhelmed? just tired?) but still gave a ringing speech calling on everyone to sacrifice and work together, even with those who did not vote for him, for he promised to be a president for all. Only one light note: He promised his kids a "new puppy" when they move to their new home, a little place they call the White House. Reportedly he nixed the idea of fireworks. Cute kids came out. Wife (in odd red and black dress) came out. Joe the Biden came out. A few waves, and so long.

So what was that music playing when Obama exited? No "The Rising," no "Signed Sealed Delivered," no "Barack and Roll Music." A *New York Times* blog reported: "Ah, one mystery solved. The music swelling in the background was 'The Patriot,' composed by John Williams." It also revealed that even as Obama spoke to the crowd, he was "texting his supporters. Amazing!" The text read: "We just made history. All of this happened because you gave your time, talent and passion to this campaign."

Obama seems to have won Virginia, Nevada and Indiana and, gasp, likely North Carolina. It's a Democratic sweep, although not crushing, in other races, with the party picking up at least five colleagues in the Senate (with four races still not decided, including the Ted Stevens fiasco and Franken-Coleman) and about 25 gains in the House.

November 5

Morning Becomes Electric
The Onion, as often true, told it best. The semi-serious editorial today: "Carrying a majority of the popular vote, Obama did especially well among

women and young voters, who polls showed were particularly sensitive to the current climate of everything being fucked." The satirical paper had a separate story titled: "Black Man Given Nation's Worst Job."

Other weightier newspapers, of course, also weighed in, including some that did not back him. Here are a few snapshots. My favorite, and shortest of all, from *The Seattle Times*: "A nation exhales."

Los Angeles Times: "The range of issues that demand the next administration's attention is almost limitless; the yearning of the country for thoughtful, conscientious leadership is nearly palpable."

The New York Times: "His triumph was decisive and sweeping, because he saw what is wrong with this country: the utter failure of government to protect its citizens."

The Wall Street Journal: "We'll now find out if the Democratic Party has learned anything since the last two times it held all the levers of power in Washington."

The Washington Post: "Mr. Obama cannot erase Mr. Bush's legacy, but he has a chance to improve America's standing in the world, ending such noxious practices as torture and indefinite detention with minimal review that have diminished this country in the eyes of its allies."

USA Today: "If the past two decades have taught anything, it's that a president and his party prosper when they involve their opponents in restoring a sense of common purpose. Obama appears to grasp how difficult and necessary that is."

Chicago Tribune: "From the moment he captured national attention with a stirring speech at the 2004 Democratic National Convention to the last day of this campaign, he reminded us that amid our often-contentious diversity, we are one nation joined in a common mission."

Houston Chronicle: "The Obama victory was forged with the help of voters in those presumed red states, and we hope that message is heard by leaders of both parties on Capitol Hill."

New York Post: "And a tip of the hat to America, too: Just two generations ago, an African-American who attempted to cast a ballot courted violent death in the dark of night - but now a black man will ascend to the highest office in the land."

Orange County (Ca.) Register: "He will be well-advised to govern as he campaigned, from somewhere close to the center of the American political spectrum."

Wasilla Hillbillies
From *Newsweek's* report on what really went on during the campaign (they are always given special access and agree not to publish a word until after the voting) comes a vignette today on Sarah Palin greeting McCain aides one day on the road in nothing but a towel around her bod and another over her hair. Also, the real dope on her clothes shopping spree, which far exceeded even what reported, including $20,000 to $40,000 just on the erstwhile First Dude.

One aide estimated that she spent "tens of thousands" more than the reported $150,000, and that $20,000 to $40,000 went to buy clothes for her husband. Some articles of clothing have apparently been lost. An angry McCainer characterized the shopping spree as "Wasilla hillbillies looting Neiman Marcus from coast to coast," and said the truth will eventually come out when the Republican Party audits its books.

Paul Mauls the 'Monsters'
The new Nobel laureate, Paul Krugman, letting it all hang out, put up this blog post today: "Last night wasn't just a victory for tolerance; it wasn't just a mandate for progressive change; it was also, I hope, the end of the monster years.

"What I mean by that is that for the past 14 years America's political life has been largely dominated by, well, monsters. Monsters like Tom DeLay, who suggested that the shootings at Columbine happened because schools teach students the theory of evolution. Monsters like Karl Rove, who declared that liberals wanted to offer 'therapy and understanding' to terrorists. Monsters like Dick Cheney, who saw 9/11 as an opportunity to start torturing people.

"And in our national discourse, we pretended that these monsters were reasonable, respectable people. To point out that the monsters were, in fact, monsters, was 'shrill.' Four years ago it seemed as if the monsters would dominate American politics for a long time to come. But for now, at least, they've been banished to the wilderness."

Did 'Bradley' Tank?
The final analysis isn't in, but it's possible that in most parts of the country the dreaded (by many) "Bradley Effect" did not materialize very much. That is, whites who tell pollsters they will vote for a black candidate but then do not. This year, the polls and exit polls in most places closely matched the actual vote totals. Also, Obama did better than John Kerry in many places, although let's not get carried away: McCain still won among whites in a landslide, by about 56% to 42%.

The *NYT* has a fascinating map at its site that shows the counties, in red, where Obama actually did worse than Kerry. These are virtually all in Appalachia or in the south (including northern Texas) – areas that didn't like or relate to Kerry *at all*, so you have to wonder what special factor might have turned them against Obama even though the country is much worse off than four years ago?

Palintology
Carl Cameron talking to Bill O'Reilly tonight on Fox revealed that McCain aides were truly "shocked" at the "gaps in knowledge" Sarah Palin displayed once they were stuck with her. He said that, in the most startling shortcoming, she actually didn't "understand that Africa was not just a country, but a continent." This led, among other things, to her asking how South Africa could be a separate country.

She also could not name all of the countries in North America, the McCain aides said, not even the NAFTA partners. And she did not know many of the basics of civics and local/state/national duties. O'Reilly pooh-poohed all of this, saying she could have been brought up to speed, but the severe "gaps" if true would explain why tensions erupted between the McCain and Palin camps.

Speaking of Fox, Chris Wallace dared to venture on *The Daily Show* tonight. Jon tried to be nice, saying that Chris put "the News in Fox News."

Then he savaged him, even though Wallace presented him with a cookie sent over by Karl Rove. Throughout he ribbed Wallace on Fox bias, ran a clip of desperate Fox attacks on Obama just in the last week, and asked if Fox, under a Democrat, would continue to argue for such things as presidential power and executive privilege.

Earlier in the show, Stewart announced that Sarah Palin, who had just flown home, had "been tagged and released into the Alaskan wilderness."

November 6

Why Obama Won #4
No one can doubt the profound role in the Obama – and national Democratic – victory played by the Netroots, with a big boost from the massive number of activists affiliated, loosely or firmly, with DailyKos. Markos Moulitsas Zuniga, the founder, has pushed, worked and raised funds for Democratic victories, beyond ideology and special interest groups, for years and, like Howard Dean, promoted the idea long ago of putting every state in play, not just the already-blueish ones, with stunning results.

In a short post at his site today he reports on Republican activists and "thinkers" holding an emergency meeting to turn things around next time – and reflects on why he helped keep the Democrats out of a certain trap: "I attended one of these for our side in early 2005, and the experience was so miserable that it ended up being a major inspiration for [his influential book] *Crashing the Gate*. It was full of the same progressive 'leaders' who had gotten us into our predicament, and their solutions were the same bullshit that had gotten us in the mess in the first place. So I left that retreat even more motivated to wage war against our party's political and issue-group establishment. Our victories in recent years have come, in large part, from our ability to bypass that crowd.

"Those early tensions are mostly erased, as a new balance has been struck by issue groups more and more aware of the need to be part of a holistic progressive movement, rather than focus obsessively and divisively on their own single pet cause. It really is night and day. But that didn't come out of that conference. And it certainly wasn't billed as a way to generate a new grassroots movement. The notion of having a bunch of top-down movement leaders create a new 'national grassroots' operation by fiat from up and above, by the same jokers who created the mess the GOP is currently in, is pretty laughable."

Markos took a wider look around in a new column at *The Hill* in explaining Obama's win, declaring that he "represented, in a very real way, the future of our nation – young and multicultural. And the exit polling suggests that Republicans are headed for some rough waters ahead if they don't recognize this." For one thing, putting it bluntly, "the GOP's best age group – those 65 and older – face…actuarial challenges."

And then there's this: "The white vote kept McCain peripherally competitive…But Republicans are tentatively holding onto a shrinking portion of the electorate, while Democrats enjoy massive advantages with the fastest growing demographics."

Turnout: The Hype and the Reality
It happens nearly every election day: The media swoon over what looks like (partly because it was predicted to be a) heavy turnout. Gosh, look at all those people standing in line! When it's over, the initial numbers seem to back that up and a "record" turnout is declared. Then the dust settles and, well, there goes any big leap forward or, usually, any leap at all. That appears to be the case again this year, with the latest report suggesting only a slight uptick – and only on the "blue" side. Which means, it did matter.

CNN quotes longtime expert Curtis Gans: "Many people were fooled by this year's increase in registration (more than 10 million added to the rolls), citizens' willingness to stand for hours even in inclement weather to vote early, the likely rise in youth and African American voting, and the extensive grassroots organizing network of the Obama campaign into believing that turnout would be substantially higher than in 2004….But we failed to realize that the registration increase was driven by Democratic and independent registration and that the long lines at the polls were mostly populated by Democrats."

November 7

Séance Isn't So
Obama's first press conference as a President-elect was a pretty somber affair as he highlighted the economic problems. He answered questions in his usual

slightly-halting delivery (now parodied on *SNL*), but he did make a couple of jokes. One referred back to Nancy Reagan and her "seances," as he claimed he was only speaking to living presidents. Also he said he might pick out the puppy for his daughters at a shelter where they have "mutts, like me." In a little payback, he did not take any questions from the Fox News reporter.

A little later he learned that it was not Nancy Reagan but Hillary Clinton who allegedly sat in on a "séance." Nancy only relied on astrology. Obama quickly called Nancy to apologize.

From *Newsweek*'s new behind-the-scenes in the campaign book comes this rather sad revelation: Another instance of Obama's extraordinary self-control. Earlier this year, on June 3rd, when Obama had finally won enough delegates to guarantee his nomination, an aide said, "You just locked up the nomination—how about a beer?" Obama started to say yes, then changed his mind. "We won't hit the ground until 3 in the morning," he replied, "and I've got AIPAC first thing—I better not."

Why Obama Won #5
If the numbers hold, Obama will end up with a comfortable popular vote margin of about 52% to 45%, and a 365-173 rout in electoral votes. Jeff Cohen, the founder of Fairness and Accuracy in Reporting (now director of the Park Center for Independent Media at Ithaca College), explores several factors behind Obama's victory at Huffington Post. He lists among others:

* Record-breaking Internet fund raising. "And without the February 1 endorsement from Netroots powerhouse MoveOn, and its infusion of energy and volunteers, Obama may well have lost the nomination to Hillary Clinton." Estimates suggest Obama may have raised over $800 million for the general election, outraising McCain by about 3-2. This helped pay for TV ads—and boots on the ground. More than 3 million individuals donated to the campaign, an unprecedented number.

* While conservative and establishment pundits still dominate TV and radio, "progressive dominance of the Internet has made it easier for media critics and bloggers to instantly rebut the kind of hoaxes and smears that so damaged Gore and Kerry. This time Swift-Boating was often countered – as when Obama refused to be eclipsed by TV clips of Rev. Wright and made his speech on race

that became the top video on You Tube....Years ago, rightwing smears would flow up the food chain from Drudge to Fox News/talk radio into mainstream media. This year, the flow of serious, accurate charges about McCain got a push from progressive media – like the story of 'McCain's Mansions,' which sailed from blogs to mainstream via the hugely successful Brave New Films viral video."

* "To succeed, robocall smears need to operate below the radar. But this year, a backlash erupted over McCain's robocalls saying Obama supported baby-killing and 'civil rights for terrorists.' Talking Points Memo blog and its active readers were quickly exposing the calls – providing sound and transcript. Several Republican senators denounced the calls."

<u>November 8</u>

Press Biased Against McCain?
Today, with the race for the White House finally over, Deborah Howell, the *Washington Post* ombudsman, examined the results of her paper's study of the fairness of its own election coverage in the past year. Soon articles relating to her piece were carrying headlines suggesting that the study had found that the *Post* had clearly "tilted" to Obama or even showed a "major tilt" (that's how Mark Halperin at his popular blog at Time.com had it, as did many others, especially conservative outlets).

On top of the widely-publicized results of the recent Project for Excellence in Journalism (PEJ) news coverage survey, this seemed to amount to a slam dunk proving press bias against McCain.

But is that really what these studies show? It's an important question because once any conventional wisdom is set, it is almost impossible to dislodge it. It may yet turn out that major, exhaustive studies will prove that the media were grossly unfair to John McCain. Bring them on. But these studies don't do that.

Both the PEJ survey, which found Obama receiving many more "favorable" stories than McCain, and the *Post's* numbers are thrown off by the fact that they found that "horse race" angles (including polling) thoroughly dominated the overall coverage – 57% of the stories in the PEJ sample and much higher than that in the *Post's* study (1,295 horse-race stories and only 594 issues stories).

This disgraceful proportion is worth its own critique about the media's priorities, but the fact is: Except for a week after the end of the GOP convention, before Palin-mania collapsed, Obama was ahead in the polls, eventually by a lot, and he always led in the fundraising (overwhelmingly), in the size of his crowds (ditto), and in putting more states in play. He couldn't help but lead in favorable coverage – if that coverage was thoroughly dominated by the horse race (which it was).

My complaint about the *Post* and PEJ handling of their own results is not that they ignored this horse race factor completely but that they did not make that key aspect clear at the very top of their analysis, not a few paragraphs down and without enough emphasis. So we will be reading for years about the strong media "bias" against McCain – look at all those "unfavorable" stories about him – when it was mainly (although perhaps not completely) a matter of Obama leading the horse race and getting credit for that by reporters who were, surprise, not deaf, dumb and blind.

Does anyone doubt that if McCain had roared to the lead in October and stayed ahead until the end that the results of the studies would have been completely different? Yes, the press is biased – in favor of recognizing who is winning and stating that perhaps too often.

Also: Can the media be faulted if one candidate is committing the major share of gaffes or (in this age of fact-check sites) making the most inaccurate statements in speeches and in ads? Is it "bias" to recognize that? Or to vet a candidate for vice president who (we now know) had not been vetted by anyone else?

Then there's this. Howell dryly relates one seemingly significant gap in the number of news stories on each candidate, going back to last November: 946 stories about Obama compared with McCain's 786. But this can be easily explained by the fact that McCain's primary race ended almost four months before Obama's! Of course, there were more stories about Obama from March to June, thanks to Hillary Clinton's spirited fight.

Howell does point this out – but buries this crucial explanation. Actually, it's amazing that the gap between Obama and McCain in this one-year period was not far wider.

What about from June 4 (when Obama clinched the nomination) to Election Day? Howell reveals, "the tally was Obama, 626 stories, and McCain,

584. Obama was on the front page 176 times, McCain, 144 times; 41 stories featured both." A "major" tilt?

And more counting: "Obama was in 311 *Post* photos and McCain in 282. Obama led 164 to 133 in color photos. In black and white photos, the nominees were about even, with McCain at 149 and Obama at 147. On Page 1, they were even at 26 each." Again: This is a "major tilt"?

Then there's this example. *The New York Times* carried a top-of-the-front page piece on Obama one morning in early October. A good thing, right? Not exactly. The lengthy story resurrected his Bill Ayers connection. That issue, dormant for months, suddenly revived and, in fact, became a focus of the McCain-Palin campaign for weeks – with the *Times* (normally hated by the GOP) cited as the authoritative source. So: a prominent story about a candidate might look swell in some of the tallies but is not necessarily a good thing in reality.

Finally: When one talks about "the media" being "in the tank" for one candidate, what is the definition of "media"? Consider that tens of millions of Americans claim they get virtually all of their news from talk radio. Others rely mainly on Web sites with clear political leanings, or *The Daily Show*, or *SNL*. Is this all "media"?

PEJ and the *Post* can claim that they can only put the tallies out there, they can't control how pundits and reporters interpret or spin them or what they write in their headlines. True enough. But those who produce the findings need to explain clearly, and right at the top, what exactly was tallied, the "horse race" context, and other crucial factors, such as providing a list of which articles were viewed as favorable or unfavorable for a candidate so others can judge their standards.

Strong bias in news coverage of the 2008 campaign may yet be shown – but it's not proven so far.

Out of the Blue, Into the Black

Brace yourself for some, or a lot, of anti-Obama racial incidents in the days, weeks and maybe years ahead. Numerous episodes, some involving physical threats or violence, have been reported since Election Day. Here's just one from AP: "A family who had supported Barack Obama's presidential campaign emerged from their home in the northwestern New Jersey town of Hardwick

Thursday morning to find the charred remnants of a 6-foot wooden cross on their front lawn. Pieces of a homemade bed sheet banner reading 'President Obama , Victory '08,' which had been stolen from the yard the night before, also were found, leading investigators to believe the banner had been wrapped around the cross before it was set afire. Lt. Gerald Lewis of the New Jersey State Police said his agency is treating the incident as a bias crime."

The parents were especially upset that their 8-year-old daughter had to experience this.

November 9

Hold the Plaudits for Parker
Kathleen Parker, the conservative syndicated columnist and frequent TV guest, earned plaudits from liberals during the fall campaign by speaking out against the Palin pick (even urging her withdrawal), which drew the wrath of many of her fans. In a column yesterday, she revealed that she wept on watching Obama declared the winner this week. Parker concluded: "The little speck of difference that kept us imperceptibly apart had been dissolved in a lovely instant of national consensus that race no longer matters."

One hates to be churlish at a time like this, but allow me to point out that this is the same woman who in a quite different column back in May strongly questioned Obama's patriotism, "DNA" and Americanism. If you want to be kind you could take that as an example of how far Parker, and maybe America, have come since then.

Peggy Noonan has joined her. Back in May we noted in this space one of her pieces in the *Wall Street Journal*. Noonan had opined: "Hillary Clinton is not Barack Obama's problem. America is Mr. Obama's problem." She wondered if Obama had ever gotten "misty-eyed" over the Wright Brothers, D-Day, George Washington or Henry Ford. "[W]hat about Obama and America?" she asked rhetorically. "Who would have taught him to love it, and what did he learn was lovable, and what does he think about it all?" She concluded: "[N]o one is questioning his patriotism, they're questioning its content, its fullness."

Now here's what Noonan wrote two days ago: "The explosion of joy in large pockets of the country Tuesday night was beautiful to see, and moving....It is a matter of profound importance that everyone in a nation know that with whatever facts they start their life, there is a clear and open route to rise. It is a less great country in which routes, and heights, are closed off or limited by things that, if you some day get to heaven, you will look back on and realize were silly, stupid: class, color, condition."

Hello Mutter, Hello Fodder
Exactly one year ago, Joe Strupp for *E&P* previewed press coverage of the upcoming 2008 race for the White House. The cover featured a Steve Brodner illustration that parodied the famous *Chicago Tribune* Truman/Dewey front page from 1948, showing Hillary Clinton flashing a newspaper that declared "PRINT Beats WEB." The kicker: Our inside spread showed a man – who looked suspiciously like blogger Chris Cillizza of *The Washington Post* – in the same pose hoisting a paper with the banner head, "WEB Beats PRINT!"

How did that work out? Well, for one thing, Cillizza got so much attention he has just been named as the paper's first Web-only official White House correspondent.

In the days following the Obama triumph numerous analysts and press pundits have weighed in on the media takeaway, sometimes a little over-the-top. Alan D. Mutter at his popular blog "Reflections of a Newsosaur" published a lengthy comment that's worth quoting. Mutter worked at the *Chicago Sun-Times* and *San Francisco Chronicle* before becoming a cable TV honcho, a top Silicon Valley executive and now an oft-quoted media and technology consultant.

His posting opened with, "The 2008 presidential election likely will go down in history as the last hurrah for the mainstream media when it comes to its influence over national politics." For one thing: "MSM haters won't let us soon forget the uncommon number of times that the common wisdom proved incorrect among the gaggle in the bubble on the bus." But the whys cut much deeper:

–"Shrinking audiences and decaying advertising revenues respectively will reduce the reach and resources that the mainstream media traditionally have enjoyed in covering presidential campaigns."

–"Any remotely competent national campaign in the future will go over the heads of the media by emulating the successful interactive tactics that Barack Obama employed to raise record campaign funding; build highly effective real and virtual networks, and energize a previously apathetic generation of young and heavily wired voters."

—"The new generation of media-savvy voters will take full advantage of the abundance of news, commentary and raw information (campaign finance reports, voting records and polling data) available to them on the Web. They not only will use those resources to educate themselves but also, in many cases, will add their voices to what is bound to become a national, 24/7, no-holds-barred town hall meeting."

But there's more and here's where it really cuts to the bone (as it were): "The last indignity for the MSM - and the one that virtually assures the decline of its future influence - will be self-inflicted. As soon as the election is over, the Washington bureaus and national desks at most newspapers, magazines and networks are almost sure to be dramatically reduced by their parent companies to offset the sustained declines they have been suffering in advertising sales. In the process, we will lose the insights and efforts of many of the talented professionals who over the years have attempted to inject a degree of honesty and balance into the inherently ill-disciplined realms of government and politics."

November 12

Cook's Tour: Why Obama Won #6
Charlie Cook, the longtime election follower for his own *Report* and now the *National Journal* weighs in on the turnout myth but with a twist: "Although young people turned out in higher numbers than they did four years ago, the increase was proportionate with the electorate as a whole. Most non-Republican voters turned out in higher numbers this year than in 2004. One key to Barack Obama's victory, however, was his overwhelming support among voters ages 18 to 29, whom he won by 34 points, 66 percent to 32 percent; and his support among those ages 30 to 44, whom he carried by 6 points, 52 percent to 46 percent. Those numbers are ominous for Republicans looking to 2010 and beyond....

"In general, in the higher-growth segments of our country, Republicans lost ground, prevailing only in small towns and rural areas. When Democrats win the suburbs, Republicans are in trouble....The question now is whether Republicans will quickly learn from their mistakes – retooling and re-branding their party soon, putting themselves in a position to capitalize on the missteps of the Obama administration and the rest of the Democratic Party – or will languish, reduced to waiting for the Democrats to collapse and for GOP candidates to win simply because they aren't Democrats.

"Those who write off the 2008 election by saying that Republican candidates weren't conservative enough are in denial. They are political ostriches, refusing to acknowledge that the country and the electorate are changing and that old recipes don't work any more."

Paying the Piper
The Palins hit a new low, allowing 7-year-old Piper to do a brief *Today* show interview, aired today. And guess what? She admits to Matt Lauer she missed "a lot" of school (while being exploited on the campaign trail) and that it is "really hard" to catch up now. Let's hope she makes out better than oldest brother (high school dropout) and oldest sister (pregnant in 11th grade, boyfriend also high school dropout).

When Lauer asks how she'd feel about hitting the campaign trail again in 2012, Piper says, "I don't know." Her mother then butts in to remind her that it was "fun" this time, huh?

A lot of dark humor in a new P.J. O'Rourke piece at *The Weekly Standard* addressing his fellow conservatives, titled "We Blew It." It opens with: "Let us bend over and kiss our ass goodbye." And closes with: "Although I must say we're doing good work on our final task–attaching the garden hose to our car's exhaust pipe and running it in through a vent window. Barack and Michelle will be by in a moment with some subsidized ethanol to top up our gas tank. And then we can turn the key."

November 13

Why Obama Won #7
Sarah Palin was roundly criticized in media quarters during the campaign for failing to hold even one press conference – surely a first in modern history. So today at the big national governor's conference, where she is starring, she finally does one. Why now? You have to give her points for honesty in this case: "The campaign is over," she explained. Perfect.

Made in the USA